CATALOGUE

OF THE

ARCHÆOLOGICAL MUSEUM

AT

MATHURA

Owing to the antiquity and rarity of this book, certain pages are regrettably absent, and readability is compromised due to the blurring of the original text. If you possess any insights regarding the availability of these missing sections, kindly inform us. Your assistance is crucial in ensuring the completion of this significant work for the benefit of future generations.

CATALOGUE

OF THE

ARCHÆOLOGICAL MUSEUM

AT

MATHURA

BY

J. PH . VOGEL

GYAN

Published by

GYAN

Gyan Publishing House
5, Ansari Road
Daryaganj, New Delhi-110002
Phone: 011-47034999, 9811692060
E-mail: books@gyanbooks.com

Distribution Network
gyanbooks.com
India, USA, Canada, UK, Australia

ISBN: 978-93-6433-838-7 (HB)
First Published, 1910

2nd Impression 2024

Printed at: Gyan Press, Delhi.

CATALOGUE OF THE ARCHÆOLOGICAL MUSEUM AT MATHURA
Author: J. PH . VOGEL

CATALOGUE

OF THE

ARCHÆOLOGICAL MUSEUM

AT

MATHURA.

BY

J. PH. VOGEL, PH.D.,

SUPERINTENDENT, ARCHÆOLOGICAL SURVEY, NORTHERN CIRCLE.

ALLAHABAD:

Printed by F. Luker, Superintendent, Government Press, United Provinces

1910.

To the Memory

of

S. S. GROWSE, Esq., I.C.S.,

This Catalogue of the Museum
founded by him at Mathura is reverently
dedicated by the author.

PREFACE.

In March 1905 I undertook to catalogue the sculptures in the Municipal Museum at Mathurā, at the request of Mr. H. C. Ferard, C.I.E., I.C.S., then Collector of the district. The time available proved insufficient to finish the work, mainly owing to the number of inscriptions, most of which had not yet been properly edited. My departmental duties and a prolonged illness prevented me from resuming the work until December 1907, when a month's stay at Mathurā enabled me to bring the catalogue to completion.

In the meanwhile the Museum had been enriched with more than a hundred Mathurā sculptures, the bulk of which came from the Allahabad Public Library. In the course of the year 1908 the collection was further increased by the addition of a large number of valuable sculptures and inscriptions which were collected in the locality by Pandit Radha Krishna, and purchased and presented to the Museum by Mr. J. H. Marshall, the Director-General of Archaeology. These also have been included in the present publication.

A few words are required to explain the arrangement of my catalogue. As in past years no proper record has been kept of the provenance of the sculptures, it was impossible to arrange them according to their find-spots. For the same reason a classification according to creeds - Buddhist, Jaina and Brahmanical—could not be adopted, except in the case of images, some illustrative bas-reliefs and a few inscribed pieces. It will be hardly necessary to add that a chronological arrangement was out of the question, as the style of the sculptures enables us only to fix in general the period to which they belong. Even those dated in Kanishka's era cannot be referred to a particular year, as the initial date of that epoch is still a matter of dispute. In these circumstances the best course seemed to me to make three main divisions consisting of images, bas-reliefs and architectural sculptures.

It is obvious that such a division is in many cases bound to be arbitrary. In Indian art images of deities are but seldom carved in the round, and have therefore in reality the character of reliefs. Most of the pieces classed as bas-reliefs, on the other hand, served the purpose of decorating some religious building and might, therefore, be called architectural. Within the three main divisions I have grouped sculptures of the same kind, as much as possible, together. This arrangement, it is hoped, will render this catalogue more convenient to consult.

The want of a list or register is to a certain extent supplemented by the papers published by Mr. Growse and by General Cunningham's archaeological reports dealing with Mathurā. A study of these publications has enabled me to ascertain the find-places of a larger number of sculptures than I had anticipated. Unfortunately, their descriptions are often vague or inaccurate, and the dimensions are but rarely given, so that in some cases it is doubtful which particular sculpture is meant.

The present catalogue contains all the information which from published accounts can be gathered regarding the provenance of these sculptures. As to their description and interpretation, a prolonged study of the Mathurā art and of the closely related Græco-Buddhist school of Gandhára has enabled me to propose a certain number of fresh identifications. In questions touching the relationship between the Mathurā and Gandhára schools, I have invariably endorsed the views put forth with great lucidity by M. Alfred Foucher in his various publications, and more especially in his standard work on Græco-Buddhist sculpture.

Here I wish to acknowledge my indebtedness to Dr. Heinrich Lüders, Professor at the Berlin University, for kindly revising my readings of the inscriptions, a complete list of which will be given in an Appendix.

Lieutenant-Colonel W. Vost, I.M.S., has rendered me great help in reading through the manuscript of my work and Mr. J. H. Marshall in revising the proofs. To Babu R. D. Banerji I owe useful notes on the sculptures and inscriptions in the Lucknow Museum which he has been engaged in cataloguing.

In my introduction I have supplied such information as will render the sculptures in the Museum more intelligible and consequently more interesting to the public. It is perhaps due to personal predilection that Buddhist art takes such a large share in this introductory treatise. But it will be admitted that not only on account of their number, but also from an artistic and historic point of view, the Buddhist sculptures form the most important part of our collection as relics of a school, which flourished during the most brilliant period of Mathurā history.

MATHURĀ :
November 1908.

J. PH. VOGEL.

Postscript.—The unavoidable delay in printing has enabled me to include in the catalogue the important acquisitions made by Pandit Radha Krishna in the course of the year 1909. These also were due to the generous assistance afforded by Mr. J. H. Marshall, Director-General of Archaeology, who supplied the money from Imperial funds. I may add that the same officer arranged for a grant-in-aid of Rs. 2,000 from the Government of India for repairs to the Museum building which have lately been completed and will serve the purpose of rendering the edifice better suited for its present use.

LAHORE :
March 1910.

J. PH. V.

CONTENTS.

INTRODUCTION.

CATALOGUE.

APPENDIX I.

APPENDIX II.

BIBLIOGRAPHY.

L. R. Stacy. *Note on the discovery of a relic of Grecian sculpture in Upper India* (with additional note by James Prinsep). Journal Asiatic Society of Bengal, Vol. V. (1836) pp. 567—570; with plate.

(Account of the so-called "Silenus" now in the Calcutta Museum.)

A. Cunningham. *Archaeological Survey Report*, Vol. I, pp. 231—244 (plates XXXIX—XL); Vol. III, pp. 13—46 (plates I—XVI); Vol. XVII, pp. 107—112 (plates XXX—XXXI) and Vol. XX, pp. 30—39 (plates II—VI).

R. L. Mitra. *Notes on Sanskrit inscriptions from Mathurā*. Journal Asiatic Society of Bengal, Vol. XXXIX (1870), pp. 117—130; with four plates.

(Discussion of twenty Mathurā inscriptions discovered about 1860).

J. Dowson. *Ancient inscriptions from Mathurā* (with additional note by A. Cunningham.) Journal Royal Asiatic Society, New Series, Vol. V (1871), pp. 182—196; with three plates.

(Discussion of twenty-nine Mathurā inscriptions collected by Cunningham who remarks (p. 194) that about one-half had been discovered by him in 1862 and 1865).

H. Blochmann. *Notes on Mathurā*. Proceedings Asiatic Society of Bengal for 1873, pp. 12—17.

(Discussion of four Persian and Hindustani inscriptions on buildings in the city of Mathurā collected by F. S. Growse).

F. S. Growse. *Mathurā, a district Memoir, with numerous illustrations*. First edition, 1874; second edition, 1880; third edition (revised and abridged), 1883. Printed at the North-Western Provinces and Oudh Government Press.

(Chapter V; The Buddhist city of Mathurā and its antiquities. Chapter VII; the city of Mathurā (concluded): its European institutions and museum).

F. S. Growse. *Supposed Greek sculpture at Mathurā*. Journal Asiatic Society of Bengal. Vol. XLIV (1875), pp. 212—215; with three plates.

(Description of the so-called "Silenus" in the Calcutta Museum and of its counterpart "the Bacchanalian group" in the Mathurā Museum. (No. C, 2; pl. XIII.)

F. S. Growse. *Mathurā Inscriptions*. Indian Antiquary. Vol. VI (1877), pp. 216—219; with plate.

(Tentative readings of eleven inscriptions in the Mathurā Museum. Nos. 2 and 7 are in the Lucknow Museum).

F. S. Growse. *Mathurā Notes.* Journal Asiatic Society of Bengal. Vol. XLVII (1878), part 1, pp. 97—133; plates IX- -XXI.

(Section 7, pp. 118—120 treats of miscellaneous antiquities in the Mathurā Museum illustrated in plates XVIII—XXI).

Transactions of the Archaeological Society of Agra (July to December 1875), Agra 1876.

(Catalogue of contents of the Museum of the Archaeological Society, Agra, pp. 30—32.)

Bhagvanlal Indraji. *The Hāthigumphā and three other inscriptions in the Udayagiri Caves near Cuttack.* Actes du sixième Congrès international des Orientalistes tenu en 1883 à Leide (Leide 1885). Part III, section II, pp. 142—144; with plate.

(Discussion of inscribed tablet of homage from Holi Gate no. Q, 2; pl. V. Cf. V.A. Smith. *Jaina Stūpa*, plate C III).

E. Curtius. *Die Griechische Kunst in Indien.* Archäologische Zeitung Vol. XXXIII (New Series, Vol. VIII) 1876, pp. 90—95; with illustrations.

J. Anderson. *Catalogue and Handbook of the archaeological collections in the Indian Museum.* Calcutta 1883.

(Description of Mathurā sculptures in the Calcutta Museum. Part I, pp. 167—192. Description of relic casket from Chaubārā mound. Part II, p. 483.)

J. F. Fleet. *Inscriptions of the early Gupta kings and their successors.* Corpus Inscriptionum Indicarum. Volume III, Calcutta 1888.

(No. 4. Mathurā stone inscription of Chandragupta II; pp. 25—28, plate III A.—No. 63. Mathurā stone image inscription of the year 135, pp. 262—264, plate XXXIX A.—No. 70. Mathurā stone image inscription of the year 230, pp. 273-274; plate XL. D.)

G. Bühler. *On the authenticity of the Jaina tradition.* Vienna Oriental Journal. Volume I (1887), pp. 165—180.

(Discussion of eight Jaina inscriptions from Mathurā.)

G. Bühler. *Further proofs of the authenticity of the Jaina tradition.* Vienna Oriental Journal. Volume II (1888), pp. 141—146; with plate.

(Discussion of Jaina inscription dated in the year 7 of Kanishka, obtained by Burgess from the Kankālī Ṭīlā).

G. Bühler. *Further proofs of the authenticity of the Jaina tradition.* Vienna Oriental Journal. Volume III (1889), pp. 233 - 240.

(Discussion of four Jaina inscriptions obtained by Führer from the Kankālī Ṭīlā).

G. Bühler. *Further proofs of the authenticity of the Jaina tradition.* Vienna Oriental Journal. Volume IV (1890), pp. 313—331.

(Discussion of Jaina inscriptions obtained by Führer from the Kankālī Ṭīlā in 1890).

G. Bühler. *New Jaina inscriptions from Mathurā.* Ibidem, pp. 169-173.

G. Bühler. *New excavations in Mathurā.* Vienna Oriental Journal. Volume V (1891), pp. 59—63.

G. Bühler. *Dr. Führer's excavations at Mathurā.* Ibidem, pp. 175—180.

G. Bühler. Almanach der Wiener Akademie der Wissenschaften. Jahrgang XXXVII, p. 206.

G. Bühler. *New Jaina inscriptions from Mathurā.* Epigraphia Indica. Vol. I (1892), pp. 371—397; with five plates.

(Discussion of thirty-five Mathurā inscriptions).

G. Bühler. *Further Jaina inscriptions from Mathurā.* Epigraphia Indica. Vol. II (1894), pp. 195—212; with three plates.

(Discussion of forty-two Mathurā inscriptions).

G. Bühler. *Specimens of Jaina sculptures from Mathurā.* Epigraphia Indica. Vol. II (1894), pp. 311—323; with four plates.

(Discussion of certain, partly inscribed, sculptures obtained by Führer from the Kaṅkālī Ṭīlā in 1890).

G. Bühler. *A Legend of the Jaina Stūpa at Mathurā.* Sitzungsberichte der Kaiserlichen Akademie der Wissenschaften in Wien 1897.

G. Bühler. *On the Indian sect of the Jainas,* translated from the German, edited by J. Burgess, London, 1903.

(Appendix A. Discussion of six inscriptions from Mathurā.)

A. Führer. *Indo-skythic architecture and sculpture of the Mathurā school.* Journal Indian Art and Industry. Vol. V (1894), p. 58; plates 85—87.

(Abstract from an unpublished report on his Mathurā excavations).

A. Führer. *The monumental antiquities and inscriptions in the North-Western Provinces and Oudh,* Allahabad 1891.

(Mathurā district, pp. 97—111).

Annual Progress Reports of the Archaeological Survey Circle, North-Western Provinces and Oudh.

V. A. Smith. *Græco-Roman influence on the civilisation of ancient India.* Journal Asiatic Society of Bengal. Volume LVIII (1889), part I. pp. 107—198; Volume LXI (1892), part I, pp. 50—76 and Vol. LXII (1893) part I, pp. 84—87.

A. Grünwedel. *Buddhistische Kunst in Indien*; mit 76 Abbildungen. Berlin 1893.—Zweite Auflage; mit 102 Abbildungen. Berlin 1900.

(See index i.v. Mathurā).

A. Grünwedel. *Buddhist Art in India,* translated by Agnes C. Gibson, revised and enlarged by Jas. Burgess; with 154 illustrations. London, 1901.

(See index i.v. Mathurā).

J. Burgess. *The ancient monuments, temples and sculptures of India.* Part I, London, 1897.

(For Mathurā sculptures see plates 55, 58—61, and 155-156. The female statue figured inplates 56-57 is now preserved in the Lahore Museum, but will be returned to Mathurā).

S. F. Oldenburg. *Notes on Buddhist art*, translated from the Russian by Leo Wiener. Journal American Oriental Society. Vol. XVIII (1897), pp. 183—201.

(Representations of *jātakas* at Bharhut, Ajāṇṭā and Boro-Boedoer).

T. Bloch. *Buddha worshipped by Indra.* Proceedings Asiatic Society of Bengal for 1898, pp. 186—189.

(Discussion of Mathurā sculpture M. 7, in the Calcutta Museum, representing Indra worshipping Buddha in the Indraśaila cave.)

V. A. Smith. *The Jain Stūpa and other antiquities of Mathurā.* Archaeological Survey of India. New Imperial series. Vol. XX. North-Western Provinces and Oudh, Vol. V. Allahabad, 1901.

(Hundred and seven plates of drawings illustrating sculptures excavated by Dr. Führer from the Kaṅkālī Ṭīlā, with brief notes. Reviewed by A. F[oucher.] Bulletin de l'école française d'Extrême-Orient. Tome I (1901) p. 375.)

A. Foucher. *L'art bouddhique dans l'Inde d'après un livre récent.* Revue de l'histoire des religions. Tome XXX (1895), pp. 319—371.

(Review of Grünwedel's *Buddhistische Kunst in Indien.*)

A. Foucher. *Étude sur l'iconographie bouddhique de l'Inde.* Paris 1900 and 1905.

(See index i. v. Matra or Mathurā).

A. Foucher. *Les bas-reliefs du stūpa de Sikri (Gandhāra).* Journal asiatique (1903) pp. 185—330.

(Reference to miniature *stūpa* no. N, 2 in Mathurā Museum, p. 323 ; see also p. 210, footnote.)

A. Foucher. *L'art gréco-bouddhique du Gandhāra.* Tome I. Paris 1905.

(On Mathurā see pp. 211, 212, 217, 222, 248, 252, 260, 494, 556, 602, 614, 615 ; figs. 93, 94, 282. Reviewed in Göttingische Gelehrte Anzeigen for 1906, pp. 533 – 552. See p. 650).

H Lüders. *Epigraphical Notes.* Indian Antiquary, Vol. XXXIII (1904), pp. 33—41 ; pp. 101—109 and pp. 149—156.

(Corrected readings of forty-four Mathurā inscriptions previously edited by Dowson, Mitra, Cunningham and Bühler).

A. Barth. *L'inscription P sur le chapiteau de lion de Mathurā.* Comptes rendus des séances de l'Académie des Inscriptions et Belles Lettres, 1907, p. 384.

The inscription P on the Mathurā Lion-capital, translated by G. Tamson in Indian Antiquary, Vol. XXXVII (1908), pp. 245—250.

F. W. Thomas. *The inscriptions on the Mathurā Lion-capital.* Epigraphia Indica, Vol. IX, pp. 135—147.

J. Ph. Vogel. *The Mathurā School of sculpture.* Annual Report Archaeological Survey, 1906-7, pp. 137—160, plates LI—LVI.

J. Ph. Vogel. *Notes de sculpture bouddhique.* Bulletin de l' École française d' Extrême-Orient. Tome VIII (1908) pp. 487—500 and IX (1909) pp. 523—532.

R. D. Banerji. *Mathurā Inscriptions in the Indian Museum* in Journal and Proceedings Asiatic Society of Bengal (New Series) Vol. V; No. 7, 1909, pp. 237—244, plates X—XI.

R. D. Banerji. *The discovery of seven new-dated Records of the Scythian Period* in Journal and Proceedings Asiatic Society of Bengal (New Series) Vol. V, no. 8, 1909, pp. 271—277.

J. Ph. Vogel. *Nāga worship in ancient Mathurā.* Annual Report, Archaeological Survey, 1908-9.

ABBREVIATIONS.

A. S. R.	...	Archaeological Survey Report.
B. E. F. E. O.	...	Bulletin de l' Ecole française d' Extrême-Orient,
Ep. Ind.	...	Epigraphia Indica.
Ind. Ant.	...	Indian Antiquary.
J. A.	...	Journal Asiatique.
J. A. O. S.	...	Journal American Oriental Society.
J. A. S. B.	...	Journal Asiatic Society of Bengal.
J. R. A. S.	...	Journal Royal Asiatic Society.
J. I. A. I.	...	Journal of Indian Art and Industry.
S. B. E.	...	Sacred Books of the East.
Z. D. M. G.	...	Zeitschrift der Deutschen Morgenländischen Gesellschaft.

PLATE I.

THE MUSEUM AT MATHURA.

INTRODUCTION.

I.—The Mathurā Museum.

The history of the building in which the Mathurā collection of sculptures is preserved, is given by Mr. Growse* in the following passage: "It was commenced by Mr. Thornhill, the Magistrate and Collector of the district, who raised the money for the purpose by public subscription, intending to make of it a rest-house for the reception of native gentlemen of rank, whenever they had occasion to visit head quarters. Though close to the Courts, which would be a convenience, it is too far from the bazar to suit native tastes, and even if it had been completed according to the original design, it is not probable that it would ever have been occupied. After an expenditure of Rs. 30,000,† the work was interrupted by the Mutiny. When order had been restored, the new Collector, Mr. Best, with a perversity by no means uncommon in the records of Indian local administration, set himself at once, not to complete, but to mutilate, his predecessor's handiwork. It was intended that the building should stand in extensive grounds of its own, where it would certainly have had a very pleasing architectural effect; but instead of this the high road was brought immediately in front of it, so as to cut it off entirely from the new public garden; the offices of the Tahsīldar were built on one side, and on the other was run up, at a most awkward angle, a high masonry wall; a rough thatched roof was thrown over its centre court; doorways were introduced in different places, where they were not wanted and only served as disfigurements and the unfortunate building was then nick-named 'Thornhill's Folly' and abandoned to utter neglect."

"It remained thus till 1874, when the idea of converting it into a Museum received the support of Sir John Strachey, who sanctioned from provincial funds a grant-in-aid of Rs. 3,500."

"The first step taken was to raise the centre court by the addition of a clerestory, with windows of reticulated stone tracery, and to cover it with a stone vault, in which (so far as constructional peculiarities are

---

**Mathurā* 2nd ed. pp. 152 ff.; 3rd ed. pp. 163 ff. Cf. also *Indian Antiquary*, Vol. VI, p. 216.

†The figure 50,000 mentioned in *Indian Antiquary*, Vol. VI, p. 216, as the amount spent before 1857, is evidently due to a misprint.

concerned), I reproduced the roof of the now ruined temple of Harideva at Gobardhan. The cost amounted to Rs. 5,336. A porch was afterwards added at a further outlay of Rs. 8,494; but for this I am not responsible. It is a beautiful design, well executed, and so far it reflects great credit on Yúsuf, the Municipal architect; but it is too delicate for an exterior façade on the side of a dusty road. Something plainer would have answered the purpose as well, besides having a more harmonious effect; and money would then have been available for the completion of the doors and windows, without which the building can scarcely be used, and for which there is now no provision, nor likely to be."

"Though the cost of the building has been so very considerable, nearly Rs. 44,000, it is only of small dimensions; but the whole wall surface in the central court is a mass of geometric and flowered decorations of the most artistic character. The bands of natural foliage, a feature introduced by Mr. Thornhill's own fancy, are very boldly cut and in themselves decidedly handsome, but they are not altogether in accord with the conventional designs of native style by which they are surrounded."

"The following Urdū inscription is worked into the cornice of the central hall":—

> 'The State having thought good to promote the ease of its subjects, gave intimation to the Magistrate and Collector; who then, by the co-operation of the chief men of Mathurā, had this house for travellers built, with the choicest carved work *. Its doors and walls are polished like a mirror; in its sculpture every kind of flower-bed appears in view; its width and height were assigned in harmonious proportion; from top to bottom it is well shaped and well balanced. It may very properly be compared to the dome of Afrasyáb, or it may justly be styled the palace of an emperor. One who saw its magnificence (*or* the poet Shaukat on seeing it) composed this *tārīkh*: So elegant a rest-house makes even the flower garden envious.'

"* Upon the word *munabbat*, which is used here to denote arabesque carving, the late Mr. Blochmann communicated the following note:—"The Arabic *nabata* means 'to plant, and the intensive form of the verb has either the same signification or that of 'causing to appear like plants,' hence *munabbat* comes to mean 'traced with flowers,' and may be compared with *mushajjar*, 'caused to appear like trees,' which is the word applied to silk with tree-patterns on it, like the more common *buta-dár*."

"As the building afforded such very scant accommodation, I proposed to make it not a general, but simply an architectural and antiquarian museum, arranging in it, in chronological series, specimens of all the different styles that have prevailed in the neighbourhood, from the reign of the Indo-Scythian Kanishka, in the century immediately before Christ, down to the Victorian period, which would be illustrated in perfection by the building itself."

A vernacular record of Accounts in the Municipal Office shows that in the year 1875 Mr. Vigram, the then Magistrate and Collector of Mathurā, received from the Raises and Zamindars of the Mathurā district a sum of Rs. 6,096 in the shape of subscriptions; and the money so raised was spent on the completion of the building. The work was done under the management of the Superintendent of the Mathurā Municipality and was finished in the year 1878.

It appears, however, that in reality the whole work was not completed until 1881. For Mr. Growse notes the following in the introduction to the second edition of his "Mathurā" which is dated Bulandshahr, June 29, 1880. "The Museum has again been taken in hand, and in the course of a year or so will, I trust, be ready for use. Noticing in one of my recent visits to Mathurā that the collection of antiquities which I had left behind me was utterly uncared for, and that some of the valuable inscriptions had disappeared, though it is possible General Cunningham may have taken them, I represented the matter to the local Government, and was thereupon allowed to submit plans for the completion of the building which have been accepted and are now being carried out." It seems, therefore, that 1881 is the year in which the Museum was opened to the public. In March 1882, when Cunningham visited Mathurā for the last time, he found the Museum established.

From Municipal records I have been able to gather only the following additional information: "In the year 1889," it is said,* "on the report of the Tehsíldar of Muttra, the Municipal Board appointed a *farrásh* on Rs. 3 a month to look after the building and keep the rooms and the images in the Museum clean and in proper order. It was from this time that the Museum building came under the control and supervision of the Municipal Board. All the expenditure incurred on repairs &c. to the building since that year has been borne by the Municipality."

* Note by Man Mohan Lal, Secretary, Municipal Board, Muttra, dated the 15th December 1899.

In 1900 it was decided by the Local Government * that the sculptures contained in the Museum also should be formally made over to the Mathurā Municipal Board "on condition that they are properly looked after." It was also stipulated that "a list of the relics should be kept in the building and a copy recorded in the Collector's Office."

It is much to be regretted that the necessity for such a list was only recognised at a time when the find-place of most of the sculptures could no longer be ascertained. Let us hope that in the future all new acquisitions will be registered and that an exact record will be kept of the circumstances of each find. Up to 1908 there was no officer specially appointed to look after the Mathurā Museum. The whole *personnel* consisted of the above-mentioned *farrāsh* on Rs. 3 a month, whose appointment apparently led to the building having come under the control of the Municipal Board.

In January, 1908, the Museum was visited by Sir John and Lady Hewett. In the same month, previous to the Lieutenant-Governor's visit, Lieutenant-Colonel W. Vost, I.M.S., had consented to act as an Honorary Curator of the Museum for the period he will be stationed at Mathurā, and Pandit Radha Krishna had declared himself willing to devote his energies to the Museum in the honorary capacity of Assistant Curator. This double appointment has proved of the greatest benefit, and there is every reason to hope that in future district officers will take a more active interest in the antiquarian treasures entrusted to their care. The value of the sculptures in the Museum has not always been fully recognised even by Government officials, as appears from the following marginal notes which I found on an official letter dating back to the time when the question of their ownership had been raised. *Query:* "To whom do the relics belong? If they were sold, who would take the proceeds?" *Reply:* "The relics were collected by Mr. Growse and Dr. Führer by digging a *tila* in the city. They belong to Government, I think, and no one would buy them as they are mostly broken."

What I have been able to gather from previous publications regarding the origin of the sculptures, I wish to discuss in a following section dealing with the archaeological explorations carried on at Mathurā. Here it will suffice to say that the bulk of the original collection consists of sculptures

---

* Government Order P. W. D. no. 294M./222, dated 5th February 1900, to the Commissioner of the Agra Division. It appears that a complaint made in November 1899 by Babu P. C. Mukharji about the neglected state of the Mathurā Museum first drew the attention of the Local Government to the matter.

and inscriptions excavated by Mr. Growse from different mounds round the city. Several of them are described by him in the various papers which he devoted to the antiquities of Mathurā. I am not aware that any of the sculptures excavated by Dr. Führer from the Kaṅkālī Ṭīlā have been placed in the Museum. All his acquisitions have gone to Lucknow.

It would seem that since the days of Mr. Growse, the collection remained stationery. Of late years I have been able to add to it four Mathurā sculptures and inscriptions which Cunningham had placed in the Lahore Museum, the female statue of the Saptarshi Ṭīlā and three inscribed Jaina sculptures which I found in the Delhi Museum and which likewise originate from Mathurā. In December, 1907, a collection of nearly a hundred Mathurā sculptures, which for many years had been lying in the Public Library at Allahābād, were, at my request, returned to the place of their origin. They belong to the sculptures excavated in 1860 from the Jamālpur (or Jail) mound.*

It is hoped that, in the course of time, other sculptures also which originate from those early excavations and have become scattered will be returned. The Mathurā sculptures which are preserved in the Calcutta and Lucknow Museums, it will be advisable to leave where they are, except in case a piece can be shown to belong to a monument of which other portions are in the Mathurā Museum. This, for instance, would apply to the Bhūtēsar railing pillars. The bulk of sculptures in the Lucknow Museum are from one site, namely, the Kaṅkālī Ṭīlā; and there is, therefore, less reason for returning them to Mathurā. But the case is different with the sculptures which reached Lucknow viâ Agra and Allahābād and which, like the Allahābād collection, are the produce of the excavation of the Jamālpur site.

At present, however, the limited space available in the Mathurā Museum, does not allow of any considerable increase of the exhibits. We can only hope that the principle will be adopted and adhered to, that all sculptures acquired in future will be kept in the local Museum. If systematic excavations at Mathurā are ever resumed and prove fruitful in their results, the question of extending the present building will have to be considered. Recently, I have made certain proposals for the improvement of the Museum building, which are intended to remedy the want of light and render it more suitable for its present purpose. Of late

* Since writing the above, the collection has been considerably extended by purchases made by Pandit Radha Krishna, the necessary funds having been placed at his disposal by Mr. J. H. Marshall, Director-General of Archaeology.

years it has been the policy of the Government to establish local Museums in important archaeological centres, such as Sārnāth, Delhi and Peshāwar. For the study of Indian archaeology such Museums are eminently useful, as their contents can be studied in connection with the topography of the find-places; and in the eyes of the general public, the vicinity of their place of origin will lend the sculptures an additional interest. The existence of a local Museum, moreover, minimises the risk of occasional finds being lost, and of valuable antiquities becoming damaged in transit. Finally a local museum commends itself to the practical mind on account of the saving of money and labour it involves. The sums spent in past years on the removal of large numbers of bulky stones from Mathurā to Agra, Lucknow, Allahābād and Calcutta would have been better used for the benefit of the local collection.

II.—Explorations.

The first discovery of sculptures recorded at Mathurā was that of the so-called Silenus* now preserved in the Indian Museum at Calcutta. It was acquired by Colonel L. R. Stacy and presented by him to the Asiatic Society of Bengal. The same officer presented to the Society a railing pillar† which likewise has reached the Calcutta Museum. It has on one side a female figure standing on the back of a dwarf and holding in her right hand a small wicker cage, the bird from which is perched on her left shoulder. On the reverse are three panels with scenes which, according to Cunningham, refer to the miracle of Rājagṛiha—Buddha subduing the elephant Nālāgiri let loose against him by his malicious cousin Devadatta. This pillar must have belonged to the same railing as the two in the Mathurā Museum (nos. J, 4 and J, 5).

In January, 1853, General Sir A. Cunningham noticed some capitals and pillars in the Kaṭrā enclosure. The first sculpture obtained by him on this site was a fragment of a railing pillar with part of a female figure standing under a tree, which he erroneously identified with Māyā standing under the *sāl* tree. At the same time he discovered a fragmentary inscription containing the genealogy of the Gupta Emperors down to Samudragupta, and which may be assigned to the reign of Chandragupta II (c. A. D. 400). Both these objects were first deposited in the Lahore Museum, but have, at my request, been returned to Mathurā

* *J. A. S. B.* Vol. V (1836) p. 567 ff. (plate). Anderson, *Catalogue.* Part I, p. 169 ff. no. M, 1. Burgess, *Ancient Monuments*, plates 60-61.

† Anderson, *Catalogue* p. 186 ff no M, 15a. Cunningham, *A. S. R.* Vol. III, p. 21, plate VII. Burgess, *Ancient Monuments*, plate 59. *Cf.* also Kittoe, *J. A. S. B.* Vol. XVI (1847) p. 335.

a. No. P, 1 ; Ht. 2'.

c. No. P, 55 ; Ht. 3'6".

d. No. P, 54 ; Ht 3 6".

b. No. P, 2 ; Ht. 2' 10".

ARCHITECTURAL FRAGMENTS.

and are now placed in the local Museum (nos. J, 40 and Q, 5). Cunningham mentions, moreover, "two large capitals of columns, one of them being no less than 3 feet in diameter, with a shaft of 23 inches diameter." These evidently were left in the Katrā square, and have since disappeared. *

In 1862 Cunningham resumed his exploration of the Katrā site and obtained a "peculiarly curved architrave of a Buddhist gateway richly sculptured on both sides with buildings, figures and trees including a representation of a gateway itself." This is evidently no. M, 1 of the Museum, which was among the sculptures returned to Mathurā from Allahābād in December 1907. (Cf. pl. XXV). The most important discovery made here was that of a standing Buddha image (height 4′ 3¼″), which was found inside a well. It bears an inscription which is dated in the Gupta year 230 (A. D. 549-50), and records that the image was dedicated by the Buddhist nun Jayabhaṭṭā to the Yaśā-vihāra.

From this it may be inferred that a Buddhist sanctuary of this name once stood on the Katrā site, and was still extant in the middle of the sixth century. On its ruins there rose in afterdays a Hindū temple dedicated to Vishṇu under the name of Kesab Dev, which apparently was seen by the travellers Tavernier, Bernier and Manucci, † but was shortly after destroyed by order of Aurangzeb, who raised a mosque over it. The plan of the temple is still traceable. The inscribed Buddha image was removed to Agra, but is now preserved in the Lucknow Provincial Museum (no. B 10).

In the same well from which the Buddha image was extracted, were found five other pieces of sculpture including a colossal arm and hand and a statuette of Buddha seated in meditation, with an incomplete inscription in Gupta characters engraved on its base.

In 1860, when the foundations of the Collector's Court-house were laid, a mound overhanging the Agra road 1¾ miles from the Holi Gate, had partly to be cleared. Growse calls it the Jamālpur mound from an adjoining hamlet of that name, whereas Cunningham refers to it as "Jail mound." The latter designation is somewhat misleading, as the present jail is nearly half a mile further down the Grand Trunk Road on the

* Cunningham, *A. S. R.* Vol. I, p. 237, and Vol. III, p. 15; plates IV and XII A and B. The inscription found by Cunningham (*A. S. R.* Vol. III, p. 37, no. 24, plate XVI) has been edited by Fleet, *Gupta Inscriptions*, p. 25 ff. no. 4.

† Tavernier, *Voyages* (Paris, 1678) Vol. II, p. 71. Bernier, *Voyages* (Amsterdam, 1699) Vol. II, p. 76. Manucci, *Storia do Mogor* (transl: Irvine) Vol. I, p. 298 f. "an ancient Hindū town called Matora (Mathurā) distant eighteen leagues from Agrah where there is an imposing temple." Cf. *Proc A. S. B.* for 1878 p. 15.

other side of the Teḥṣīl and Museum buildings. I have, therefore, adopted the name "Jamālpur mound." It proved to contain sculptural remains in large quantity such as statues, bas-reliefs, pillars, portions of railings, small stone *stūpas* and umbrellas. Cunningham mentions the left hand of a statue measuring 1′ across the palm (no. A, 23), two colossal standing Buddha statues, 7½′ in height, two seated ones of life size, and one somewhat smaller in size. The most remarkable piece of sculpture which came to light here was, according to Cunningham, a female figure, which from its attitude reminded him of the Venus of the Capitol. It is now preserved in the Lucknow Museum.

Three statues of lions (ht. 3′) similar to those in the Mathurā Museum (nos. O, 1-7) were also discovered on this occasion. Exceedingly numerous were the railing pillars which exhibit three different types, 4′ 6″, 3′ 8″ and 2′ 9″ respectively in height, and consequently seem to have belonged to three different railings. Among the six specimens of the smallest type, two were found to be marked with the numerals 118 * and 129. Moreover a fragment of a cross-bar (Sanskrit *sūchi*) turned up, which must have made part of the medium-size railing, and a coping-stone, ornamented on both faces with semi-circular panels or niches containing figures and flowers. Among the sculptures discovered in the Jamālpur mound there were several bearing inscriptions. According to Growse, three were dated in the reign of Kanishka and several in that of Huvishka. In this connection I must also mention the discovery of thirty bases of columns, fifteen of them inscribed with dedicatory inscriptions. Growse mentions that the whole collection of sculptures discovered in the Jamālpur (or Jail) mound was removed to Agra and thence to Allahābād. The bulk ultimately found a resting place in the Lucknow Museum. An exception, however, was made with the thirty pillar bases; of these ten were sent to the Calcutta Museum, while the rest remained at Mathurā and are now in the local Museum. †

After Mr. Growse's transfer from the district ‡ the Jamālpur mound was completely levelled at a cost of Rs. 7,236. This was done as a famine work under the supervision of his successor.† Some of the

* That marked with the numeral 118 is no. J, 15 of the Mathurā Museum, the other is at Lucknow (no. B 91).

†See beneath nos. P, 20-53.

‡Mr. Growse was Joint Magistrate under Mr. Hardinge whom he succeeded as Collector. (The "Hardinge Gate" is dated A.D. 1870). He was transferred to Bulandshahr early in 1877. The excavation was probably done in the famine year 1877-8.

sculptures obtained on this occasion are now in the Calcutta Museum; the others apparently remained at Mathurā. One at least is now in the local Museum, namely, the beautiful standing Buddha statue (no. A, 5). The inscription on its base records that it was dedicated by the Buddhist friar Yaśadinna; judging from the script, it must belong to the fifth century of our era. (Cf. pl. IX).

The inscribed pedestal dated in the Gupta year 135 (A. D.454-55), which was among the sculptures in the Allahābād Institute and is now in the Museum (no. A, 48), is also said to originate from this site.*

Growse speaks of an inscription of some length commencing with the words :—*Mahārājasya Devaputrasya Huvishkasya saṁvatsare* 51 *Hemanta-māsa* 1 *div*. . . . It is not among the inscriptions edited by Cunningham and others; it is now at Lucknow (no. B, 3). A third inscribed slab is recorded by Growse to have been found after Cunningham's visit, beginning with the word *Siddham* followed by a date, and consisting of at least seven lines of writing. This appears to be the slab erected "at the place sacred to the Lord, the Nāga king Dadhikarṇa" which is now in the Lucknow Museum (no. 56). †

Here I may also mention a fragmentary inscription now in the Mathurā Museum (no. A, 49), which was found by Growse in the compound of the Magistrate's Court-house and which, as he supposes, was excavated from the Jamālpur mound in 1860, but thrown aside as of no value. It is dated in the year 28, and in the reign of a king whose name is partly lost. Growse assumed that it was to be assigned to the reign of Kanishka, but Professor Lüders has pointed out that more probably the name is to be restored as *Hushka*.

In a small mound half a mile due west of the Jamālpur mound Growse discovered the lower portions of two large seated figures. The one was a Buddha image with a partly obliterated inscription, of which the only legible words were *varsha māse 2 divas 6*‡. The other is described by Growse as "a woman with her left hand clasping an infant in her lap. One foot rests on an elaborately ornamented stool, the other is doubled under her body. There are five small accessory figures, one in front and two on either side at the back."

---

* Cunningham. *A.S.R.* Vol. III, p. 36, no. 22 and Fleet, *Gupta Inscr.* p. 262 ff. no. 63.

† Bühler, *Ep. Ind.* Vol. I, p. 390, no. XVIII, where it is erroneously stated that the slab was found in the Kaṅkālī Ṭīlā. *Cf.* Growse, *Mathurā*, 2nd ed. p. 108 and facsimile.

‡ It is in the Lucknow Museum (no. B, 18).

Growse states definitely that in 1860, in digging the foundations of the Magistrate's court-house (*kachahri*), thirty bases of columns were found, partly inscribed with dedicatory inscriptions. According to Cunningham the number of inscribed bases amounted to fifteen. Ten out of these thirty pillar bases were presented to the Asiatic Society of Bengal on the 3rd September 1862 by the Honourable G. F. Edmonstone, Lieutenant-Governor of the North-Western (now United) Provinces. *

The inscriptions on these bases were simultaneously edited by Dowson and Mitra. The number published by Mitra is fourteen, that of Dowson fifteen, which agrees with the figure mentioned by Cunningham. Evidently the inscriptions are the same, though the readings differ considerably. Mitra notes of eight out of the fourteen inscriptions that they were deposited in the Museum of the Asiatic Society.

What became of the twenty remaining pillar bases is not distinctly stated. When in 1881-2 Cunningham inspected the Mathurā Museum, he found not twenty but thirty bases of Indo-Scythian pillars. Twenty-seven of these were lying outside the building, and this was still the case in April, 1905, when I had them placed inside. Fourteen of them are inscribed. We must assume that in addition to the thirty specimens discovered in 1860 several more had come to light in 1877-8, when the Jamālpur mound was levelled. But of this "excavation" no record is available.

Cunningham† mentions that a few were still "lying about" at Agra and Allahābād. Among the sculptures in the Allahābād Public Library I found indeed two such bases, one of which bears an inscription. These have now been returned to the Mathurā Museum. One more was discovered by my photographer in a wall at the entrance of the Teḥṣīl building. The Museum now contains thirty-four specimens, one is in the Lucknow Museum and two were recently discovered by Mr. Marshall at the Tāj at Agra, where they had been used as supports of modern lamp-posts. It is intended to return these also to Mathurā.

The total number of these bases, including the Calcutta ones, amounts, therefore, to forty-seven, of which at least thirty-one bear votive inscriptions. These epigraphs are of exceptional interest, as one of them

---

* *A. S. R.* Vol. I, p. 239. Anderson, *Catalogue*, part I, pp. 176—179. The inscriptions on these ten pillar-bases have lately been re-edited by Babu R. D. Banerji in *Journal and Proceedings Asiatic Society of Bengal* (New Series) Vol. V, no. 7; 1909, p. 237f.

† *A. S. R.* Vol. XVII, p. 107.

contains the name of the monastery to which they belonged, while four supply the date of its construction. It is much to be deplored, however, that at the time of their discovery no notice was taken of their position, and no plan was made of the building in which they were found. Any interesting information they might have supplied regarding the architecture of the Indo-Scythian period has thus been lost.

When in March and November 1871 Cunningham revisited Mathurā, he devoted his attention mainly to two other important sites: the Kaṅkālī Ṭīlā and the Chaubārā mounds. The former, situated half a mile to the south of the Kaṭrā, has proved the most prolific of all the sites around Mathurā. The first discovery of sculptures* had been made some years previously by men digging for bricks. Subsequently the mound was partially trenched by Mr. Hardinge and two colossal standing Buddha (?) images (ht. 7′ 6″) came to light, which apparently were sent to Agra and thence to Allahābād. (Cf. above p. 8).

In the course of his excavations at the western end of the Kaṅkālī Ṭīlā, Cunningham obtained many broken statues of Tīrthaṁkaras, some of which were inscribed, as well as pillars and cross-bars of railings. He speaks also of brick walls and pavements, but unfortunately no drawings of these structural remains are now available. They prove, as Cunningham remarks, that the Kaṅkālī Ṭīlā was the site of some important Jaina building which existed during the rule of the Indo-Scythians. The twelve inscriptions discussed by him range in date from the year 5 in the reign of Kanishka to the year 98 in that of Vāsudeva. To these is to be added an inscription of the year 39 in Huvishka's reign inscribed on an elephant capital which Cunningham discovered in a garden near the Kaṅkālī Ṭīlā and which has since disappeared. That the Jain establishment, which once occupied this site, existed down to the Muhammadan period, is proved by inscribed Jina images dated in the 12th century of the Vikrama era †

In the space between the Kaṅkālī Ṭīlā and the Kaṭrā, stands a temple dedicated to Śiva under the name of Bhūtēsar (Sanskrit *Bhūteśvara*

* Growse, *Mathurā* 2nd ed. p. 109, gives a list of eight sculptures discovered in the Kaṅkālī Ṭīlā, some of which are now in the Museum. The northern portion of the mound was apparently examined by Mr. Growse in 1875.

† Growse, *Mathurā* p. 119, mentions an image dated *saṁvat* 1134; Führer, *Provincial Museum Report* 1888-9 "four basements of Jina statues inscribed *saṁvat* 1134" and in that for 1890-1 "two colossal images with the dates *saṁvat* 1036 (*read* 1038) and 1134 found in 1889 and another donative inscription dated *saṁvat* 1080." These three are in the Lucknow Museum.

"Lord of Demons"). At the back of this shrine there rises a high mound of limited circumference. The large railing pillar (no. J,1) in the Mathurā Museum once stood on the top of this mound and was thence removed by Mr. Growse. It is carved with the nearly life-size figure of a female parasol-bearer. Over it is a bas-relief with a scene presumably relating to some *jātaka*. The railing to which this pillar, as the mortices at the sides indicate, belonged, must have been one of unusual size. Cunningham noticed on it the symbol for 100 and inferred from it that the railing consisted of no less than a hundred similar posts.*

To the south of the Bhūtēsar temple is a tank known as Balbhadar Kuṇḍ. In the enclosing wall Growse noticed eleven cross-bars of a railing, measuring 1′ 3″ in length and ornamented with a rosette, a lotus, a winged monster and similar devices. Four were removed by Cunningham, the others were left on the spot. From an adjoining well was recovered a plain pillar measuring 4′ 7″ in height by 11″ in width and carved with two rosettes. This is probably no. J, 3 of the Museum collection, though it should be noted that the height is in reality 6′ 2½″.

An important discovery was made on the same site. Built into the verandah of a native rest-house (*dharmsālā* or *chaupāl*) were found five well-preserved railing pillars, two of which are now in the Museum (nos. J, 4 and 5). They are 4′ 8″ high and 11″ wide; the front of each is carved with a nearly nude female figure standing on a prostrate dwarf. Above is shown a balcony, over which two smaller figures are partly visible. The back of each pillar is carved with three bas-reliefs. In one case (no. J, 4) the scenes evidently refer to the birth-story of Viśvantara (*Viśvantara-jātaka*), and in the other instance (no. J,5) to that of the tigress (*Vyāghrī-jātaka*).

Not only do these five pillars belong to the same railing, but the one previously acquired by Colonel Stacy, which exhibits a similar type, may safely be added to their number. Cunningham makes, moreover, mention of two fragments which he assigns to the same monument.

Two of the five pillars discovered in 1871 were sent to Calcutta, where they are now preserved in the Indian Museum together with the one of Colonel Stacy. The remaining three specimens were intended by Mr. Growse to be placed in his Museum; but at present only two

* *A. S. R.*, Vol. III, p. 21, Growse, *Mathurā*, 3rd ed. p. 120. The numeral in question appears to me to be 30.

a. No. J, 24; Ht. 1' 7".

c. No. J, 18; Ht. 2' 4'.

RAILING PILLAR FRAGMENTS.

may be seen here. The third has reached the Lucknow Provincial Museum, presumably *viâ* Agra and Allahābād.

It is much to be regretted that these pillars, which originate from one monument, have thus been injudiciously dispersed. The intention evidently was to have specimens in various Museums. But it should be noticed that these pillars, though similar in type, are by no means identical. Only if placed side by side, as on the photograph published by Dr. Burgess,* do they give us some idea of the effect they produced in their original position. Besides, it is a fact not at once recognised, that the bas-reliefs carved on the back relate to *jātaka* stories divided in a series of scenes over different pillars. No. J, 4, for instance, contains only one passage of the story of Viśvantara. The distribution of these pillars over various Museums is almost as bad as the Indian practice of dividing a valuable manuscript among the heirs of its deceased owner.

Another important site explored by Cunningham in 1871 is that of Chaubārā or Chauvārā†, consisting of a group of some twelve mounds situated about a mile to the south-west of the Kaṭrā. In 1868, when the Sonkh road was laid through one of these mounds (D), a gold reliquary had come to light. It was presented to Mr. Growse and apparently remained in his possession. Cunningham opened another of these mounds (A) and discovered in its centre a steatite relic casket, which is now in the Calcutta Museum. In mound B he unearthed a Persepolitan capital (ht. 2′) formed by four recumbent animals with human faces, curved-down horns and wings. This remarkable sculpture is now preserved in the Calcutta Museum (M,14).‡

A fourth mound (C) yielded a colossal head (ht. 14″) and the right knee of a seated figure with the left foot on the calf of the leg. Both fragments evidently belong to a Buddha statue of nearly double life-size. Growse mentions that a knee of a colossal statue found by Cunningham was placed in the Mathurā Museum. Presumably it is the one just referred to, and no. A, 24 of the collection. At the foot of the same mound Cunningham found part of a seated image with the left hand resting on the left knee. The missing right hand must have

---

* *Ancient Monuments*, plates 58-59.

† According to Growse (*Mathurā* p. 122) the site is named after a rest-house (*chauvārā*) which once stood on this spot.

‡ *A. S. R.*, Vol. III, p. 18, plate III, Anderson, *Catalogue*, part I, p. 186.

been raised towards the shoulder in the attitude of protection *(abhaya-mudrā.)*

Subsequently to Cunningham's visit Growse explored one of the Chaubārā mounds, apparently the same which had yielded the steatite relic vase. His researches resulted in the discovery of a colossal head "of very Egyptian cast of features," with a round hole in its forehead, probably meant to contain a precious stone as indication of the *ūrṇā*. It must be no. A, 27 of the Museum. He also acquired the lower portion of a large-size seated Buddha (Lucknow Museum no. B, 2) with an inscription dated in the year 33 and in Huvishka's reign, several pillars and cross-bars of railings and "a great number of small fragments of male and female figures, animals, grotesques and decorative patterns." Sculpture no. J, 7 in the Mathurā Museum was also found on this occasion; the description of it given by Growse is somewhat misleading. Another sculpture he describes as representing "a capacious throne resembling a garden chair of rustic wood-work, with a foot-stool in front of it and some drapery spread over the seat, on which is placed a relic casket. In the background are two figures leaning over the high back of the chair."*

Some twenty paces from the base of the mound in which these discoveries had been made, Growse came upon a pavement with three large, square, graduated pedestals, of which apparently two were *in situ*. He surmises that the Persepolitan capital, found by Cunningham, formed part of a pillar to which one of these pedestals belonged. They were placed in the local Museum.† On the margin of an ancient tank adjoining the mound, Growse found a stone fragment inscribed with three letters in ancient Brāhmī, which he read : *Dānaṁ chha*.

Besides the main sites mentioned above, Growse speaks of several extensive mounds, in nearly all of which he made some trial excavation. In one of them, situated between the Chaubārā mounds and the Kaṅkālī Ṭīlā, he discovered "a few arabesque fragments, and, at a depth of six feet below the surface, a small pediment containing in a niche, flanked by fabulous monsters and surmounted by the mystic wheel, a figure of Buddha, canopied by a many-headed serpent and seated on a lion throne." It must be identical with our no. B, 26; but it should be noted that the central figure is not a Buddha, but a Tīrthaṁkara.

---

* *Mathurā*, 2nd ed. p. 114 and *J. A. S. B.* Vol. XLVII p. 119, plate XX. The fragment is no longer traceable. It is also shown on no. 841 of the photographic negatives of the Indian Museum (Dr. Bloch's *List*, p. 35).

† They may perhaps be identified with nos. R, 33 and 34.

A mound near the boundary pillar of Mathurā, Mahōlī and Pālī-khēṛā, due south of the Kaṅkālī Ṭīlā and east of the Girdharpur mound produced "a strange squat figure of a dwarf, 3′ 9″ high and 2′ broad," which may safely be identified with no. C, 3 of the Mathurā Museum. (Cf. pl. XIV).

In another mound just outside the Pālī-khēṛā village an important find was made by Growse in the cold weather of 1873-4. It is the so-called Bacchanalian group, one of the most remarkable sculptures in the Mathurā Museum (no. C, 2). It may be compared with Colonel Stacy's "Silenus" in the Calcutta Museum, but as the latter is smaller in size (ht. 3′ 8″), there is no reason to assume that the two sculptures are counterparts and belonged to the same monument. (Cf. pl. XIII).

In the same mound Growse discovered *in situ* "three bell-shaped bases of large columns at 13 feet distance from one another, at the three corners of a square." This would seem to indicate that the Pālī-khēṛā mound marks the site of a temple. In the space between the pillar-bases were found "some small figures of baked clay, glazed, of a bluish colour, similar in character to the toys still sold at Hindu fairs; also a few small fragments of carved stone and some corroded pieces of metal bangles." These objects do not seem to have been preserved. The pillar-bases are still on the spot where Growse discovered them.

In addition to the antiquities obtained in the course of his explorations, Mr. Growse rescued for the Museum some sculptures and inscriptions, which had been found accidentally and were being misused.

The base of a large-seated statue (no. B, 29 of the Mathurā Museum), bearing an inscription dated in the year 50 and in Huvishka's reign, he found set up by a subordinate in the Public Works department to protect a culvert on the high road through cantonments. An inscribed pillar base (no. P, 22) had been plastered and whitewashed and embedded in one of the side pillars of the Teḥṣīl Gateway.*

Finally, I may mention the figure of the Nāga (no. C, 15) which Growse obtained from the village of Kukargāma in the Sa'dābād *parganā* of the Mathurā district.†

Cunningham's last visit to Mathurā in March 1882 had as chief object the inspection of the newly-established Museum.‡

---

*Growse, *Mathurā* 2nd ed. p. 154, 3rd ed. p. 165 and *Ind. Ant.* Vol. VI, p. 217.

†Growse, *Mathurā* p. 169 and *J. A. S. B.* Vol. XLIV (1875), part I, p. 214 f; plate XIV. The identification of this sculpture with Balarāma, proposed by Growse, cannot be maintained.

‡*A. S. R.*, Vol. XVII, p. 107 *ff.* plates XXX and XXXI and Vol. XX p. 30 ff.

In the court-yard he found, as already stated, twenty-seven bases of Indo-Scythian pillars and inside three more, making in all thirty bases which are still in the Museum (nos. P, 20—53). In his report he discusses the inscriptions found on some of these bases and three other epigraphs.

On the occasion of this visit, Cunningham discovered the curious sculpture of "Herakles strangling the Nemaean lion" (ht. 2′ 5″) which he presented to the Calcutta Museum in October of the same year.*

In examining the site of the old fort on the bank of the Jamnā above Sītalā Ghāṭī, he noticed "a broken Jaina figure, naked, with an Indo-Scythian inscription, dated in the year 57 both in words and figures," which Mr. Growse placed in the local Museum (no. B, 15).†

To the north-west of the Sītalā Ghāṭī site there is another mound named after the Arjunpura Maḥalla. Cunningham noticed here numerous fragments of sculptures and large-sized bricks (18″ by 10″ by 2½″). The antiquity of this site is indicated by the discovery of a railing(?) pillar decorated with lotus-flowers and inscribed with an inscription in three lines in Brāhmī character of the Maurya period which Cunningham read: *Amogharakkhitaye dānaṁ*. The original is no longer traceable. It will be noticed that no other inscription of so early a date has yet been discovered at Mathurā, except the Parkham image. Whenever excavations are resumed, the Arjunpura site would deserve full exploration.

In Rāṇī-kī-maṇḍi, north of Arjunpura, Cunningham obtained an inscribed Jina pedestal which had been found in a well fifteen years before. It is dated in the year 62, in the 3rd month of summer, the 5th day. The stone was sent to the Calcutta Museum. It is the sculpture marked M, 12 in that collection, which is described as "a pedestal of a statue in red speckled sandstone with an inscription in four lines; the feet of the statue alone remaining, size 17″×13″×4″. It was presented by the Archaeological Survey of India in December 1882."‡

The last archaeological explorations at Mathurā were those carried out by Dr. A. Führer, in the three seasons 1888—91, at the Kaṅkālī Ṭīlā and in February-March 1896, on the Kaṭrā site. On these important excavations no other information is available than the brief notes contained in Dr. Führer's *Annual Progress Reports* and in the *Museum Reports* for

---

*Anderson, *Catalogue*, part I, p. 190 no. M, 17.

†*A. S. R.* Vol. XX, p. 36. *Cf.* Growse, *Ind. Ant.* Vol. VI, p. 218.

‡Anderson, *Catalogue* Part I, p. 185. *J. A. S. B.* (N. S.) Vol. V, no. 7, 1909, p. 239 no. III.

those years.* In the Kankālī Ṭīlā were discovered a brick *stūpa* of 47′ in diameter and two Jaina temples. Unfortunately, no proper drawings of these monuments have been made, and the few photographs taken in the course of the work fail to convey an idea of what they were like. At present, no remnants of any buildings are traceable on the spot.

Dr. Führer's excavations were remarkably fruitful in results, as regards the acquisition of sculptures and inscriptions. In the season 1890-1 alone no less than 737 pieces of sculpture came to light. All the finds were placed in the Lucknow Museum, which thus has become the principal depository of Mathurā sculptures. It appears from the Museum Report that Dr. Führer's explorations of the season 1889-90 were partly carried out at the expense of the Mathurā Municipality, but the local Museum has not benefited by it. It is distinctly stated that "all the newly unearthed treasures" were sent to Lucknow. I may mention in passing that among the acquisitions of the Lucknow Museum for the year 1888-9, † I find, besides numerous sculptures from the Kankālī Ṭīlā "a collection of ornamental plinths, string-courses, door-sills, door-jambs, pillars and pilasters of the original temple of Keśava-deva, destroyed by Aurangzeb in A.D. 1661, excavated from the Kaṭrā mound," and "five large columns, beautifully carved and inscribed *samvat* 1226 (read 1227), from the Assi Khambhā temple at Mahāban." It is much to be regretted that, in disposing of these antiquities, so intimately connected with the history of Mathurā, the claims of the local Museum were so entirely overlooked.

On account of their exceptional interest, I quote the following passage in full from Dr. Führer's Progress Report ‡ regarding his last explorations of 1896 on the Kaṭrā site.

"During the months of February and March 1896, I was enabled to resume the explorations at Mathurā, which in 1889—91 had yielded the splendid collection of important Jaina sculptures and inscriptions, on which a detailed monograph, illustrated by 103 plates, is now in the Press. With the sanction of the Local Government, Rs. 380 were spent partly on 'prospecting operations' in the large Kaṭrā

---

* The passages regarding the Kankālī Ṭīlā from the *Museum Reports* will be found in V. A. Smith, *The Jain Stūpa of Mathurā* pp. 2—4.

† *Minutes of the Managing Committee, Provincial Museum, Lucknow*, 1888-9, pp. 136-137, 1889-90, pp. 102-103 and pp. 232-233.

‡ *Annual Progress Report of the Archaeological Survey, Circle North-Western Provinces and Oudh, for the year ending 30th June* 1906, pp. 1-2.

mound, which is believed to conceal the ruins of Keśava Deva's ancient temple, destroyed by Aurangzeb in A.D. 1669, and partly on diggings in some unexplored portions of the Kaṅkāli Ṭilā, which mound in former years had furnished numerous Jaina sculptures and epigraphical documents."

"The Kaṭrā is an oblong brick enclosure, built like a *sarāi*, measuring 404 feet in length and 653 feet in breadth. In its centre is a raised terrace, 72 feet long and 86 feet broad, upon which stands Aurangzeb's Masjid, occupying its entire length, but only 60 feet of its breadth; about 5 feet lower is another terrace, measuring 286 feet by 268, into the pavement of which are let some short votive Sanskrit inscriptions, dated *Saṁvat* 1713 and 1720, corresponding to A. D. 1656 and 1663. At the back of the Masjid, and running at right angles to it for a distance of about 163 feet, may be traced the plinth of some old brick sub-structure, which, according to the popular belief, marks the ground floor of the sanctum of the once famous and imposing temple of Keśava visited and described by the French travellers Tavernier (1650) and Bernier (1663). About 50 paces to the north west of this plinth I dug a trial trench, 80 feet long, 20 feet broad and 25 feet deep, in the hope of exposing the foundations and some of the sculptures of this ancient Keśava temple. However, none of the hoped for Brahmanical sculptures and inscriptions were discovered, but only fragments belonging to an ancient Buddhist *stūpa*. At a depth of 20 feet I came across a portion of the circular procession-path leading round this *stūpa*. On the pavement, composed of large red sandstone slabs, a short dedicatory inscription was discovered, according to which this *stūpa* was repaired in *saṁvat* 76 by the Kushaṇa King Vasushka; unfortunately, I was unable to continue the work and lay bare the whole procession-path, as the walls of the brick sub-structure, adjoining the Masjid, are built right across the middle of this *stūpa*."

Thus the Mathurā explorations ended in 1896 on the same spot, the Kaṭrā site, where they had been begun in 1853. The results obtained in the course of these forty-four years' research have been very considerable. An imposing series of epigraphical records of great palaeographical, linguistic and historical interest has come to light. In them we can follow the transition of the script of Aśoka's edicts to that of the imperial Guptas, which has finally developed into the alphabets of modern India. In these inscriptions we see the ancient Prakrits gradually superseded by Sanskrit, which henceforward becomes the sole language used in epigraphical documents. The Mathurā inscriptions have supplied dates for the great Kushaṇa rulers of India, and thus enabled us to fix their order of succession and the approximate duration of their reigns. When once the difficult problem of the era used in these epigraphs has been definitely solved, they will form the basis for the chronology of the Indo-Scythian period. The past explorations have further revealed the existence of a Mathurā school of sculpture which flourished in the Kushaṇa period.

The importance of this Mathurā school in the history of Indian art as a link between old-Indian and Mediaeval sculpture and its close affinity with the Græco-Buddhist school of Gandhāra will be treated in a following chapter.

III.—The Monuments of Ancient Mathurā.

When about A.D. 400 the Chinese pilgrim Fa-hien travelled through the country of Mathurā, he counted no less than twenty Buddhist monasteries which stood on both banks of the Jamnā and contained some three thousand monks. Hiuen Tsiang, who visited Mathurā in the first half of the 7th century, found the same number of monasteries, but estimates that of the residing priests at only two thousand. He mentions, besides, five Brahmanical or Deva temples. When the Chinese pilgrims speak of monasteries, the word is not to be taken in the sense of a single dwelling-house for monks or nuns. It means a monastic establishment, consisting of a group of sacred buildings including convents, temples and *stūpas*.

The scattered and mutilated remnants of these Buddhist sanctuaries, now preserved in the Mathurā Museum, still convey some faint idea of their former splendour. They call to our imagination monuments of imposing dimensions, covered with ornamental carvings and possessing numerous statues, some of gigantic size. It is less easy to form a more exact idea of the appearance of those buildings, of the plans on which they were designed and of their architectural features. The broken bas-reliefs and headless images leave no doubt that they met with a violent end at the hands of some enemy of the Buddhist faith. Who this enemy was, it is difficult to decide. The destruction of these buildings probably happened many centuries before the Muhammadans made their appearance in India. For the latest Buddhist inscriptions hitherto found at Mathurā belong to the Gupta period. There would, therefore, be reason to assume that the Huns are responsible for the ruin of the Buddhist monuments of Mathurā. We know from Hiuen Tsiang that their king

Mihir Gul or Mihiragula (c. A. D. 475) was a bitter enemy of the Buddhists, and "issued an edict to destroy all the priests through the five Indies, to overthrow the law of Buddha, and leave nothing remaining." This assumption, however, seems incompatible with the existence of twenty monasteries and the flourishing state of Buddhism at Mathurā at the time of the pilgrim's visit.

However, it is certain that at the time when the remnants of these monasteries were excavated, hardly any walls were found standing, so that Growse even doubted whether on the site of the Kankāli Ṭīlā there had ever existed a building at all and whether perhaps the mass of images found on the spot had been collected from somewhere else.* It is, however, not very difficult to account for the complete disappearance of structural remains. The walls were built of bricks, and these have been gradually dug up and used as materials for later buildings. This is the common fate of ancient monuments which, like those of Mathurā, are situated in the neighbourhood of a large town. I must, however, add that Dr. Führer, in the course of his subsequent excavations, did find distinct remains of buildings. It can hardly be doubted that, if explorations at the various ancient sites round the city had been carried on more systematically, and if the results had been published in detailed and illustrated accounts, our knowledge of the architecture of ancient Mathurā would have been much greater than it is now.

As it is, we have largely to depend on the evidence of the sculptures themselves and on the testimony of Buddhist monuments elsewhere. We know that three classes of such monuments existed in India: the *stūpa*, the temple and the convent. The last-mentioned class can be safely left out of discussion, as the convent, used as a dwelling-place for the monks, was usually not of a highly decorative character, though it often, if not always, comprised a chapel with an image of Buddha.

The Buddhist convent assumed the shape of a square block formed by four rows of cells built along the sides of an inner courtyard. It had indeed the same type as the *sarai* of modern India, with this difference that the larger convents consisted of several storeys. Along the inner courtyard there was usually a verandah supported on pillars. It is not impossible that the pillar-bases, thirty-four of which are preserved in the Museum (nos. P, 20-53), belong to such a building. From an inscription on one of them, now in Calcutta, it appears that it belonged to the *vihāra* of the Mahārājā Huvishka, which once stood on the site of the

* Growse, *Mathurā*, p. 118.

Magistrate's court-house. The word *vihāra*, however, means both a monastery and a temple, so that the inscription affords no certainty regarding the point under discussion.

It is very probable that highly ornamental pillars and pilasters, like nos. P, 54 and 55, formed part of a temple, and that the two carved stones, nos. P, 1 and 2, also belonged to such a building. But regarding the temple architecture of that period little is known. On the fragment of a railing pillar (no. J, 24) we find a building which seems to represent a temple. It has a high conical roof which apparently is provided with several cornices. The lowermost cornice rests on four pillars or pilasters. Between the two inner pillars is an arched doorway and at each side a square window. The building is unfortunately shown on so small a scale that it is impossible to judge of the details, and the carving is, moreover, much defaced. Its spire looks very similar to that of the temple of Bhitargaon (Cawnpore district), which is the oldest brick temple existing in this province. (Pl. II and III a.)

We are better informed about the third and most important class of Buddhist monuments—the *stūpa* or tope*. *Stūpas* are solid structures of brick or stone, often of enormous size, consisting of a basement of one or more square terraces *(medhi)* approached by a flight of stairs *(sopāna)*, a circular drum and dome *(aṇḍa)* and a cube *(harmikā)*† surmounted by a range of parasols *(chhattrāvalī.)* These parasols *(chhattra)* were attached to a metal mast *(yashṭi)* on the top of which a "rain vase" *(varsha-sthāla)* was placed. In the oldest *stūpas* there is no drum; the dome stands immediately on a circular base. In the latter examples, this base has, as it were, become a drum, and the whole structure is raised on a square plinth, sometimes consisting of several terraces. The dome at the same time becomes more elevated and the whole structure assumes the character of a "tower," the name by which *stūpas* are usually designated by the Chinese pilgrims. They are in the first instance raised to contain relics of Buddha himself and of his chief disciples. Next they were built to commemorate some important event in his life or in one of his previous existences. Finally *stūpas* were erected merely for the sake of merit and specimens of miniature size were given as votive offerings.

---

* *Cf.* Foucher, *L'art gréco-bouddhique du Gandhâra*, Vol I, pp. 45—98. Fergusson, *History of Indian and Eastern Architecture* (London 1899) chapter III, pp. 57—104.

† For this member we use the Burmese term *htt.*

The Mathurā Museum possesses a specimen of such a votive *stūpa* (no. N, 1; pl. IV) inscribed with a dedicatory inscription. It will convey some idea of the shape and decoration of the monumental *stūpa* of the period. It should, however, be remarked that this *stūpa* model is not complete, as both the lowermost and uppermost members are missing. It consists merely of a drum and a dome. On the top of this dome we still find the mortice which was meant to receive the tenon of the *hti* and the bottom of the stone has a flange showing that it fitted on to a basement. The remaining portion, however, is sufficient to show that this *stūpa* belongs to the later type; and this is of special interest, as, on account of the inscription, we may assign it to the flourishing period of Mathurā architecture—that of the Kushaṇas.

The shape of the *hti* placed on the top of the *stūpa* dome can be best seen from no. I, 9—the upper portion of a bas-relief on which evidently two Nāgas were shown worshipping a *stūpa*. Complete *stūpas* may also be seen on the reverse of some railing pillars, such as nos. J, 10 and 11 (pl. XXIII.)

The Museum possesses two fragments of large stone parasols (nos. N, 10 and 11), carved with concentric decorative borders. These may have belonged to the pinnacles of *stūpas*; but it is also possible that they were placed over statues of colossal size. That this was the custom is evident from the two inscribed Bodhisattva statues which have been found at Sahēṭh (Bahraich district) and at Sārnāth near Benares. The inscriptions, the latter dated in the 3rd year of Mahārājā Kanishka, state definitely that these images were dedicated together with parasols; and at Sārnāth a carved parasol with inscribed post was found near the image.

One of the most interesting objects in the Museum is no. N, 2—the drum of a miniature *stūpa* from Dhruva Ṭīlā*. It will be seen that it is carved with eight scenes of Buddha's life. Thus it helps us to understand how fragments like no. H, 7, which exhibit similar scenes, were used to decorate *stūpas* of larger size. But as these fragments are not curved but straight, they must have belonged to the square basement and not to the drum of some small-sized *stūpa*. The bracketed cornice of this *stūpa* drum (no. N, 2) deserves also notice not only on account of its debased classical style, but also because it explains the use of fragments like nos. N, 4—6.

---

* *Cf.* V. A. Smith, *Jain Stūpa* plates CV—CVII, and my *Notes de sculpture bouddhique*, *B.E.F.E.O.* Vol. VIII (1908) pp. 492—500.

Plate IV.

No. N, 1; Ht. 1' 7".

Votive Stūpa; Kushaṇa Period.

There is one decorative detail in the votive *stūpa* (no. N, 1) which deserves special mention. It will be seen that the top of its drum is decorated with a garland carried by little figures. The same device we find on the bas-reliefs nos. I, 2—6, and there is, therefore, reason to assume that these stones once formed part of the facing of a *stūpa*. It will, however, be noticed that they cannot have belonged to the drum, but adorned some flat surface. The special interest of these garland-carrying figures in the history of Buddhist art will be pointed out in the next chapter.

It is well known that the famous *stūpas* of Barāhat (Bharhut), Sānchi and Amarāvatī were enclosed within stone railings of a highly ornamental character. The procession-path thus formed round the *stūpa* was approached through four gateways (*toraṇa*), facing the four cardinal points and adorned with profuse carvings. Railings and gateways of the same type existed round the *stūpas* of ancient Mathurā. On a so-called tablet of homage (*āyāgapaṭa*)* which was recovered near the Holi Gate (no. Q, 2; pl. V.), we find the complete representation of a *stūpa* with the staircase leading up to the terrace which is surrounded by a railing. At the top of the flight of steps we notice the gateway with its three architraves, similar in shape to those of Barāhat and Sānchi. This alone would suffice to show that the gateways of the Mathurā *stūpas* were derived from such old-Indian examples. I must remark here that the tablet of homage just mentioned is not Buddhist but Jain, as appears from its inscription. But this is immaterial for our present purpose. The Buddhist and Jain *stūpas* were similar in appearance, so that according to a curious legend preserved in a Chinese text † even the great Indo-Scythian King Kanishka, who was a fervent Buddhist, could mistake the one for the other.

The type of a so-called Buddhist railing‡ can be best seen on the fragment no. I, 32 where we distinguish three elements; first, the pillar (Sanskrit *stambha*) decorated with a human figure; second, the coping-stone, and, third, the cross-bar or transom (Sanskrit *sūchi*). Detached specimens of these three members of a Buddhist railing, varying in size

* V.A. Smith, *The Jain Stūpa of Mathurā*, plate CIII. *Cf.* also Plate XII, which shows a similar tablet of which the upper portion is missing. It is now in the Lucknow Museum.

† *Ind. Ant.* Vol. XXXII (1903) p. 385.

‡ On the Mathurā railings *cf.* Cunningham, *A.S.R.* Vol. III, pp. 23—25. The Sanskrit-Pali term for a railing appears to be *vedi*, *vedikā* cf. *A. S. R.* Vol. III, p. 36, no. 21, plate XVI and *Mahāvanso* (ed. Turnour) p. 228.

and ornament, have been found in great numbers on the ancient sites of Mathurā. Nos. K, 1—6 of the Museum collection are portions of coping stones. The carving on no. K, 1-2 is similar to that on the fragment no. I, 32. The cross-bars are usually decorated on both sides with a medallion.* "In the ornamentation of the bosses or medallions," Cunningham says, "the choice of subjects seems to have been left entirely to the artist. Here, accordingly, we see him display his taste in the variety of his flowers, or letting his fancy revel almost wildly in the creation of fabulous animals. We see fish-tailed lions, both with and without wings; a crocodile or *magar*, and an alligator or *gariāl*, each with only two feet."

Of greater interest are the railing-pillars†, of which the Museum possesses a representative number, varying in size from the large pillar no. J, 1 (ht. 6′ 8½″) which once stood in front of the Bhūtēsar temple, to the miniature specimen no. J, 15 (ht. 2′ 8½″). First of all we notice that all these pillars are provided with a tenon at the top which fitted in the coping-stone, and with three mortices on each side to receive the cross-bars. It is noteworthy that, whatever the size of the pillar may be, the number of cross-bars is invariably three. The railing pillars are all carved on two sides except only nos. J, 1-3.

On one side, we usually find a nude female figure, standing on a prostrate dwarf, either under a tree, of which she clasps a branch, or under a balcony, over which one or two smaller figures are partly visible. These female pillar figures, which are typical of Mathurā sculpture, have sometimes been identified with Māyā standing under the *sāl* tree, but are mostly designated as dancing-girls. The prostrate dwarfs, however, on which they are commonly placed, do not admit of either interpretation. On the railing pillars of the Barāhat *stūpa*, we find figures standing on animals in the same position, and these are marked by inscriptions as semi-divine beings.

There is, to my mind, little doubt that the Mathurā pillar figures, which are derived from old-Indian examples, have the same meaning and represent fairies or nymphs (*Yakshī*), which were supposed to guard the sacred monument round which they were arrayed. The lascivious attitude of several of these figures, does not militate against this interpretation. On the other hand, it should be noted that in some cases they are armed (no. J, 63), and assume the distinct character of guardians. They

---

* *Cf.* V. A. Smith, *op. cit.* plates LXV-LXXVI for cross-bars, and plates LXXVII-LXXXIV for coping-stones.

† *Cf.* V. A. Smith, *op. cit.* plates LII-LXIV.

evidently occupy the same function as the door-keepers (Sanskrit *dvārapāla*) of the Brahmanical temples and of the Rākshasas placed at the entrance of Javanese shrines.

The female figures just described, are by far the most common on the railing-pillars of Mathurā. We find, however, sometimes male figures. It is interesting that some of these wear Scythian dress—a conical cap, a long coat, trousers and heavy boots—exactly as it is found on the coins of the Kushaṇa kings. Apart from epigraphical evidence, these figures point to the Indo-Scythian period as the flourishing time of Mathurā sculpture. In other railing figures we recognise Bodhisattvas (pl. III).

The reverse of the Mathurā railing-pillars, is carved in two different ways. The older method followed on the railings of Barāhat is to decorate them with medallions containing a conventional flower, a sacred symbol or a phantastical animal. But on some of the Mathurā pillars, for instance those from the Bhūtēsar site, we find the reverse divided in three panels placed one over the other, and carved with various scenes. Sometimes these scenes seem merely to represent devotional subjects, such as the worship of a *stūpa* or sacred tree. But in other cases they refer to some *jātaka.**

We have noticed that one of the Bhūtēsar pillars (no. J, 4) contains three scenes of the *Viśvantara-jātaka,* in which the future Buddha in his existence as prince Viśvantara performs the extraordinary act of giving away his own children in charity.

The other Bhūtēsar railing-pillar in the Museum (no. J, 5) contains three scenes which seem to refer to the *jātaka* in which the Bodhisattva gave his own body to feed a hungry tigress. On a fragment of a railing-pillar of unknown origin (no. J, 36) we find the concluding scene of the *jātaka* of the loquacious tortoise, and on another fragment (no. J, 41) there are two monkeys pouring out water over the head of an owl, which must refer to the *jātaka* of the owl *(Ulūka-jātaka).*†

I may mention here that on the large railing-pillar (no. J, 1) there is a curious bas-relief, which apparently also represents a *jātaka* in which two monkeys, an ogre and an owl are the actors, but which has not yet been identified. On the large pillar no. J, 2 also, we find a medallion

---

* A *jātaka* or "*birth-story*" is a story relating to some previous existence of the Buddha. They form a special section of the Pali canon and have also been preserved in a Sanskrit collection known as *Jātakamālā*.

† *Cf. A. S. R.* for 1906-7, pp. 155—157 pl. LI and *B. E. F. E. O.* Vol. VIII (1908) pp. 528—530.

which possibly refers to some birth-story. It is noteworthy that in both cases the *jātaka* scene is carved not on the back of the post, but over the pillar figure.

There remains one point to be mentioned with regard to the decoration of a Buddhist *stūpa*. The Museum contains several specimens of lion figures (section O), most of which consist only of the front portion of the animal. In the Trans-Indus country—the ancient Gandhāra—such half engaged lions were used to decorate the basements of *stūpas* which they were supposed to support. We may assume that at Mathurā they served the same purpose. "Le lion" says M. Foucher*, "bien qu'il achève seulement de s'éteindre dans l'Inde a été traité dans un style assez conventionnel, et sa crinière soigneusement peignée ou bouclée se sent des modes d'Assyrie. Le plus souvent, il orne les coins des bases (à défaut de balustrades) des *stūpa* en attendant qu'il supporte le trône *(simhāsana)* du Bienheureux. Que son avant-train seulement soit dégagé de la pierre, comme sur les exemples de Sanghao (Peshāvar) et de Mathurā, ou qu'il soit complètement détaché comme à Amarāvatī, le mouvement indique d'habitude qu'il est assis sur les pattes de derrière, exactement tel qu'il se dresse, langue pendante, au haut de l'un des piliers d'Aśoka." It deserves notice that the Museum contains lion figures of the two kinds described by M. Foucher—viz. half-engaged and detached. In this respect also Mathurā forms a link between Gandhāra and Amarāvatī.

The names of only a very few of the ancient monuments of Mathurā have been preserved in inscriptions. We have already noticed that on the site of the Magistrate's court-house, there once stood a Buddhist Convent founded by the Indo-Scythian king Huvishka and evidently named after him. The sculptural remains found on the spot still attest its royal magnificence. It is curious that side by side with this sanctuary there existed once a shrine dedicated to the Nāga king Dadhikarṇa. Another important Buddhist establishment occupied the site of Aurangzeb's mosque. It must have comprised several edifices including a fane of the name of Yaśā-vihāra and a *stūpa* restored by a king Vāsushka. The mounds on the bank of the Jamnā to the south of the modern city, seem to mark the spot of a third group of Buddhist buildings, which existed in the days of the Satraps, and comprised a sanctuary of the name of Guhā-vihāra and a *stūpa* founded by the Chief Queen of the Great Satrap Rājūla.†

---

*A. Foucher, *L'art gréco-bouddhique du Gandhâra*, p. 216, f. fig. 93.

† *Ep. Ind.* Vol. IX pp. 141 and 146.

No. Q. 2 ; Ht. 2' 4".

TABLET OF HOMAGE FROM HOLI GATE.

The Chaubārā mounds are undoubtedly the remnants of Buddhist *stūpas* and thus represent a fourth group. An inscription found here mentions a locality Mādhuravaṇaka.*

The Jain community of ancient Mathurā had its main sanctuary on the site of the Kaṅkālī Ṭīlā. In the days of the Kushaṇa rulers there existed here a monument called in an inscription "the *Vodva Stūpa*, built by the gods." From this we may infer that even at that time its origin was lost in obscurity. From other inscriptions we know that the great Jain establishment of the Kaṅkālī Ṭīlā existed till the time of the Muhammadan conquest, when all Buddhist monuments of Mathurā had long since fallen into ruins.

Thus we can still imagine the ancient city of Mathurā, as it revealed itself to the wondering eyes of the pilgrims, with the glittering domes of its *stūpas*—enclosed by elaborate railings and surmounted by rows of parasols, with the dazzling splendour of its temples, in which gigantic Buddhas silently received the homage of the faithful, and with its massive convents thronged by hundreds of yellow-robed monks.

IV.—The Mathurā School of Sculpture.†

The vast amount of sculptural remains discovered at Mathurā would suffice to show the importance of this place in the history of Indian art. One of the very few statues in the whole of India which can be assigned to the Maurya period is the colossal image (no. C, 1; pl. XII) which once stood at Parkham, a village 14 miles from Mathurā on the road to Agra. That it belongs to so early a period is proved by its inscription written in the character of the Aśoka edicts. The Śaka satraps who ruled in Mathurā in the first century B. C. were patrons of Buddhism and Buddhist art, as appears from the Kharoshṭhī inscriptions on the lion-capital. The great flourishing period of the Mathurā school of sculpture coincides with the reign of the great Indo-Scythian rulers Kanishka, Huvishka and Vāsudeva. The bulk of the inscriptions found on or in connection with Mathurā sculptures are written in Brāhmī character of the Kushaṇa type, and several of them are dated in the reign of one of those three kings. We have seen that the Buddhist monastery which once stood on the site of the Collector's court-house was founded by Huvishka himself in the 47th year of Kanishka's era. Buddhist tradition pictures us Kanishka the

***Ep. Ind.* Vol. VIII, p. 182.

†*Cf.* my paper *The Mathurā School of Sculpture* in the *Annual Report of the Archaeological Survey for* 1906-7, pp. 137—160.

influence, received its classical inspiration indirect through Gandhāra. The influence of the Græco-Buddhist school on all later Buddhist art has so clearly been shown in M. Foucher's standard-work that no doubt can now subsist on this point. Mathurā, owing to its geographical position and—I may add—to its political importance during the Kushaṇa epoch, was the first to feel that influence. This explains the mixed character of the Mathurā school in which we find, on the one hand, a direct continuation of the old-Indian art of Barāhat and Sānchi and, on the other hand, the classical influence derived from Gandhāra.

The most important point in which the Mathurā school differs from the old-Indian school is the Buddha image. During the Maurya period, representations of Buddha, either as detached statues or in bas-reliefs, are wholly unknown. In scenes dealing with episodes of his life, his presence is indicated by some sacred symbol. At Mathurā, on the contrary, images of Buddha are exceedingly numerous, and we find him figured both in illustrative and decorative bas-reliefs. This innovation is, no doubt, due to influence from the North-West; for all evidence points to the fact that the Buddha image is a creation of the Hellenistic sculptors of Gandhāra. This point I wish to discuss more fully in the next chapter.

The Mathurā Museum possesses a number of sculptures with scenes of Buddha's life. Here Gandhāra influence is evident not only from the occurrence of the Buddha figure, but also from the treatment of such scenes. The episodes of Buddha's life are far less numerous and varied than in Græco-Buddhist sculpture. Most frequent are the four main events of his existence: his birth, enlightenment, first sermon and death. These we find on the slab of the Rāj Ghāṭ (no. H, 1; pl. VIa) and on the *stūpa* drum of the Dhruv Ṭīlā (no. N, 2). The birth scene we find combined with that of the first bath in which the new-born Buddha (or better Bodhisattva) is being worshipped by the two Nāga kings, Nanda and Upananda, who are shown emerging half-way from masonry wells. This treatment seems to be peculiar to the Mathurā school. It is true that on Sārnāth sculptures also the first bath is usually shown together with the birth. But there we see the two Nāgas standing in the air and pouring water over the head of the holy infant.

Besides the four main events of Buddha's life, there are four episodes of secondary importance which form a favourite subject of Indian art. These are:—the descent from the Heaven of the thirty-three gods, the subjugating of the elephant Nālāgiri, the offering of honey by the monkey, and the miracle of Śrāvastī. On the *stūpa* drum of Dhruv Ṭīlā we find, be-

No. H, 1 ; Ht. 2' 2".
Slab from Rāj Ghāṭ.

No. H, 11 ; Ht. 1' 6".
Slab repr. Buddha visited by Indra.

sides the four main events, four scenes, which, however, only partly agree with those four minor episodes. It would seem that at the time when the Mathurā school flourished, the choice of the four minor scenes had not yet been definitely fixed. It is surprising that representations of the offering of the monkey are wholly absent, as this event, according to Hiuen Tsiang, was located not only at Vaiśālī but also at Mathurā.

On the *stūpa* drum of Dhruv Ṭīlā these two scenes are replaced by the offering of the four bowls by the Lokapālas and by Indra's visit to Buddha in the Indraśaila Cave. Of this last scene the Museum possesses two very full representations—one on the *toraṇa* lintel no. M, 2, and another on the bas-relief no. H, 11 (pl. VIb). There are certain details in the latter sculpture which leave no doubt that it is an imitation of Græco-Buddhist work. The peacock over the Buddha figure and the two wild animals in their caves are especially remarkable. On the other hand it should be noticed that the Mathurā school has introduced a new element in this scene—Indra's elephant Airāvaṭa, which is also found on the replica in the Calcutta Museum. This points again to the truly Indian character of the Mathurā school. A comparison of the bas-reliefs in the Mathurā Museum and the exquisite bas-relief of Loriyān Tangai (Swāt) in the Calcutta collection will, notwithstanding the points of similarity, serve to emphasise the wide gulf between the Gandhāra and Mathurā schools, as regards artistic merit. In Gandhāra the classical influence is still obvious in the harmonious arrangement of the figures and in the variety of their attitude and expression. At Mathurā the figures are reduced to a few fixed types, and the bas-reliefs representing scenes of Buddha's life, bear distinct evidence of being only clumsy imitations of their Gandhāran prototypes.

These points are also evident in the decorative elements which Mathurā borrowed from Gandhāra. Here I wish first of all to draw attention to the friezes with garland-carrying figures of which the Museum possesses several specimens (nos. I, 2-6). These figures are ultimately derived from the garland-carrying Cupids which are found on the sarcophagi of Hellenistic and Roman art. On the Buddhist monuments of the North-West they are extremely common. "They are represented," Grünwedel says, "on string courses, plinths or friezes, as boyish figures carrying garlands or playing between garlands. In the intervening portions lotus-flowers are sometimes introduced, or the intervals are filled in with symbols, animals or birds."*

* *Buddhist Art in India*, p. 148.

Grünwedel was the first to point out that the same device, in a modified form, is found on the rail coping of the Amarāvatī *stūpa*. Here "the boys at play have turned into men who, bearing huge snake-like bodies, advance in studied and graceful attitudes." A connecting link between Gandhāra and Amarāvatī is supplied at Mathurā, where we find the garland-carriers in an intermediate stage of their development—less classical than in Gandhāra and less indianised than at Amarāvatī. It has been noticed above that this device occurs not only in detached fragments of friezes of various sizes preserved in the Mathurā Museum, but also on the miniature *stūpa* (no. N, 1; pl. IV). This proves that at Mathurā such friezes were indeed used for *stūpa* decoration in exactly the same manner as in Gandhāra.

Another curious instance in which influence of the Græco-Buddhist school of Gandhāra is plainly visible is no. I, 1 of the Mathurā Museum. Among Gandhāra sculptures we often meet with semi-circular or curvilinear pediments divided into various compartments by means of concentric arches. The centre of each lunulate area thus formed, is occupied by a seated Buddha or Bodhisattva figure, by an alms-bowl or some other object of worship, whilst on both sides we find an equal number of standing or kneeling figures of devotees. At the end of each group of worshippers there is usually a winged Triton, the coil of whose snake-like body effectively fills the narrow end of the lunulate space.

If we compare our no. I, 1, it will be evident that it is derived from such pediments, though its shape is different and it cannot have served the same structural purpose. Each side is divided into three lunulate spaces; in the centre we find Buddha and Bodhisattva figures, Buddha's alms-bowl and head-dress each approached on both sides by worshipping figures. But here the latter have become flying Devas of a thoroughly Indian type, and at the end of each group there is a yawning crocodile, which has replaced the classical Triton. The spandrils are occupied by conventionalised Garuḍas. Here again we notice how the Mathurā school, in copying Gandhāra examples, has replaced many classical elements by typical Indian motives. With the bas-relief in question may also be compared the remarkable sculpture excavated by Dr. Führer from the Kaṅkālī Ṭīlā and discussed by Professor Bühler.* It evidently served the same purpose, but is much more elaborately carved.

It is clear that in the instance just quoted, there is no question of direct Greek or even Hellenistic influence. The sculpture is thoroughly

* *Ep. Ind.* Vol. II, p. 319, also V. A. Smith, *Jain Stūpa*, plates XIX and XX.

Indian, both in its general conception and decorative details. But the influence of the Græco-Buddhist school is unmistakeable. In other instances Mathurā has preserved some of the classical elements which characterise that school, but usually in a more indianised form, so that without the connecting link in Gandhāra, their true origin would be hardly discernible. This applies also to the garland-carrying figures.

It is true that Mathurā has produced a few sculptures, such as the Bacchanalian group and the so-called Herakles, of a distinctly classical parentage, though no immediate prototypes can be pointed out in the North-West. It is, however, by no means improbable that some day such prototypes will be found. Those few sculptures which have hitherto received so much attention do not justify us in assuming a direct Greek or Hellenistic influence or even the existence of a body of Bactrian sculptors in ancient Mathurā, as Cunningham suggested. It is not impossible that the men who fashioned those so-called Grecian sculpture had inherited their skill from some Greek or Bactrian ancestor. But that they were European Greeks, nobody will assert who has once set his eyes on a Greek sculpture.

A study of Mathurā sculpture as a whole only confirms the fundamentally Indian character of this school which followed the traditions set by the sculptors of Barāhat and Sānchi. At the same time it received its inspiration partly from the North-West, but here its activity resulted in thoroughly indianising the creations of Gandhāra. Not only the *stūpa* drum of Dhruv Ṭīlā, the friezes of garland-carrying figures, but every Buddha or Bodhisattva image which Mathurā has produced, bears testimony to this process.

Apart from the style of the sculptures, there is some more tangible evidence of Gandhāra influence having been at work in ancient Mathurā. One sculpture has been found which is not only thoroughly Gandhārian in style, but which is made of the blue schist universally used for Gandhāra sculptures. It is the female statue discovered by Bhagvanlal Indraji in the Saptarshi mound and recently returned to Mathurā. There can be no doubt that this sculpture was made in Gandhāra and was brought from there to Mathurā. We may perhaps connect it with the inscribed lion-capital, which apparently was found on the same site, and dates back to the time when Mathurā was ruled by foreign satraps. The close relationship between these satraps and those of Taxila must have favoured the intercourse of artists from both places, and we may well assume that the Gandhāra figure just mentioned was sent to Mathurā by order of the

Court. Anyhow, it is evident that the sculptors of Mathurā had actual Gandhāra sculptures at hand, which they could imitate on the spot.

It is not a little curious that in the beginning of Kanishka's reign we find Mathurā, in its turn, sending down images to the sacred sites of the Gangetic Plains, thus setting examples to the sculptors of Benares and Gayā.

V.—Iconography.*

The name *Buddha* was the title given to Siddhārtha or Gautama, the founder of the Buddhist religion. It is a Sanskrit word meaning "awakened" or "enlightened." Other titles of Gautama Buddha are *Śākyamuni* and *Śākyasiṁha*, "the Sage or the Lion of the Śākya race." The Śākyas were a clan who were settled in the Nepāl Tarai, and Buddha's father was a Śākya chieftain, Śuddhodana by name, whose capital was Kapilavastu. It is related that his queen Māyā gave birth to the future Buddha in the Lumbinī garden not far from Śuddhodana's capital. The site of Buddha's Nativity is marked by an Asoka pillar which was discovered by Dr. Führer in 1896 near the village of Rummindei in Nepāl territory at a distance of 5 miles from the British border. It can best be reached from Dulhā in the Bastī district. From the inscription on the pillar it is clear that as far back as B.C. 250—the tradition of the Buddha's birth was associated with this spot.

Gautama did not really become "Buddha" until the moment when he attained enlightenment (Sanskrit *Bodhi*) under the pipal tree of Bōdh Gayā. Up to that time the Buddhist texts designate him as *Bodhisattva*, viz. a person predestined to become a Buddha. In the texts, Buddha is described as a being of supernatural powers, to whom the gods and demi-gods of ancient India were subject. He is called the Lord *(Bhagavān)*, the Omniscient *(Sarvajña)*, the Supreme *(Anuttara)* and the god of gods *(Devātideva)*.† He received the worship due to a deity, and this explains the multitude of Buddha statues found all over India. It must, however, be remembered that the first images of Buddha were made several centuries after his death. In the monuments of the Maurya period, as noted above, the Buddha is invariably represented by a symbol. It is curious that in all probability the Buddha image originated with the Hellenistic sculptors of Gandhāra, the present Peshāwar dis-

---

* Cf.—Grünw del-Burgess, *Buddhist Art in India* (London 1901) pp. 158—177 and Foucher, *Etude sur l'iconographie bouddhique de l'Inde* (Paris 1900) pp. 76—95.

† Cf.—Kern, *Manual of Indian Buddhism* (Strassburg 1896) p. 63.

No. A, 1 ; Ht. 2' 3¼"

BODHISATTVA STATUETTE FROM KATRA.

trict, who apparently, in fashioning his face, took the Greek sun-god as an example.

In any case, the Buddha type found in sculpture, is purely conventional. It is, however, partly based on the Buddhist texts in attributing to Buddha, the thirty-two bodily marks peculiar to a great man (Sanskrit *mahā-purusha*). To these belong the protuberance of the skull (Sanskrit *ushṇīsha*)—apparently a kind of bump of intelligence—on the top of the head, and the circular mark between the eye-brows (Sanskrit *ūrṇā*) which, at first sight, one might take for a *ṭīkā* or sect-mark. The treatment of the hair—arranged in schematic little curls turned to the right—is also in accordance with the characteristics of the *mahā-purusha*, though it would have been more natural to represent Buddha with a shaven head like a Buddhist monk. There are indeed Buddha images of the Kushaṇa period in which this is the case (nos. A, 1 and 4; pl. VII & XV a), but from the Gupta period onwards we meet only with the curly-headed Buddha. Among the peculiar marks of the Buddha, are also to be reckoned the symbols of the wheel (Sanskrit *chakra*) and of the three jewels (Sanskrit *triratna*) visible in the palms and on the soles of the feet.

The dress of the Buddha is that of a Buddhist monk*. It consists of three pieces (Sanskrit *trichīvara*): first, the lower garment *(antaravāsaka)*, something like a petticoat, hanging low down and bound to the loins with a girdle; second, the upper garment *(uttarāsaṅga)*, which covers the breast and shoulders and reaches below the knees; and third, the cloak *(saṅghāṭi)* worn over the two under-garments. On the images, the long folded cloak is naturally most prominent; but the lower garment is also shown over the lower portion of the legs, and in images of the Gupta period, the girdle is mostly skilfully indicated under the folds of the *saṅghāṭi* (cf. nos. A, 3 and 6-10). The treatment of the drapery is of particular interest, as it was evidently derived from classical art through Gandhāra. The indication of the drapery is indeed foreign to Indian art. Though very common in the Buddha images of Gandhāra and Mathurā, it is seldom found on those of the Gupta period and of the Middle Ages. In Mathurā art the treatment of the robe is much more schematic than in Gandhāra, which received its Hellenistic influence more directly.

Another feature which the Buddha figure has borrowed from the West is the nimbus. It does not, however, appear in classical art until the time of Alexander, and belongs originally to astral deities. Professor

---

* Kern, *op. cit.* pp. 79-80.

Grünwedel * remarks that "the nimbus is a purely pictorial element which, executed in stone, presents a strange appearance, and points in the clearest way to an old school of painting." Strangest it seems, if associated with recumbent figures of Buddha in the scene of his Nirvāṇa (nos. H, 1 and 7). The fact that Buddha is always pourtrayed with a halo, points also to his divine rank. It deserves notice that in Gandhāra sculpture the nimbus is plain: to this rule there are but few exceptions.† In the Mathurā images of the Kushaṇa period we find regularly a halo with a simple scalloped border (pl. XV), whereas those of the Gupta epoch are distinguished by elaborately carved haloes, which however have retained the scalloped border of the earlier type. A fine specimen of such an ornamental nimbus will be noticed on the standing Buddha image (no. A, 5; pl. IX) which on the strength of its inscription may be assigned to the time of the Guptas.‡ On a torso (no. A, 13), apparently of the same period, we find remnants of a halo, enveloping not only the head, but the whole figure.

Buddha images are invariably executed in certain conventional attitudes (Sanskrit *mudrā*, literally "a seal, mark or stamp") of symbolical meaning. In Mathurā sculpture these attitudes are practically limited to two. The standing statues are invariably shown with the right hand raised towards the shoulder, the open palm turned outward. This *mudrā* is known as that of imparting protection (Sanskrit *abhaya-mudrā*). Several of the seated ones have the same attitude. It will be remarked that in the statues of the Gupta period (no. A, 5) this attitude is much more graceful and easy than in those of the earlier Kushaṇa epoch (no. A, 4). In the latter it should be noticed that the stone between the raised hand and the shoulder is not cut away, but carved in a decorative fashion so as to assume the appearance of a cushion. In the images of the Gupta time we find the hand regularly free from the shoulder. Evidently the sculptors of India had then become familiar with the execution of detached statues. Another point of difference, which may here be noted, is that the Kushaṇa images are usually carved in the round, while the later ones are always carved in relief projecting from a back-slab.

---

* *Buddhistische Kunst in Indien* (Berlin 1900) p. 83. The passage has been misinterpreted in the English version, p. 86 f. Cf. also Drouin, *Revue numismatique*, series IV, Vol. V. 1901, pp. 154—166 (transl. *Ind. Ant.* Vol. XXXII (1903) pp. 427—432).

† Cf. *Buddhist Art in India*, fig. 143.

‡ Another specimen from Sārnāth is reproduced *A. S. R.* 1904-5, plate XXIXc.

Other seated Buddha images assume the attitude of meditation *(dhyāna-mudrā)*. They are sitting cross-legged with the soles of the feet turned upward and the two hands resting in the lap, the one upon the other.

Besides these two, there are the *mudrās* of touching the earth (Sanskrit *bhūmi-sparśa-mudrā*) and that of expounding the law *(dharma-chakra-mudrā.)* The latter particularly symbolizes Buddha's first sermon at Benares and is consequently very common in the sculptures of Sārnāth, but at Mathurā I do not know of a single instance. In the representation of the first sermon on the miniature *stūpa* drum of Dhruv Ṭīlā (no. N, 2 o) we find the Buddha seated in the act of turning a wheel placed at his side. In the previous scene *(b)* of his enlightenment, Buddha is rightly shown touching the earth with his right hand in order to call her to bear witness to his meritorious deeds, but it is the only instance of this *mudrā* known in Mathurā sculpture.* Apparently the canon of these *mudrās* was not yet fixed at the time when the Mathurā school flourished.

As early as the time of Aśoka, there existed among Buddhists the belief that previous to Gautama, there had been a number of other Buddhas, who, like him, had preached the law to save mankind from suffering. Both the northern and southern texts mention six predecessors of Gautama, and at Niglīva in the Nepāl Tarai an Aśoka pillar has been found which was erected at the reputed birth-place of one of these previous Buddhas. At the same time, it was believed that after Gautama Buddha there was to be another Buddha of the name of Maitreya. This future Saviour became very soon an important figure in Buddhist worship.

In later Buddhist iconography, the various Buddhas are all similar in appearance. They are only distinguished by their gesture *(mudrā)* and by a peculiar cognizance. But from the above remark it will be clear that no such distinction existed at Mathurā, so that it is impossible to tell whether a certain image represents Gautama or some other Buddha.

With the future Buddha Maitreya, however, the case stands different. He is still a Bodhisattva and is therefore represented not in monk's dress but in royal attire. We know that Gautama was a prince before he became a Buddha; it is, therefore, only natural that the future Buddha Maitreya should be represented under the same aspect. He is, moreover, usually distinguished by an attribute—a small vessel in his left

* There is another instance in a sculpture no. B 208 of the Lucknow Museum, ht. 1' 10½" width 4' 1½" representing a series of scenes, namely, 1. The sun god on a chariot with four horses, 2. The *Bodhi*, 3. The first sermon, 4. Indra's visit. Rest missing.

hand. This has been explained as an ointment vessel to mark his royal rank. The same attribute is sometimes held by the Bodhisattva figures of Gandhāra. We find it also in the left hand of a statuette (no. A, 43; pl. XV a) in the Mathurā Museum, and for this reason I feel inclined to identify it with the future Buddha Maitreya.

Both the Northern and Southern Buddhists, recognize Maitreya the future Buddha, but it is a distinguishing feature of the Northern school that it has adopted a plurality of celestial Bodhisattvas, among whom Avalokiteśvara takes a prominent place. In mediaeval Buddhist sculpture Gautama Buddha is usually attended by Maitreya and Avalokiteśvara, and numerous images of these and other Bodhisattvas found at Bōdh Gayā, Sārnāth and other important Buddhist sites show the great popularity of these divinities in mediaeval Buddhism.

The Mathurā sculptures, however, point to the fact that during the Kushaṇa period this Bodhisattva cult was not yet developed. The statuettes, no. A, 43 and 68 of the Mathurā Museum are the only figures which can be identified with Maitreya. I do not know of any representation of Avalokiteśvara, not to speak of other less popular Bodhisattvas. Even those well-known groups of a seated Buddha between two standing Bodhisattvas, so common in later Buddhist art, do not seem to occur at Mathurā. This is the more remarkable, as such triads were already known in Gandhāra.

In a previous chapter I have mentioned the two colossal statues of Sārnāth and Sahēṭh-Mahēṭh, which were erected at those places by Bala, a Buddhist friar from Mathurā. In the inscriptions on these images they are distinctly marked as Bodhisattvas, but their aspect is totally different from that of the celestial Bodhisattvas of later Buddhist art. They wear a very plain dress, consisting of a kind of petticoat and a thin upper garment thrown over the left shoulder, and have neither diadem nor ornaments. They have indeed the appearance of Buddha figures without a monk's robe.

The fact that these two colossal statues were set up at places intimately connected with the legend of Gautama Buddha "on the Promenade of the Lord" *(Bhagavato Chaṅkrame)*, as the inscriptions say, makes it highly probable that they were meant for the historical Bodhisattva Gautama before he attained Buddha-hood. The Sārnāth image has a small lion figure between its feet, and we may assume that this refers to his appellation *Śākyasiṁha* "the lion among the Śākyas." I may note that standing Bodhisattva images of the Kushaṇa period frequently have such symbols, placed between their feet, the meaning of which remains as yet unexplained.

Among the sculptures preserved in the Mathurā Museum there is a statue (no. A, 40) which in its style and attitude betrays a close affinity to the Bodhisattvas of Sārnāth and Sahēṭh-Mahēṭh. Unfortunately, the head and arms of this image are missing, but there can be little doubt that it likewise represents a Bodhisattva and belongs to the Kushaṇa period. Whether it is meant for Gautama, Maitreya or some other Bodhisattva, it is impossible to decide, but it is noteworthy that, unlike the Bodhisattvas of Sārnāth and Sahēṭh-Mahēṭh, the figure wears ornaments.

With these figures may also be compared a life-size statue said to have been found among the ruins of Gaṇēśra about 3 miles north-west of Mathurā and now in the Lucknow Museum.* The head and feet are lost, but both the arms are preserved. They exhibit the stiff posture peculiar to the Bodhisattvas of Sārnāth and Sahēṭh-Mahēṭh : the left fist is placed against the hip and the right hand is raised at the height of the shoulder, the palm turned outward. It is the gesture which in Buddhist iconography symbolises, as we saw, the granting of protection. We notice here also this peculiarity that the right hand is not carved in the round, but connected with the shoulder, the stone being carved so as to assume the appearance of a cushion against which the hand seems to rest. The Lucknow image wears a necklace and bracelets ; the dress consists of a *dhōtī* and an upper garment arranged in the same fashion as on Bodhisattva figures like no. A, 40 of the Mathurā Museum. But the girdle here assumes the aspect of a thick cord tied together in front and hanging down between the knees in a decorative tassel. A similar girdle is peculiar to the Bodhisattva figures of Gandhāra. The similarity in attitude and dress also makes it highly probable that these were the prototypes from which the Bodhisattva images of Mathurā are ultimately derived.

The Gaṇēśrā image was supposed by Dr. Führer to represent the Tīrthaṁkara Vardhamāna, but Mr. V. A. Smith rightly points out that there is no foundation for this identification. I have little doubt that this figure also is a Bodhisattva image, though I do not venture to suggest the name of any particular Bodhisattva. Possibly another statue† at

* V. A. Smith, *op. cit.* plate LXXXVII. The village of Gaṇēśrā lies some 3 miles due west of the Katra, north of the Govardhan road. The sculptural remains found there are distinctly Buddhist.

† V. A. Smith, *op. cit.* plate LXXXIX.

Lucknow, said to originate from the Kaṅkālī Ṭīlā, represents a Bodhisattva, though the attitude is different (*vara-mudrā*) and the apparel of a much richer kind.

The evidence afforded by the standing images would seem to justify us in framing the following rule: images in full monk's [illegible]

It is clad in an ample robe which covers both shoulders, and may, therefore, safely be identified as a Buddha. The most interesting feature is the pedestal on which we find a seated Bodhisattva with figures of worshippers standing on both sides. Such a devotional scene is commonly found on Buddha images from Gandhāra, and we cannot but conclude that here we have another element borrowed from the North-West.

The Bodhisattva type in secular attire is also represented by a seated statuette (no. A, 45; pl. X), the head and right arm of which are unfortunately broken. It is represented in the attitude of meditation *(dhyāna-mudrā)*, as indicated by the position of the hands resting in the lap. The soles of the feet are marked with the symbols found in Buddha figures, while a circular halo with scalloped border is still traceable, The dress is similar to that of standing Bodhisattva figures, particularly to that of the Gaṇēśra statue. We notice the cord-like girdle, the tasseled ends of which are displayed on the top of the pedestal. Especially interesting are the ornaments—the flat torque, the heavy necklace with a clasp of *makara* heads, the string of amulet-holders passing under the right arm, and the bracelets with plâques bearing a figure of Vishṇu (?) astride on a Garuḍa.

I now wish to offer a few remarks regarding images of Jinas or Tīrthaṁkaras, the patriarchs—twenty-four in number—of the Jainas. As stated above, the great Jaina site of Mathurā is the Kaṅkālī Ṭīlā, where Dr. Führer excavated a large number of Tīrthaṁkara figures varying in size and in date. These have all been deposited in the Lucknow Museum. The Mathurā collection contains more than eighty pieces (Section B), but they are mostly broken or defaced.

The Tīrthaṁkara image is in all probability a purely Indian creation; at least it does not bear any mark of classical influence and we find such figures on "tablets of homage" which, from their inscriptions, appear to belong to a time anterior to Kushaṇa rule*. The most striking feature of the Tīrthaṁkara figure is its nudity, by which it can easily be distinguished from Buddha and Bodhisattva images. This remark, however, is only true with regard to images of the Digambara or "Sky-clad" sect, whereas the Śvetāmbaras represent theirs as clothed and decorate them with crowns and ornaments. Those in the Mathurā Museum belong all to the former class. The Jina has symbols not only on the palms and soles, but also in the centre of the breast. The hair is usually arranged in short curls in the shape of spirals turned

* V. A. Smith, *Jain Stūpa*, plates VII, IX and X.

towards the right, as is also the case with most Buddha images. But in the earlier specimens we find sometimes a different treatment: the hair assumes the appearance of a periwig, or it hangs down on the shoulders in straight locks. In the latter instance we have probably to deal with a particular patriarch. In contradistinction with the Buddhas, the earlier Tīrthaṁkaras have neither *ushṇīsha* nor *ūrṇā*, but those of the later part of the Middle-Ages have a distinct excrescence on the top of the head.

The attitude of the seated images is invariably that of meditation *(dhyāna-mudrā)*, the hands being placed in the lap. In artistic merit these Jain images are far inferior to those of the Buddhists; their conventionalism and uniformity will appall even the most enthusiastic admirer of Indian art. This does not imply that in the course of time they have undergone no change.

A specimen of the earlier type is no. B, 4 (pl. XI), which bears an inscription dated in the reign of the Kushaṇa king Vāsudeva. The pedestal, on which the inscription is incised, deserves special notice. Between the two lions, which, as usual, are placed at both sides to indicate the throne or "lion-seat," there is a bas-relief representing a wheel of the law and a number of worshippers arranged in two groups at both sides of it. Such devotional scenes are commonly found on the pedestals of Tīrthaṁkara figures of the Kushaṇa period. They occur also on the bases of Buddha images, as appears from the instance above quoted, in which, however, the object of worship in the centre is not a wheel, but a Bodhisattva. There is some reason to assume that in both cases the figures of devotees carved on the pedestal represent the actual donors of the sculpture.

A Tīrthaṁkara image of a somewhat later date is the seated colossus no. B, 1, the provenance of which is unknown. It displays the same characteristics as the one of Vāsudeva's reign just described; but the elaborate nimbus leads me to attribute it to the Gupta period.

The standing Jain images are, if possible, even more devoid of grace and expression than the seated ones. The treatment of the arms, stretched out along the body, is particularly stiff and inartistic. I must make special mention of the four-fold Jaina figures (the inscriptions designate them as *pratimā sarvato bhadrikā* "an image auspicious on every side"), of which the Museum possesses several specimens.* They consist of a block, square in section, on each of the four faces

(*) Cf. Smith, *op. cit.* plate X c.

carved with a Tīrthaṁkara either seated or standing. The four corners of the pedestal are often occupied by figurines of human devotees. It deserves notice that usually one of the four Jinas is distinguished by a snake-hood expanded over his head, and another by long hair falling down on the shoulders in straight locks, whereas the remaining two have the usual type with curly hair and nimbus. The figure with the snake-hood must represent either Supārśva the 7th or Pārśvanātha the 23rd Tīrthaṁkara*

It should be noticed that in the earlier Jain sculptures of the Kushaṇa and Gupta periods there is nothing to distinguish the individual Tīrthaṁkaras, except the snake-hood in the case of Supārśva and Pārśvanātha. The name of the pontiff represented is, however, sometimes recorded in the inscription incised on the base of the statue.

In mediaeval sculpture there is usually a symbol or cognizance (Sanskrit *chihna*, *lāñchhana*) carved on the pedestal, to show which Tīrthaṁkara the image represents.† Thus we find a bull as emblem of Ṛishabhanātha or Ādinātha the first Tīrthaṁkara (no. B, 21). The Jain sculptures of this period are often very elaborate, the main figure being surrounded by numerous attendants—*chaurī* bearers standing at his sides, kneeling devotees and crouching goblins *(Yaksha)* with the usual lions on the pedestal and garland-carrying celestials and elephant-riders on both sides of the triple umbrella placed over his head. Very often we find twenty-three miniature Tīrthaṁkaras, arranged along the sides and top of the back-slab, which together with the main figure complete the full number of Jain patriarchs.‡

Finally, a few words may be said about the representations of the demi-gods, called Yakshas and Nāgas, which form the third section (C) of the Mathurā collection. The Yakshas are comparable with the goblins of Western mythology. They are misshapen dwarfs who guard the treasures of the northern mountains, and their king is Kubera, the god of wealth. They are usually malignant of disposition and sometimes even feeding on human flesh; but the benign influence of the Buddha's teaching makes them forego their cruel habits. In architecture they appear frequently as Atlantes, for instance on one of the *toraṇas* of Sānchi. A

(*) In later Jain iconography Supārśva has a five-fold and Pārśva a seven-fold snake-hood.

†Cf. Burgess, *Digambara Jaina Iconography*, *Ind. Ant.* Vol. XXXII, pp. 459—464 and *Progress Report*, *Archl. Survey*, *Northern Circle*, for 1903-4, p. 61 f.

‡Cf. Smith, *op. cit.* plates XCIV and XCVIII.

good specimen of a Yaksha is the crouching figure (no. C, 3; pl. XIV) of the Museum collection. We may perhaps assume that the colossal Parkham statue (no. C, 1; pl. XII) also represents a Yaksha, though it is not designated as such in the inscription. In the famous Bacchanalian sculpture (no. C, 2; pl. XIII), I recognise groups of Yakshas and Yakshīs (female Yakshas), the corpulent figure seated on a low rock (Kailāsa?) being their king Kubera. This I infer from certain statuettes (nos. C, 4 and 5), apparently later in date but similar in subject, in which the main figure holds a moneybag, the typical attribute of the god of wealth. It is not impossible that the Faun-like figures standing under trees (nos. C, 18 and J, 7; pl. XXII a), one of which seems to hold a bag, represent Yakshas, though of a much more pleasing appearance than the deformed dwarfs figured elsewhere. The changeable mood of these mountain spirits is thus apparently expressed in plastic art also.

The Yakshīs lived certainly in the imagination of ancient India as beings of beauty. In the Mahābhārata* we hear the messenger of the wicked king of Sindh address Draupadī, the spouse of the five Pāṇḍavas, in the following terms: "Who art thou that, bending down the branch of the *kadamba* tree, shinest lonely in the hermitage, sparkling like, at night, a flame of fire shaken by the breeze, oh well-browed one! Exceedingly art thou vested with beauty, yet nothing fearest thou here in the forest. Art thou a goddess or a Yakshī or a Dānavī or a celestial nymph or a fair Daitya damsel or a beautious maiden of the Nāga king or a night-wandering (Rākshasī) woman wandering in the wood?" On the gates of Barāhat there are female figures which the inscriptions describe as Yakshīs, and it is not unlikely that the lascivious nymphs standing on dwarfs which decorate the railing pillars of Mathurā are also meant for such semi-divine beauties. It will be noticed that their attitude is exactly that of Draupadī "bending down a branch of the *kadamba* tree."

In this connection I may draw attention to a railing pillar (no. J, 55) carved with a female figure leaning in a graceful attitude against the trunk of a flowering *aśoka* tree. It seems that the sculptor has intended here to illustrate the poetical conception, frequently referred to in old Indian lyrics, of the *aśoka* tree induced to burst into bloom by the touch of the left foot of a fair woman. It will be seen that on the sculpture the figure stands with her left foot placed against the trunk of the tree.

---

* Bopp, *Diluvium cum tribus aliis Mahâbhârati praestantissimis episodiis* (Berlin, 1892) Pt. I, p. 51.

Kālidāsa alludes to it when in his "Cloud Messenger" he makes the exiled Yaksha say :*

> "Profuse *aśoka* sheds its radiant flower,
> And budding *kesara* adorns the bower;
> These are my rivals, for the one would greet,
> As I would willingly, my charmer's feet,
> And with my fondness, would the other sip,
> The grateful nectar of her honied lip."

It should be remembered that in this passage there is question of a Yakshī, though in Sanskrit poetry *e.g.*, in the play "Mālavikā and Agnimitra" the ceremony of "kicking the *aśoka*" is usually performed by mortal women.

The Nāgas play a not less conspicuous part in Indian lore than the Yakshas. The name Nāga is usually rendered by "Snake-god" or "Serpent-god." But, though in sculpture they are almost invariably figured with a snake-hood expanded over their head, they have the character of water-spirits both in the ancient legends and in the popular worship of to-day.† They are believed to dwell in springs, lakes and tanks, and have the power to yield rain. In this respect they are benevolent deities. But, if roused to anger, they hurl down rocks from the mountain tops and destroy fair cities garlanded with grain.

Nāga images can easily be recognised from the canopy of five or seven snake heads, but it has already been noticed that the Tīrthaṁkaras Supārśva and Pārśva wear the same emblem. The Museum possesses a life-size statue (no. C, 13) which in an inscription incised on the back is denoted as a Nāga. It was erected during the reign of Huvishka and in the 40th year of Kanishka's era. The Nāga is figured with his right hand raised over the head, as if about to strike. The left hand, which is broken, must have held a cup. This we may infer from a comparison with another smaller Nāga image (no. C,15) which Mr. Growse erroneously identified as Balarāma, the elder brother of Kṛishṇa. Mr. Growse was led to this identification by the circumstance that such ancient Nāga figures are now-a-days regularly worshipped as Dāu-jī, the popular appellation of Balarāma. It is not a little curious that modern images of this deity, such as the white marble statuette (no. D, 36) which was manufac-

---

* *Meghadūta* stanza 75 (ed. Stenzler, p. 16). I have quoted Wilson's version. Cf. also *Raghuvaṁśa* VIII 62 and Böhtlingk, *Indische Sprüche* 1st. ed. 2580 (*Kāvyaprakāśa* 105).

† For a different theory see C. F. Oldham, *Serpent Worship in India*, *J. R. A. S.* for 1891, pp. 361—392.

tured at Brindāban, are exact copies of the Nāgas of the Kushaṇa period. In this connection it is interesting to note that, according to the Puranic accounts, Balarāma was an incarnation of Śesha-nāga, and that at the time of his death a large show-white snake was seen issuing from his mouth. Are we to assume that the elder brother of Kṛishṇa started his career as a simple "Snake-god?"

CATALOGUE.

A—G.—IMAGES.

A.—BUDDHA AND BODHISATTVA IMAGES.

* A 1[1].—Statuette (ht. 2′ 3¼″ or 0 m. 692; width 1′ 8″ or 0 m. 51) in black sandstone, representing a Bodhisattva, presumably Śākyamuni, seated cross-legged with his left hand resting on his knee and his right hand raised to the shoulder in the attitude of imparting security (Skr. *abhaya-mudrā*). The hand is connected with the back-slab by means of a projection carved with a decorative pattern. The figure is clad in a garment which leaves the right shoulder and breast bare. The folds of the drapery are indicated in a conventional fashion on the left shoulder and arm and beneath the legs. The palm of the right hand is marked with the symbol of the wheel, and the soles of the feet with the wheel and three-jewel symbols. The toes are each marked with a *svastika*. The treatment of the hair deserves special notice. It is not carved in curls, but is only indicated by a line over the forehead, so as to give the impression that the head is shaven. The protuberance of the skull (Skr. *ushṇīsha*) has the shape of a snail-shell (Skr. *kaparda*). The *ūrṇā* is indicated between the eyebrows. It is curious that, though the image thus possesses the marks of a Buddha, it is designated in its inscription as a Bodhisattva.

The head is encircled by a halo with scolloped border, around which the foliage of the Bodhi tree is shown. The circumstance of the foliage being that of the *pīpal* tree (*ficus religiosa*) renders it highly probable that the image represents indeed Śākyamuni before the attainment of Buddhahood. To the right and the left of the Bodhisattva stands an attendant, wearing royal attire and waving a fly-whisk in his right hand.

Over these two attendants are two flying figurines, presumably Devas, showering flowers over the Bodhisattva. One of these figures, that to the proper left, is slightly damaged. For the rest the sculpture is in excellent preservation. The pedestal is supported by three seated lions; the one in the centre facing, the other two, placed at the sides, turned outward. On the three raised rims of the pedestal is a Prākrit inscription in three lines, measuring 15¼″, 10½″ and 7½″ respectively. I read it [2]:

---

[1] Inscribed sculptures are marked with an asterisk.

[2] In a preliminary note on this inscription (*Annual Progress Report* for 1907-08, p. 37) I read *Śaka-vihāre* "in the Śaka-Monastery," but this reading is to be abandoned.

(1) *Budharakhitasa mātare Amohā-āsiye Bodhisacho [1] patiṭhāpito* (2) *sahā mātāpitihi sake vihāre* (3) *saravasatvānā hitasukhāye.*

Or rendered in Sanskrit:

Buddharakshitasya mātrā Amohāsyā Bodhisattvaḥ pratishṭhāpitaḥ saha mātāpitṛibhyām svake vihāre sarvasattvānām hitasukhāya. "Budharakhita's mother Amohā-āsī has erected [this] Bodhisattva together with her parents in her own convent (or temple) for the welfare and happiness of all sentient beings."

Palaeographical evidence points to the sculpture belonging to the early Kushaṇa period. It is with the Buddha image of Anyor (No. A 2) the oldest representation of Śākyamuni of which the date can approximately be fixed by an inscription, and must be one of the first Buddhist images made in Mathurā. On account of its artistic merit and excellent preservation also this Bodhisattva is one of the most remarkable sculptures preserved in the Museum.

The statuette was purchased for the Museum by Pandit Radha Krishna from a Brahmin who is said to have found it in digging a well on the Kaṭrā site, and who worshipped it as Viśvāmitra, while assuming that the four attending figures represented Rāma and his three brothers Lakshmaṇa, Bharata and Śatrughna (Plate VII). On loan from the Government of India.

* A2.—Image (ht. 2′ 9″ or 0 m. 838; width 2′ 1″ or 0 m. 634) of a Buddha seated cross-legged with his left hand resting on his knee. The right arm is lost, but the hand was evidently raised to the shoulder in the attitude of imparting security (Skr. *abhaya-mudrā*). The head is lost; it was provided with a circular halo, which is partly extant. On both sides of the halo is the foliage of the Bodhi tree (*ficus religiosa*). The figure is clad in an upper garment which leaves the right shoulder and breast bare. The turned-up soles of the feet are marked with the wheel and three-jewel symbols. The image is placed on a pedestal decorated on the sides with a pair of seated lions turned outward. The central portion of the pedestal appears to be defaced and may have contained a third lion, as is found on the Kaṭrā Bodhisattva (cf. above A 1). Along the raised upper rim of the pedestal is an inscription in two lines of 23″ and 17½″ respectively. It reads:

1. *Upāsakasya Sushasya Hārushasya dāna[*ṁ] Bu[*d]dha-prat[i]mā Uttarasya H[ā]rusha[sya]*

2. *vihāre sahā mātā-pitihi sarvasatvāna[ā]ṁ hita-sukh[ā]rtha[ṁ].*

---

[1] With the form *Bodhisacho* for *Bodhisattva* cf. *chachchara* for *chatvara*, *pahuchchai* for *prabhutvati*, and *kichcha* for *kṛitvā* which occurs in Ardhamāgadhī and connected dialects.

PLATE IX.

No. A, 5 ; Ht. 7' 2½".

BUDDHA STATUE FROM JAMĀLPUR MOUND ; GUPTA PERIOD.

"Gift of the lay-member Susha of Harusha[1], a Buddha image at the convent of Uttara of Harusha together with his parents for the sake of the welfare and happiness of all sentient beings."

It deserves notice that the language is much more sanskritic than that of the Kaṭrā Bodhisattva inscription. It may be assigned to the early Kushaṇa period on account of the character which agrees closely with that of the Sārnāth Bodhisattva inscriptions of the 3rd year of Kanishka.

The image is the oldest Buddha figure designated as such in an inscription and must, therefore, be one of the first representations of Buddha found in India, excluding Gandhāra. It was discovered by General Cunningham in 1882-83 at the village of Anyor at the south-eastern foot of the Girirāj or Govardhan hill and acquired for the Museum in January 1903 by Pandit Radha Krishna. (Plate VIII. Cf. *A. S. R.*, Vol. XX, p. 49; plate V, No. 5) On loan from the Government of India.

A 3.—Image (ht. 1′ 11″ or 0 m. 602) of a Buddha[2] seated cross-legged, with his right hand raised to the shoulder in the attitude of imparting protection. The right hand is broken; the head and left arm are missing. Part of the halo is preserved. The robe leaves the right shoulder uncovered and is tied to the loins by means of a girdle ending in two tassels which are visible below the feet. This image was standing at the entrance of the Damdama or Sarāi-Jamālpur now occupied by the Police lines. Possibly it originates from the neighbouring Jamālpur site.

A 4.—Image (ht. 2′ 8″ or 0 m. 81) of a standing Buddha. Feet and pedestal missing. The head is provided with a circular halo with scolloped border. The hair is treated so as to simulate the shaven head of a monk; the protuberance of the skull is conical in shape. Circular mark (Skr. *ūrṇā*) between the eye-brows. Protruding lips. The right hand is raised to the height of the shoulder; the open palm is marked with the symbol of the wheel (Skr. *chakra*). The stone connecting the hand and the halo is carved so as to present the appearance of a cushion. The left hand lifts the hem of the robe (Skr. *saṅghāṭi*) to the level of the shoulder. The robe covers both shoulders. The general attitude of the image is similar to that of some Gandhāra images, but the style is typical for the Mathurā school. Find-place unknown. (Plate XVa. Cf. Grünwedel, *Buddhist Art*, fig. 117).

*A 5.—Statue (ht. 7′ 2½″ or 2 m. 20, width across shoulders 2′ or 0 m. 61) of a standing Buddha clad in a well-carved upper garment (Skr.

[1] The geographical (?) name Harusha I am unable to identify.

[2] I have designated all images in monk's robes as Buddha figures, though, like No. A 1, they possibly represent Śākyamuni before the *Bodhi*, in which case they would be correctly named Bodhisattvas.

saṅghāṭi) which covers both shoulders. Round the waist we notice he indication of a girdle which holds up the lower garment visible above the ankles. The right hand which is broken was raised in the attitude of protection (Skr. *abhaya-mudrā*). The left hand holds the hem of the upper garment. The hair, in agreement with the canon, is arranged in schematic little curls turned to the right. The protuberance on the top of the skull (Skr. *ushnīsha*), a characteristic of the Buddhas, is clearly marked. But there is no trace of the mark on the forehead (Skr. *ūrṇā*), another sign of the *bodhi*. The nose and elongated ears are slightly injured. The head is adorned with a magnificently carved halo (diameter 3′ or 0 m. 915), circular in shape, consisting of concentric, decorative bands of various design.

At the feet of the statue we find two kneeling figurines, partly broken, which represent a couple of human worshippers, presumably the donors of the sculpture. On the front of the base a Sanskrit inscription is cut, consisting of two lines in Gupta character of the fifth century :—*Deyadharmo yaṁ śākyabhiksho* (*r**) *Yaśadinnasya. Yad atra puṇyaṁ tad bhavatu mā* (2) *tā-pittro āchāry-opādhyā* (*dhyā*)*yānāṁ cha sarvva-satvā* (*ttvā*)-*nuttara-jñāna*(*nā*)-*vāptaye.* " This is the pious gift of the Buddhist monk Yaśadinna. Whatsoever merit [there is] in this [gift], let it be for the attainment of supreme knowledge of [his] parents, teachers and preceptors and of all sentient beings.'

The sculpture was discovered in the course of the excavation of the Jamālpur (or Jail) mound. It was found broken in two pieces by a fracture above the ankles. Apart from the missing right hand, it is in an excellent state of preservation. (Plate IX. Cf. Growse, *Mathurā*, p. 115 and plate facing p. 172. and *J. A. S. B.*, Vol. XLVII (1878), Part I. p. 130 ; plate XXI. G. le Bon, *Les Civilisations de l' Inde* (Paris 1887) fig. 94).

A 6.—Statue (ht. 4′ 9″ or 1 m. 47) of a Buddha standing in the attitude of imparting security (Skr. *abhaya-mudrā*). Head and two hands broken. The drapery of the robe which covers both shoulders is indicated by schematic folds. At the feet of the Buddha are two kneeling figurines of worshippers. Judging from the style, the image belongs to the Gupta period. The statue is broken in two pieces across the knees. It was preserved in the Allahabad Library up to December 1907, and perhaps came from the Jamālpur site.

A 7.—Torso (ht. 4′ 4″ or 1 m. 33) of a Buddha statue of which the head, hands and feet are missing. The draping of the robe which covers both shoulders is marked by schematic folds. The image stands in the attitude of imparting security (Skr. *abhaya-mudrā*). Over the left shoulders part of an ornamental halo. On account of the style, the image can be assigned to the Gupta period. It was kept in the Allahabad Library up to December 1907, and perhaps came from the Jamālpur site.

A 8.—Torso (ht. 3' 8" or 1 m. 11) of a Buddha statue standing in the attitude of imparting protection (Skr. *abhaya-mudrā*). Head, right hand and feet with pedestal missing. The drapery of the robe which covers both shoulders is marked in schematic folds. Under the upper garment the girdle is shown with which the lower garment is fastened round the loins. On account of its style, the sculpture may be attributed to the Gupta period. It was preserved in the Allahabad Library up to December 1907, and perhaps originates from the Jamālpur site.

A 9.—Torso (ht. 3' 6" or 1 m. 075) of a standing Buddha draped in a foldy robe which covers both shoulders. The girdle (Skr. *kāyabandhana*), by means of which the lower garment is fastened to the loins, assumes the appearance of a double, flat belt. The head, which must have been provided with a halo, is missing. The arms are broken off at the elbows. Evidently the right hand was raised to the shoulder and the open palm turned outward in the gesture expressing protection (Skr. *abhaya-mudrā*). The left hand probably held the hem of the monk's robe. On account of its similarity in style with no. A 5, the image may be assigned to the Gupta period. Find-place unknown.

A 10.—Torso (ht. 3' 3" or 0 m. 99) of a Buddha statue standing in the attitude of imparting protection (Skr. *abhaya-mudrā*). Head, hands and feet with pedestal missing. The drapery of the robe which covers both shoulders is disposed in schematic folds. Judging from the style, the image belongs to the Gupta period. It was preserved in the Allahabad Library up to December 1907 and perhaps originates from the Jamālpur site.

A 11.—Torso (ht. 3' 3" or 0 m. 99) of a Buddha image standing in the attitude of imparting protection (Skr. *abhaya-mudrā*). Head, hands and feet with pedestal missing. Carving defaced. Drapery of the robe, which covers both shoulders, is arranged in schematic folds. The style of the image is that of the Gupta period. It was preserved in the Allahabad Library up to December 1907 and perhaps came from the Jamālpur site.

A 12.—Lower portion (ht. 2' 8" or 0 m. 825) of a standing Buddha image. Feet with pedestal missing. Drapery indicated in the usual fashion. It was preserved in the Allahabad Library up to December 1907 and perhaps originates from the Jamālpur site.

A13.—Torso (ht. 2' 5" or 0 m.72) of a Buddha statuette standing in the attitude of imparting protection (Skr. *abhaya-mudrā*). Head, hands and feet with pedestal missing. The robe which covers both shoulders is schematically treated. On both sides of the figure remnants of an ornamental halo. It was preserved in the Allahabad Library up to December 1907 and was perhaps excavated on the Jamālpur site.

A 14.—Image (ht. 3′ or 0 m. 925) of a Buddha seated cross-legged on a throne or lion-seat (Skr. *siṁhāsana*), his right hand raised in the attitude of protection (Skr. *abhaya-mudrā*). Head and left arm missing. The well-draped robe covers both shoulders. Wheel (Skr. *chakra*) and three-jewel (Skr. *triratna*) symbols on the soles of both feet. Lion on proper right side of pedestal missing. The image was preserved in the Allahabad Library up to December 1907 and perhaps came originally from the Jamālpur site.

A15.—Image (ht. 2' 8" or 0 m. 81) of a Buddha seated cross-legged. Head and both arms broken. Remnant of a halo with scolloped border under the right arm. The right hand was probably raised in the attitude of protection (Skr. *abhaya-mudrā*), whilst the left held the hem of the garment. The well-draped robe leaves the right shoulder bare. Wheel (Skr. *chakra*) and three-jewel (Skr. *triratna*) symbols on the sole of each foot. The image was kept in the Allahabad Library up to December 1907 and was perhaps unearthed on the Jamālpur site.

A16.—Image (ht. 2′ 6" or 0 m. 76) of a Buddha seated cross-legged. Head and arms missing. The left hand is preserved and rests on the knee. Right shoulder bare. The drapery is slightly indicated on the left shoulder. The lower garment is fastened to the loins by means of a double girdle. The right hand was perhaps raised to the level of the shoulder in the attitude of protection (Skr. *abhaya-mudrā*). The wheel (Skr. *chaka*) and three-jewel (Skr. *triratna*) symbols are marked on the soles of the feet. The image is perhaps identical with the mutilated figure found by Growse in one of the Chaubārā mounds together with an inscribed image. (*Ind. Ant.*, Vol. VI, p. 217.)

A17.—Statuette (ht. 1′ 6" or 0 m.45) of a Buddha seated cross-legged. The head is missing and both arms are broken. The attitude was probably that of imparting protection (Skr. *abhaya-mudrā*) expressed by the right hand, still traceable, being raised towards the shoulder, the open palm turned outwards. The left holds the hem of the monk's robe which covers both shoulders. The beginning of the halo is visible near the right shoulder. Find-place unknown.

A 18.—Statuette (ht. 1′ 1½″ or 0 m.204) of a Buddha seated cross-legged on a throne, on which is a wheel between two lions couchant with their heads turned back The head of the Buddha figure with most of the ornamental nimbus is lost. The right hand, which is also missing, was raised in the attitude of imparting security (Skr. *abhaya-mudrā.*) The other hand holds the hem of the monk's robe which covers both shoulders. The soles are marked with the wheel (Skr. *chakra*) and three-jewel (Skr. *triratna*) symbols. Find-place unknown.

A 19.—Statuette (ht. 1′ or 0 m. 304) of a Buddha seated cross-legged in the attitude of meditation. The robe covers both shoulders. Head and right knee missing. At the side of the left knee is a projecting piece of stone. The image was preserved at the Allahabad Library up to December 1907 and perhaps originates from the Jamālpur site.

A 20.—Statuette (ht. 7½″ or 0 m. 19) of a Buddha (?) seated cross-legged in meditation on a throne between two attendants. On the front of the pedestal is a wheel placed between two seated female figures; two lions couchant occupy the corners. It was found in clearing a well at Jamālpur[1] and was made over to the Museum by Lieutenant-Colonel W. Vost, I.M.S.

A 21.—Statuette (ht. 1′ 5½″ or 0 m. 444) of a Buddha seated cross-legged on a cushion placed on a throne supported by standing lions. The head which was detached has been refixed. The two arms are broken, but evidently the right hand was raised in the attitude of imparting protection, whilst the left held the hem of the garment, as appears from the drapery displayed over the left knee. The robe covers both shoulders. Over the left shoulder is a remnant of an ornamental halo. In front of the throne between the two lions is a relief representing a seated figurine with halo, presumably a Bodhisattva, with four figures of devotees, two on each side, approaching him with offerings. The figure on the proper left end is a woman. Part of the pedestal with the lower portion of these five figures is defaced. The scene on the front relief is evidently derived from similar devotional scenes commonly found on the pedestals of the Buddha and Bodhisattva images of Gandhāra. (Cf. *A. S. R.*, 1903-04, pp. 255—257 and plate LXVII.) On the proper left side are traces of an inscription. I found the statuette set up near a shrine at Sītalā-Ghāṭī in Mathurā city, where it was being worshipped, and purchased it for the Museum. (Plate XVI.) On loan from the Government of India.

---

[1] The site of the hamlet of Jamālpur is now used as an encamping ground for civil officers.

A 22.—Statuette (ht. 7″ or 0 m. 165) of a Buddha (?) seated crosslegged on a throne supported by two lions. In front of the throne is a figurine with halo seated in the attitude of meditation between two standing figures. (Cf. above No. A 21.) Find-place unknown.

A 23.—Fragment (length 1′ 11″ or 0 m. 584, with 1′ 3½″ or 0 m. 394) consisting of the left hand of a Buddha statue of colossal size. The statue was evidently standing in the attitude of imparting security (Skr. *abhaya-mudrā*), the left hand holding the hem of the garment. Symbol of wheel (Skr. *chakra*) partly visible beneath drapery. The fragment must be identical with "the stone hand, measuring a foot across the palm, which must have belonged to a statue not less than 20 to 24 feet in height" and which, according to Growse, was excavated from the Jamālpur (or Jail) mound in 1860. It was preserved at the Allahabad Library till December 1907. (*Mathurā* p. 107.)

A 24.—Fragment (ht. 1′ 5″ or 0 m. 432) consisting of part of the right leg and a portion of the left foot of a colossal Buddha (?) figure seated cross-legged. Drapery indicated. The symbol of the wheel (Skr. *chakra*) is partly preserved on the sole of the foot. The toes are marked with five different symbols, including the mystic cross (Skr. *svastika*). This fragment must be identical with that described by Cunningham as "the right knee of a squatted colossal draped figure, with the left foot resting on the calf of the leg." It was found in the Chaubārā mound C which also yielded a colossal Buddha head (A 28 ?) believed by Cunningham to belong to the same statue. (*A. S. R.*, Vol. III, p. 18; cf. *Mathurā*, p. 124, where the fragment is said to come from Chaubārā mound B.)

A 25.—Fragment (ht. 1′ 8″ or 0 m. 508) of a Buddha image consisting of a portion of the left shoulder and arm draped in a monk's robe. Find-place unknown.

A 26.—Bust (ht. 5½″ or 0 m. 14) of a Buddha statuette clad in a well-draped robe which covers both shoulders.

A 27.—Head (ht. 1′ 10½″ or 0 m. 57) of a Buddha image of colossal size. Nose broken. Shaven head. *Ushṇīsha* distinctly marked in the shape of a snail shell. *Ūrṇā* indicated by a circular hole between the eyebrows, evidently meant to contain a precious stone. This head is no doubt identical with "the head of a colossal figure of very Egyptian cast of features with a round hole in its forehead, in which was once set a ruby or other precious stone." It was found by Mr. Growse in one of the Chaubārā mounds, the same which yielded the steatite relic casket now in the Calcutta Museum and the railing pillar No. J 7. (*Mathurā*, p. 123.)

A 28.—Head (ht. 1′ 5″ or 0 m. 432) of a Buddha image of colossal size. *Ushṇīsha* distinct. Forehead, nose, chin and ears broken. Cheeks and chin round and full. Pupils not indicated. Find-place unknown.

A 29.—Head (ht. 1′ 4″ or 0 m. 403) of a Buddha image of colossal size. Nose missing; ears damaged. Hair arranged in rows of schematic waves. Protuberance of the skull (Skr. *ushṇīsha*) damaged. Mark on forehead (Skr. *ūrṇā*) indicated by a slightly raised disc. Three mortices, two over the ears and one behind the *ushṇīsha*. Find-place unknown.

A 30.—Head (ht. 1′ 2″ or 0 m. 355) of a Buddha image of life-size. Nose broken. Forehead, chin and ears damaged. Hole on proper right side. Hair arranged in schematic curls. *Ushṇīsha* distinctly marked. The head was preserved at the Allahabad Library till December 1907. Perhaps from the Jamālpur site.

A 31.—Head (ht. 1′ 2″ or 0 m. 355) of a Buddha image of life-size, with portions of the draped shoulders and of the plain halo. Nose and *ushṇīsha* broken; eyes damaged. Hair arranged in schematic curls. It was found in clearing a well at the village of Jamālpur and made over to the Museum by Lieutenant-Colonel W. Vost, I.M.S.

A 32.—Head (ht. 1′ 1″ or 0 m. 33) of a Buddha or Bodhisattva image of life-size. Nose missing, ears and chin damaged and surface generally disintegrated. There are traces of an *ushṇīsha*, but not of an *ūrṇā*. On the top behind the *ushṇīsha* are two holes, evidently meant to receive iron clamps or hooks. This head was found on the Anyor Buddha image to which it had been attached with mud plaster by the inhabitants of the village who used to worship the image. It is, however, obvious that this head belongs to an image of much larger size than that on which it was placed. The head was acquired for the Museum by Pandit Radha Krishna at the same time with the Buddha image. On loan from the Government of India.

A 33.—Head (ht. 11″ or 0 m. 28) of a Buddha (?) image of life-size. Nose, right eye and *ushṇīsha* broken. Hair indicated by a line over the forehead. It was preserved at the Allahabad Library till December 1907, and perhaps came originally from the Jamālpur site.

A 34.—Head (ht. 10″ or 0 m. 253) of a Buddha (?) image of less than life-size. *Ushṇīsha* broken; nose damaged. Hair indicated by a line over the forehead. *Ūrṇā* between the eye-brows. The head was kept at the Allahabad Library till December 1907, and perhaps originates from the Jamālpur site.

A 35.—Head (ht. 10″ or 0 m. 254) of a Buddha (?) image of life-size. Back of head broken off; nose missing. No trace of an *ushṇīsha*. *Ūrṇā* marked between the eye-brows. Hair arranged in schematic curls. It was found in clearing a well at Jamālpur and made over to the Museum by Lieutenant-Colonel W. Vost, I.M.S.

A 36.—Head (ht. 10" or 0 m. 254) of a Buddha (?) image of less than life-size. Nose and *ushṇīsha* broken. Ears damaged. No *ūrṇā*. The head was preserved at the Allahabad Library till December 1907, and was perhaps excavated on the Jamālpur site.

A 37.—Head (ht. 11" or 0 m. 28) of a Buddha image of life-size. Half of the face is broken off. Hair arranged in conventional curls. *Ushṇīsha* partly preserved. It was kept at the Allahabad Library till December 1907, and perhaps originates from the Jamālpur site.

A 38.—Head (ht. 5¼" or 0 m. 133) of a Buddha figure. Find-place unknown.

A 39.—Head (ht. 5½" or 0 m. 14) of a small Buddha (?) image. Nose broken. Hair arranged in short, schematic curls. *Ushṇīsha* on top. No *ūrṇā*. Pupil in left eye indicated; right eye, lips and chin slightly injured. Elongated ears, the lobes touching the shoulders; ears broken.

A 40.—Statue (ht. 6′ 7" or 2 m. including tenon) of a Bodhisattva standing. Head and arms missing. The left hand probably rested on the hip, where the stone is broken. The upper part of the body is nude, except for a torque and flat necklace. A scarf thrown over the left shoulder passes round the right leg beneath the knee. It was probably held at the hip with the missing left hand. The lower garment which covers the legs is fastened round the loins by means of a double flat belt, the upper one being knotted over the right thigh. It has the appearance of a *dhōtī* with its ample folds hanging down between the legs. On both sides of the feet are traces of a kneeling figurine. These presumably represent the donors of the statue. The image shows a marked affinity to the Bodhisattva of the third year of Kanishka excavated by Mr. Oertel at Sārnāth in March 1905 and to the one previously discovered by Cunningham at Sahēṭh-Mahēṭh, the site of the ancient city of Śrāvastī. (Cf. *A. S. R.* for 1904-05, pp. 78 ff., plate XXVI.) We may, therefore, assume that the pose of the present Bodhisattva was the same, the right hand being raised towards the right shoulder, and that the image belongs to the Kushaṇa period. A comparison with the Bodhisattva statuette A 43 will show what the image was like when entire. (Cf. also *A. S. R.*, Vol. III, plate XI D.) Find-place unknown.

A 41.—Life-size statue (ht. 4′ 5" or 1 m. 342) of a standing Bodhisattva, of which the head and feet are broken off. Near the right shoulder are traces of a circular halo with scolloped border. The right arm is missing; the hand was probably raised to the level of the shoulder in the attitude of imparting protection. The left hand rests on the hip. The figure is clad in a thin upper garment, of which the drapery is indicated on the left arm and breast, and in a *dhōtī* fastened to the loins by means of a flat girdle tied in a knot over the right thigh. The *dhōtī* falls down in ample folds between the legs. The statue is of exactly the same type as the Bodhisattva statues of Sārnāth and Sahēṭh-Mahēṭh and, on that account, may be attributed to the Kushaṇa period. I found it in December 1907 lying at the side of the *kachchā* road at the foot of the Menāgaṛ Ṭīlā close to the garden known as the Bangalanvālī Bāghīchī. On loan from the Government of India

A 42.—This head, which was lying in front of a house on the top of the Menāgaṛ Ṭīlā, was said to have been found at the same time as the image A 41, but it is doubtful whether it belongs to it. The image represents a Bodhisattva, whereas the head with its conventional little curls and *ushṇisha* must have belonged to a Buddha image. Its style is of the Kushaṇa period. The nose and ears are broken.

A 43.—Statuette (ht. 1′ 5″ or 0 m. 43) of a Bodhisattva, presumably Maitreya. Right arm broken. It has a plain halo with scolloped border, an elaborate head-dress and the usual ornaments. It wears a scarf over the left shoulder and arm, and holds an ointment vessel between the fore-finger and the middle finger of the left hand, the palm of the hand being turned foreward. The figure is clad in a *dhōtī* fastened to the loins by means of a double flat girdle tied in a knot above the right thigh. The statuette has a marked resemblance to the headless statues A 40 and 41, and must belong to the Kushaṇa period. The Bodhisattva type represented by these figures seems to be derived from the Graeco-Buddhist art of Gandhāra. Find-place unknown. (Plate XV *b*.)

A 44.—Fragment (ht. 1′ 5½″ or 0 m. 444, including tenon) of a standing Bodhisattva (?) statuette of which only the lower half remains. Between the legs is a portion of the drapery of a *dhōtī*. Cf. Nos. A 40, 41 and 43. The sculpture was preserved at the Allahabad Library till December 1907 and perhaps originates from the Jamālpur site. I found it broken in two pieces.

A 45.—Image (ht. 2′ 2″ or 0 m. 68) of a Bodhisattva seated cross-legged in the attitude of meditation (Skr. *dhyāna-mudrā*). Head missing and right arm broken; the halo with scolloped border is partly preserved. The soles of the feet are marked with the wheel and three-jewel symbols,

The figure wears a scarf thrown over the left shoulder and arm, and a *dhōtī*, the end of which is spread out in front on the pedestal together with the tassels of the cord with which it is fastened to the loins. The breast and arms are decorated with profuse ornaments. We notice particularly the broad necklace fastened with buckles in the shape of animal-heads and the string of amulet-holders[1] under the right arm which are commonly found on the Bodhisattvas of Gandhāra. The bracelets on the upper arms are embellished with plâques on which we observe a human figure riding on a conventional bird, probably a Garuḍa or a peacock. The spread-out tail of the bird forms, as it were, an ornamental halo round the rider. The image was found inside a well near the village of Ganēsrā five miles from Mathurā on the Gōvardhan road and was placed in the Museum in 1908. (Plate X.) On loan from the Government of India.

A 46.—Torso (ht. 2′ 2″ or 0 m. 66) of a male figure of colossal size, perhaps a Bodhisattva, profusely adorned with various ornaments. Over a string of beads and two flat torques a heavy beaded necklace hangs down between the breasts. This necklace is very curiously decorated with four *makara* heads. These are evidently copied from the Bodhisattva figures of Gandhāra which generally wear necklaces with clasps in the shape of animal heads. But in the present instance the meaning of this ornament seems to have been misunderstood. In the centre of the chest we notice a disk with nine tassels attached to a thin cord which passes round the neck. To another cord, passing under the right arm, four amulet-holders are attached, such as are peculiar to the Bodhisattva figures of Gandhāra. Finally we notice the long locks falling down on both shoulders. Pandit Radha Krishna obtained this torso for the Museum at the same time with the seated Buddha image A3 which had been placed at the entrance of the Damdama or Jamālpur Sarāi. There is reason to suppose that both sculptures originate from the neighbouring Buddhist site, now occupied by the Collector's Court House.

A 47.—Fragment (ht. 2′ 5½″ or 0 m. 745) consisting of the lower portion of a Bodhisattva figure seated in European fashion on an ornamental stool of wickerwork. The sandaled left foot is placed on a foot-stool, on which the other empty sandal lies. The right leg, now missing, must have been drawn up in the attitude peculiar to Bodhisattva images of the Graeco-Buddhist school (Cf. *A.S.R.*, 1903-04, p. 254, plate LXVIII c and 1906-7, p. 151, plate LII*b*).

---

[1] The British Museum contains a similar amulet-holder of gold set with jewels which was discovered by Mr. W. Simson in the Ahīn-Pōsh Stūpa near Jalālābād. Cf. *Proc. A. S. B.* for 1879, pp. 77—79, and 122 ff, and *Archaeologia*, Vol. LVIII (1902), p. 261 and plate 16.

No. A. 45; Ht. 2' 2".

BODHISATTVA (?) STATUETTE

*A 48.—Pedestal (ht. 1′ 3½″ or 0 m. 39 including the square tenon) of a standing Buddha (?) image of which only the bare feet remain. Outside the feet are kneeling figurines of which the upper portions are lost. These two figures, male and female, probably represent the donors of the image. The front of the pedestal has an inscription in four lines, first deciphered by Professor J. Dowson and re-edited by Dr. J. F. Fleet, who gives the following transcript and translation :—

1. *Saṁvvatsara-śa'e paṁcha-stris (triṁś)-ottaratame* 135, *Pushya-māse divase vi[ṁ]ś[e] di* 20. *Deyadharm[o] yaṁ vihāra-svāminy[ā]*

2. *Devtāyā (Devatāyāḥ) Yad atra puṇyaṁ tad bhavatu mātā-pitroḥ sarvva-sat [t*]vānāñ cha anuttara-jñānāptaye.*

3. *Saubhāgyaṁ pratirūpatā guṇavatī kīrttis sapatna-kshayaḥ śrīmanto vibhavāthavā [ḥ*] sukha-phalā nirvvāṇam aṁte śivam*

4. *Astabdhāni bhavanti dāna-niratau chittaṁ niyojyaikada* — — — ⏑*vitāraṇa*⏑ ⏑*dhiyāṁ* — — ⏑ — — ⏑*yām.*

"In a century of years increased by the thirty-fifth [year], [or in figures] 135; in the month Pushya; on the twentieth day [or in figures] the day 20. This is the appropriate religious gift of the abbess[1] Devatā. Whatever religious merit [there is] in this act, let it be for the acquisition of supreme knowledge by [her] parents and by all sentient beings.

Good fortune; the condition of being a model [worthy of imitation], abounding in virtuous qualities; fame; the destruction of the enemies [of religion]; riches abounding in prosperity; births that result in happiness; [and] finally, an auspicious *nirvāṇa*; [all these] are not permanent (?); having once fixed the thoughts upon the happiness of making gifts ;... ......"

The date of this inscription, if referred to the Gupta era, corresponds to A.D. 454-5. The pedestal was found in the Jamālpur (or Jail) mound probably in the course of the excavations carried on by Mr. Hardinge in 1877-8. It was removed presumably first to Agra and then to Allahabad where Dr. Fleet examined it in "the Government Museum" shortly before 1888. I found it in 1904 in the Allahabad Public Library and arranged in December 1907 for its return to Mathurā together with the other sculptures from this place.

(Cf. Dowson, *J. R. A. S.*, N. S., Vol. V, p. 184, No. 8; Cunningham, *A. S. R.*, Vol. III, p. 36; plate XVI, no. 22; *Corpus Inscr. Ind.*, Vol. III, pp. 262-263, no. 63; plate XXXIX A.)

[1] I do not quite agree with Dr. Fleet regarding the interpretation of the word "*vihāra-svāminī*" which I believe to mean "an abbess or female superior of a nunnery" and not "the wife of a Vihārasvāmin." The latter was no doubt a *bhikshu* and as such had to take the vow of celibacy.

* A 49.—Fragment (ht. 5″ or 0 m. 127 ; width 1′ 3½″ or 0 m. 393) apparently belonging to a seated Buddha image. Only some drapery of the robe is preserved. The flat surface beneath the drapery is inscribed with a fragmentary inscription in one line of which the beginning and concluding portions are lost. It reads : ......*shkasya rājya-saṁvatsare* 28 *hemanta* 3 *di*......" In the 28th year of the reign of......shka, in the third month of winter, on the.... day...." It was discovered by Mr. Growse in the courtyard of the Magistrate's Court House and had probably been brought to light in 1860 when the foundations of this building were laid. Growse presumed that the name of the king is to be restored as that of Kanishka. Professor Lüders, however, has pointed out that the stroke preceding the syllable *shka* is in favour of the restoration *Hushkasya*. (Cf. Growse *Mathurā* (2nd ed.), p. 106, with plate ; *Ind. Ant.*, Vol. VI, p. 217, no. 1 with plate ; and Lüders, *Ind. Ant.*, Vol. XXXIII, pp. 38-39, no. 8).

*A 50.—Pedestal (ht. 1′ or 0 m. 314) of a seated Buddha (?) image of which only the left foot, marked with the wheel symbol, together with the drapery beneath the legs is preserved. On this drapery we notice two tassels apparently belonging to a girdle. In the centre of the pedestal is a wheel placed on a pillar between two standing figures of worshippers, apparently each carrying a garland and a bunch of flowers. On the proper left end is a lion turned outward ; the corresponding lion figure to the right is lost. On the upper and lower rims of the pedestal is a mostly defaced inscription in two lines which I read :—

1. ....*vih*[*ā*]*r*[*e*]..................
2. ....[*pra*]*t*[*i*]*m*[*ā*] *p*[*r*]*atish*[*ṭhā*]*pit*[*ā*]

Pandit Radha Krishna obtained this inscribed fragment from the village of Naugavā, 4½ miles west of the City south of the Govardhan road. On loan from the Government of India.

A 51.—Pedestal (ht. 11″ or 0 m. 28, including tenon) of a standing Buddha (?) image of which only the bare feet remain standing on a kind of cushion, perhaps meant for a lotus-flower. At the right foot there is the lower portion of a miniature kneeling figure, probably the donor of the image. It was preserved at the Allahabad Library till December 1907 and perhaps came originally from the Jamālpur site.

A 52.—Pedestal (ht. 1′ 10″ or 0 m. 557, including square tenon) of a standing Bodhisattva (?) image of which only the bare feet remain. On each side a kneeling figurine, presumably a human devotee, can be traced. The fragment was brought to the Museum from the Joint Magistrate's bungalow. Its find-place is unknown.

A 53.—Fragment (ht. 1′ 2″ or 0 m. 355, including square tenon) of a standing Bodhisattva (?) image, of which only the bare feet remain. Between the feet is a cluster of lotus-buds surmounted by a full-blown lotus-flower. At the sides of the image are two figurines, male and female, both standing and holding a wreath in their right and some other offering in their left hands. These figures probably represent the donors of the image. It was brought to the Museum from bungalow no. 14 in Cantonments. Its find-place is unknown.

A 54.—Fragment (ht. 1′ 5″ or 0 m. 431, including square tenon) of a standing Bodhisattva (?) image, of which only the bare feet remain. Between the feet is a cluster of lotus-buds. It was brought to the Museum from the same bungalow as A 53. Its find-place is unknown.

A 55.—Fragment (ht. 1′ 3″ or 0 m. 38, including tenon) of a standing Bodhisattva (?) of which only the bare feet remain. Between the feet is a projection which perhaps was part of the *dhōtī*. To the proper right is a figurine of a male devotee, to the left a woman and a child. These three figures, which are much defaced, probably represent the donors of the image. The sculpture was brought to the Museum from the same bungalow as A 53. Its find-place is unknown.

•A 56.—Fragment (ht. 10″ or 0 m. 255) of a pedestal of a standing Bodhisattva (?) image of which only one foot remains. On the front of the pedestal are traces of two lines of an inscription in Brāhmī of the Kushaṇa type.

A 57.—Bust (ht. 6½″ or 0 m. 165) of a Bodhisattva (?) figure wearing a torque and flat necklace similar to that of the Bodhisattva (?) images A 42 and 43. The fragment was brought to the Museum from the Joint Magistrate's bungalow. Its find-place is unknown.

A 58.—Fragment (ht. 8¾″ or 0 m. 223) carved with drapery, probably belonging to a Buddha image. Find-place unknown.

A 59.—Fragment (ht. 11½″ or 0 m. 292) carved with drapery, probably belonging to a Bodhisattva image. Find-place unknown.

A 60.—Statuette (ht. 6¼″ or 0 m. 163) of a Buddha seated cross-legged on a lion-throne in the attitude of meditation. Four miniature figures are to his right, one of which is a chowrie carrier. The other side is broken. The sculpture which is much worn was obtained by Pandit Radha Krishna from a weaver in the City. On loan from the Government of India

A 61.—Bas-relief (ht. 12½″ or 0 m. 321) representing a Bodhisattva, perhaps Maitreya, seated cross-legged on a throne decorated with a wheel and two lions. He raises his right hand to the shoulder and holds a vessel in his left hand. On each side stands an attendant chowrie-carrier. The sculpture which is much defaced was purchased from a *Chamār* who worshipped it as Bundēlā Bābā. On loan from the Government of India.

A 62.—Life-size statue (ht. 6′ 8½″ or 2 m. 04, including tenon) of a Bodhisattva standing. Head and arms missing; pedestal defaced. Between the feet is a cluster of lotus-flowers. The style of the image which must belong to the Kushaṇa period is the same as that of A 40. It was found in two pieces at the Bharatpur Gate, the larger fragment being used as a wheelguard, and taken to the Museum in December 1908. On loan from the Government of India.

*A 63.—Life-size statue (height 6′ 4″ or 1 m. 926, including tenon) of a Bodhisattva standing. It is broken in two; the head and right arm are lost. The right hand was most probably raised to the shoulder, the attitude of the image being the same as that of the Bodhisattva statue of Sārnāth. The dress also is similar. It consists of a *dhōtī* fastened to the loins by means of a flat girdle and an upper garment thrown over the left arm and shoulder. The front of the pedestal is cut off with part of the feet. Between the feet we notice a cluster of lotus-buds. On the top of the pedestal is a fragmentary inscription of one line which reads: *Siddha*[*ṁ*] *Maharajasya Devaputrasya Huvishkasya sa*[*ṁ*] *35 hemata* ...... "Success! In the year 35 of the King, His Majesty, Huvishka ...." The image was acquired by Pandit Radha Krishna from Likhanu, Hathras *parganā*, Alīgaṛh district. On loan from the Government of India.

*A 64.—Fragment (ht. 1′ 2½″ or 0 m. 368) of the pedestal of a seated Buddha figure of which only the legs are preserved with indication of the clothing and legs of attendant standing behind left knee. On the front of the pedestal is a relief similar to that on No. A 50 representing a dwarf pillar with wheel (?) in the centre, and a worshipping figure standing on each side, that to the proper left a female holding a garland in her right hand, whilst of the other, male (?) figure only the head and left arm remain. There is a lion rampant on the proper left end. The pedestal bears a fragmentary inscription, apparently consisting of four lines, of which two are placed above and two beneath the front-relief.

It reads (1) ...... *d*[*i*]*vas*[*e*] *30 eta*[*sya*] (2) [*purvā yāṁ*].
.... *pa śa vadhu*[*ye*] *Devarakshi*. (3)
.... [*sarva-*]*satva-hi* (4) [*tasukhāya*].

The character is Brāhmī of the Kushaṇa period. The fragment was acquired from the Dhūnsarpārā Quarter in Mathurā city. On loan from the Government of India.

*A 65.—Statuette (ht. 1′ 2″ or 0 m. 355) of a Buddha seated cross-legged with his right hand raised in the attitude of imparting protection (Skr. *abhaya-mudrā*), whilst the left holds the hem of the robe which covers both shoulders. The drapery is indicated in a schematic manner. The halo is broken. On the front of the pedestal is a bas-relief representing a Buddha seated in the attitude of meditation between two devotees standing at his sides. Both ends are occupied by lion figures. The workmanship, both of the Buddha and of the pedestal is clumsy. There is an indistinct inscription of two lines cut on the raised rims above and beneath the bas-relief. It is dated Sa 51 g[ri] 3. On loan from the Government of India.

The sculpture was discovered by Pandit Radha Krishna at Anyor near Gōvardhan, where it was being worshipped as the Goddess Durgā by the Malkhāna Ṭhākurs (Moslims !) who inhabit the village.

*A 66.—Fragment (ht. 1′ or 0 m. 305) of a seated Bodhisattva (?) image of which only the left leg, right foot and left hand remain, together with the left leg of an attendant standing on his left side and part of the pedestal. From the little that remains of the image we may conjecture that it was similar in attitude and style to the Anyor Bodhisattva (No. A 1). It certainly belongs to the same period, as appears from the character used in the inscription. The front of the pedestal was evidently cut in three facets, the side ones measuring 3″ in width and receding 1″. The central facet is carved with a female figure standing turned to the proper right and raising both hands to the forehead in token of respectful salutation. From the position of this figure—apparently a female devotee—we may surmise that the centre of the pedestal was occupied by a Buddha or Bodhisattva figure. The corner of the rim over the central part of the front face is supported by a standing winged lion. The inscription in Kushaṇa Brāhmī is cut on the two rims (1st) above, and (2nd) beneath the bas-relief, (3rd) on the rim and (4th) on the facet under the attendant. It reads:—

— — — —[*upāsi*]*kaye Naṁdāye kshatrapa sa*

(2) — — — —[*Bo*]*dhisat* [*va*] *visa* — *ta*[*re*].

(3) *savasatānāṁ hitasu*[*khā*]*rtha* [*ṁ*].

(4) *Śavasthi*[**vā*] *diyānaṁ parigṛihe.*

The inscription is too fragmentary to allow of a consecutive translation of it being given. It seems that the donor of the image was a female relative of a satrap. We further find the usual formula: "For the sake of the welfare and happiness of all sentient beings." Finally the image is said to be an object of homage (*parigṛiha*) of the Sarvāstivādins, if at least we may assume that this is meant by the expression *śāvasthidiyānaṁ*.

The fragment was obtained by Pandit Radha Krishna from a shrine known as Galatēsvar Mahādēv Maṭh near the Kaṭrā where it was inserted in a wall. It is said to have been unearthed from a small mound in the neighbourhood. On loan from the Government of India.

A 67. Life-size image (ht. 5' 11" or 1 m. 80 including tenon) of a Bodhisattva standing. Head, right shoulder and arm and left hand missing and carving generally obliterated. The right hand was probably raised to the shoulder and the left hand either rested on the hip or held an alabastron. The figure wears a *dhōtī* fastened with a girdle, and an upper garment hanging down from the left shoulder. The upper part of the body is decorated with several necklaces and other ornaments similar to those of the torso A 46. Between the feet we notice a cluster of lotus-buds and next to the left foot a female figurine standing to front and holding in her right hand a garland as an offering, whilst the left hand is placed on the hip. Of a corresponding figure standing on the proper right side of the image, only the feet are left. These two figurines presumably represent the donors of the statue.

The image which must belong to the Kushaṇa period was found by Pandit Radha Krishna at the Kaṅkōr Ṭīlā near the village of Jaisiṅghpura 3 miles north of Mathurā, west of the road to Brindāban. It was being worshipped as the guardian-god of the village. On loan from the Government of India.

A 68. Statuette (ht. 2' or 0 m. 61) of a Bodhisattva, probably Maitreya, to judge from the alabastron or ointment vessel in his left hand. The right arm and part of the halo are missing, also the feet with the pedestal. The halo shows traces of a zigzag border. The hair is arranged in curls schematically treated. The figure is dressed in a long robe which leaves the right breast and shoulder bare. A loose upper garment hangs down from the left shoulder and from the left hand. The Bodhisattva wears ear-pendants, a flat torque and necklace, and two bracelets round the left arm. The present figure is in some respects similar to the Maitreya statuette No. A 43, but is decidedly superior artistically. This is particularly noticeable in the position of the legs and in the treatment of the hand with the alabastron. The statuette is carved in the round which is another indication of its early date. It may be safely assigned to the early Kushaṇa period. It was obtained from the Shāh-ganj mound near the Brindāban Gate of the city. On loan from the Government of India.

A 69. Image (ht. 2' 5" or 0 m. 736) of a seated Buddha clad in a monk's robe, much worn. Obtained from a *bāghīcha* opposite the Bhūtēsar mound. On loan from the Government of India.

A 70. Head (ht. 7″ or 0 m. 179) of a Buddha image with *ūrṇā* and pronounced *ushṇisha*. Hair arranged in curls. From Chāmuṇḍā Maṭh at 'Āzampur Sarāi, 3 miles from Mathurā on the Delhi road. On loan from the Government of India.

*A 71. Fragment (ht. 9″ or 0 m. 228) consisting of a pedestal with the lower portion of a Buddha figure seated cross-legged. Indication of drapery on right leg. The face of the pedestal is carved with a relief, partly defaced, consisting of two seated lions which occupy the corners and two human figurines, probably worshippers, standing on both sides of a wheel-pillar (?) On the rim above there is an inscription in one line which commences with the name of Huvishka and appears to be dated in the year 31. The sculpture was acquired from the mound of Rāl-Bhaḍār, 8 miles north-west of Mathurā. On loan from the Government of India.

B. Jina or Tirthamkara Images.

B 1.—Image (ht. 4′ 7½″ or 1 m. 103) of a Jina of colossal size seated cross-legged in the attitude of meditation (Skr. *dhyāna-mudrā*) with both hands resting in the lap. The lower portion of both arms is broken as is also the upper portion of the elaborate halo, decorated with concentric bands of various design. The nose is broken; the lips and elongated ears are slightly injured. The hair is arranged in short schematic curls turned to the right. There is the *śrīvatsa* symbol in the centre of the chest. The palms of the hands and soles of the feet are marked with the symbol of the wheel. The image probably belongs to the Gupta period on account of its ornamental halo and the treatment of the hair. Find-place unknown.

*B 2.—Image (ht. 3′ 3½″ or 1 m.) of a Jina seated cross-legged in meditation (Skr. *dhyāna-mudrā*). Head and left arm missing. *Śrīvatsa* symbol in centre of chest and symbols in the palms of the hands and on the soles of the feet. Relief on front of pedestal defaced. Inscription in two lines on rim over front relief. It was first published by Professor Dowson, corrected by Cunningham and re-edited by Professor Lüders who reads:

1. *Siddhaṁ Mahārājasya Vāsudevasya saṁ* 83 *gri*. 2 *di*. 16 *etasya purvvaye Senasya*

2. *[dhi]tu Dattasya vadhuye Vya . . cha . . sya gandhikasya Kuṭumbiniye Jinadāsiya pratimā dhar[rma]dānaṁ.*

"Success! In the year 83 of Mahārāja Vāsudeva, in the second [month of] summer, on the 16th day, on that [date specified as] above, an image, the pious gift of Jinadāsī, the daughter of Sena, the daughter-in-law of Datta, the wife of the perfumer Vya . . cha . . ."

The image was preserved at the Allahabad Public Library till December 1907 and perhaps originates from the Kaṅkālī Ṭīlā.

(Dowson, *J. R. A. S.* N. S., Vol. V, p. 184, No. 6; Cunningham, *A. S. R.*, Vol. III, p. 34, No. 16; Bühler *V. O. J.*, Vol. IV, p. 324; Lüders, *Ind. Ant.* Vol. XXXIII, p. 107, No. 21.)

*B 3.—Image (ht. 2′ 8½″ or 0 m. 82) of a Jina seated cross-legged in meditation. Head and left arm missing. *Śrīvatsa* symbol in centre of chest and symbols on the palms of the hands and soles of the feet. Relief on front of pedestal defaced. Fragmentary inscription in one line on rim over front relief. It was read by Cunningham: *Saṁ*. 83. *gri*. 2, *di*. 25 [*etaye purvvaye*] ... ... "In the year 83, in the second [month of] summer, on the 25th day ...." The date proves that the image was made in the reign of the Kushaṇa king Vāsudeva. Cf. above sub B.2.

No. B. 4 ; Ht. 2' 10".

TIRTHAṀKARA STATUETTE FROM BALBHADAR KUṆḌ ; KUSHĀNA PERIOD.

It was preserved at the Allahabad Public Library and came perhaps originally from the Kaṅkālī Ṭīlā.

(Cunningham, *A. S. R.*, Vol. III, p. 34, No. 17.)

*B 4.—Image (ht. 2′ 10″ or 0 m. 89) of the Jina Ādinātha or Ṛishabha-nātha seated cross-legged in meditation. Head and arms missing. Halo with scolloped border partly preserved. *Śrīvatsa* symbol in centre of chest, and wheel symbols on the palms of the hands and soles of the feet. The relief on the front face of the pedestal represents a wheel of the law (Skr. *dharma-chakra*) placed on a pillar. It is being worshipped by ten human devotees, both male and female, of whom two are kneeling at the foot of the pillar, whilst the others are standing, some carrying flowers as offerings and others folding their hands in the attitude of adoration. The two ends of the relief are occupied by lions standing.

The sculpture was carved in the reign of the Kushaṇa king Vāsudeva, as appears from the inscription of three lines, two above and one beneath the front relief. It reads :—

1. *Siddha[ṁ] Mahār[ā]jasya r[ājā]tir[ā]jasya Devaputrasya [Shāhi] V[ā]sudevasya rājya-sa[ṁ]vatsare* 84 *grishmamāse dvi* 2

2. *di* 5 *etasya pur[vā]yāṁ Bhaṭadattasya Ugabhinakasya vadhūs* — — *sya kuṭubinie.*

3. *Bhagavato Arhato Ṛishabhasya pratimā pratishṭhāpitā Dharasahasya kuṭub[i]nie —mi—gutta-Kumāra[da]ttasya nirvarttana.*

"Success! In the reign of the king, the king of kings, His Majesty [Shāhi] Vāsudeva, in the year 84, the 2nd month of summer, the 5th day, on that [date specified] above, — — — the wife of — — — the daughter-in-law of Bhaṭadatta Ugabhinaka has erected an image of the Lord the Arhat Ṛishabha at the request of Kumāradatta — — — — —.

This image was discovered in November 1908 by Pandit Radha Krishna on the bank of the Balabhadra Kuṇḍ, where it was being used as a grinding stone. He subsequently secured it for the Museum. (Plate XI. Cf. *J. A. S. B.* N. S., Vol. V., p. 6, no. VIII). On loan from the Government of India.

*B 5.—Image (ht. 2′ 7½″ or 0 m. 77) of a Jina seated cross-legged in meditation (Skr. *dhyāna-mudrā*). Head and arms broken; sculpture otherwise damaged. Symbol of wheel on the palms of the hands and soles of the feet. On front of the pedestal is a relief representing a wheel placed on a trident which is being worshipped by six monks (?), of whom the two nearest it are kneeling, while the others are standing. At the sides a lion couchant with head turned outward. On the pedestal there is an inscription, considerably mutilated, which consists of two lines (2′ 2″ in length), one over and the other under the relief. Some more letters are traceable beneath the second line.

The inscription was first edited by Cunningham and subsequently by Bühler. Cunningham's facsimile proves that some letters have disappeared since its discovery. These I have placed between round brackets.

1. *Sava* (90 *va.*) ...... *[Ku]ṭu[ṁ]banie D(i)nasya vadhūya*

2. *Ko[ṭṭiyāto] ga(ṇā)to [Pa]va(ha)kāto kulāto Majhamato śākhā(to) sanikaya Bhatibalāe (tha)bhani—*

3. *ye d[ā]na[ṁ].*

According to Cunningham, this image was found in the Kaṅkālī Ṭīlā (*A. S. R.*, Vol. III, p. 33, No. 19; Bühler, *Ep. Ind.*, Vol. II, p. 205, No. 22.)

B 6.—Image (ht. 3′ 5″ or 1 m. 04) of a Jina seated cross-legged in the attitude of meditation (Skr. *dhyāna-mudrā*). Head missing. Ornamental halo and locks partly preserved. On each side stands a male attendant, holding a fly-wisk in his right hand. The sculpture is perhaps identical with " the life-size seated figure with an elaborately carved nimbus and long hair flowing over the shoulders and down the back " excavated by Mr. Growse from the Kaṅkālī Ṭīlā (*Mathurā*, p. 117).

B 7.—Statuette (ht. 2′ 5″ or 0 m. 737) of a Jina seated cross-legged in meditation on a cushion which is placed on a throne (Skr. *siṁhāsana*) supported by a pair of lions. In the centre is a wheel between two figurines of meditating Jinas, both defaced. The head of the main figure is missing, but the long straight hair is still visible on both shoulders. An attendant chowrie-bearer stands on a lotus-flower on each side; the left one is missing. Find-place unknown.

B 8.—Image (ht. 2′ 5″ or 1 m. 04) of a Jina (?) image seated cross-legged in the attitute of meditation (Skr. *dhyāna-mudrā*). Find-place unknown.

B 9.—Torso (ht. 1′ 10½″ or 0 m. 56) of a Jina (?) image seated cross-legged in the attitude of meditation (Skr. *dhyāna-mudrā*). Find-place unknown.

B 10.—Lower portion (ht. 1′ 3″ or 0 m. 39) of the figure of a Jina seated cross-legged in the attitude of meditation. Brought from the Joint Magistrate's bungalow.

B 11.—Image (ht. 2′ 6″ or 0 m. 74) of a Jina seated cross-legged in the attitude of meditation. Head missing. Symbol in the palms of the hands and on the soles of the feet. Pedestal defaced. Find-place unknown.

B 12.—Image (ht. 1′ 11″ or 0 m. 584) of a Jina seated cross-legged in meditation (Skr. *dhyāna-mudrā*). Head missing. On front of pedestal a devotional scene, a wheel placed on a pillar, worshipped by three men, four women and a child. On both ends a lion to front. Find-place unknown.

B 13.—Image (ht. 1′ 7½″ or 0 m. 495) of a Jina seated cross-legged in meditation (Skr. *dhyāna-mudrā*). Head missing. Arms broken. On front of pedestal a relief, much defaced, representing a wheel being worshipped by male and female devotees. On each end a lion to front; that to the proper left broken. Over relief traces of an inscription. The image probably belongs to the Kushaṇa period. Find-place unknown.

*B 14.—Fragment (ht. 7″ or 0 m. 18) of a statuette of a Jina (?) seated cross-legged in the attitude of meditation (Skr. *dhyāna-mudrā*) on a throne (Skr. *siṁhāsana*), supported by two lions standing to front. Between these lions a devotional scene representing a wheel on a pillar with three figures of human worshippers standing on each side. Over this an inscription in one line 6¼″ long. It was published by Mr. Growse and re-edited by Professor Lüders who reads: *Siddhaṁ Vāchakasya Datta-śishyasya Sīhasya ni[vartanā]* ..... "Success! [At the request] of the preacher Sīha (Skr. Siṁha) the pupil of Datta ....
The remaining portion was evidently on the lower rim which is broken.

There are also a few letters on the proper left side of the pedestal. On palæographical grounds the sculpture is to be assigned to the later Kushaṇa period. It was found at the Kaṅkālī Ṭīlā. (Growse, *Mathurā* p. 118; *Ind. Ant.*, Vol. VI., p. 219, No. 8; *J. A. S B.*, Vol. XLVII, (1878) Pt. I., p. 119; plate XX [inscription erroneously described as that of No. B 15] Bühler, *Ep. Ind.*, Vol. I., p. 383, note 60; Lüders, *Ind. Ant.* Vol. XXXIII, p. 154, No. 33).

*B 15.—Statuette (ht. 1′ 7″ or 0 m. 482) of a Jina seated cross-legged in the attitude of meditation. (Skr. *dhyāna-mudrā*.) The head is lost, but remnants of a radiating halo are still extant. An attendant on each side; but one to the left broken. The one to the right stands in the attitude of adoration (Skr. *namaskāra*) and wears a snake-hood, showing him to be a Nāga. On the front of the base is a relief representing eight human worshippers including three women and two children, standing in the attitude of adoration on both sides of a wheel placed on a pillar. Similar devotional scenes are commonly found on the bases of Gandhāra images. On both sides of the relief are defaced lions. On the pedestal over the relief is an inscription in two lines, each 7″ in length, which was first edited by Growse and re-edited by Bühler. It reads:—

1. *Saṁvatsare saptapañchāśe* 57 *hemanta-tri(tri)tī—*

2. *ye divase trayodaśe sya pūrvvāyāṁ* .....

"In the fifty-seventh (57th) year, in the third month of winter, on the thirteenth day; on that [date specified as] above. ......"

Professor Lüders refers this date to the Kushaṇa era; but on account of the character I feel inclined to refer it to the Gupta era, in which case it would correspond to A.D. 376-7.

Evidently this sculpture is the same as "the broken Jaina figure naked with an Indo-Scythian inscription dated in the year 57, both in words and in figures"; which was obtained by Cunningham from the Sītalā-ghāṭī mound on the bank of the Jamnā and placed by Growse in the local museum. But Growse says that it had been built up into a mud wall in the Manoharpur Quarter of the city and that his attention was first called to it by General Cunningham. (Cunningham, *A. S. R.*, Vol. XX, p. 36; Growse, *Ind. Ant.*, Vol. VI., p. 218, No. 5, and plate; Bühler, *Ep. Ind.*, Vol. II., p. 210, No. 38 and plate.)

B 16.—Statuette (ht. 1′ 4½″ or 0 m. 418) of a Tīrthaṁkara seated cross-legged in the attitude of meditation on a throne supported by a pair of lions. Between these lions are four figures, mostly defaced, worshipping a wheel. The main figure has a circular halo with scolloped border round the head, and the *śrīvatsa* symbol in the centre of the chest. The soles of the feet also are marked with symbols. On each side stands an attendant figure, with an elaborate head-dress.

It was purchased by Pandit Radha Krishna from a Khattri, Girdhar Lal by name, who is said to have found it in the Jamnā near the Gōkaraṇ Mahādēv Temple. On loan from the Government of India.

*B 17.—Statuette (ht. 10′ or 0 m. 255) of a Jina (?) seated cross-legged in the attitude of meditation. (Skr. *dhyāna-mudrā*) on a throne supported by two lions. Between these lions are two male and two female figurines worshipping a wheel which is placed on a pillar. On the rim over this relief is an inscription in one line, 8″ long. It reads .... *ja da sa* .... *sa* [*Dha*]*mam*[*i*] *trasa vadh*[*vye*].

*B 18.—Statuette (ht. 10″ or 0 m. 255) of a Jina seated cross-legged in the attitude of meditation. (Skr. *dhyāna-mudrā*) on a throne supported by two lions. Between these lions are two male and two female figurines worshipping a wheel which is placed on a pillar. On the rim over this relief is an inscription in one line, 6½″ long. It reads :— *Koṭṭikato gaṇāto Vachhalikato kulato vadha* . . "Out of the Koṭiya *gaṇa*, out of the Vachchhaliya *kula* . . . ." The inscription was evidently continued on the lower rim which is defaced. It shows the statuette to be Jaina and to belong to the Kushaṇa period [1]. There are some more letters on the side of the proper left lion. The image was found at the Mātā Maṭh inside the Holi (or Hardinge) Gate, where it was being worshipped. It was obtained for the Museum by Pandit Radha Krishna On loan from the Government of India.

B 19.—Image (ht. 2′ 2″ or 0 m. 66) of a Jina (?) seated cross-legged in the attitude of meditation. (Skr. *dhyāna-mudrā*). *Ushṇīsha* on top of head and *śrīvatsa* symbol in centre of the chest. On each side a miniature attendant standing on a lotus and waving a fly-wisk (Sanskrit *chāmara*, Hindī *chaurī*). In the two upper corners two flying figures, apparently carrying garlands. The relief is enclosed between two pillars indicating a chapel in which the image was supposed to be placed. The stone was at the Allahabad Library up to December 1907; it is doubtful if it originates from Mathurā.

B 20.—Image (ht. 2′ 2″ or 0 m. 66) of a Jina seated cross-legged in the attitude of meditation (Skr. *dhyāna-mudrā*) on a low triangular cushion, with ornamented front. Head missing and arms broken. The nipples are marked by wheel symbols. In the centre of the chest is a *śrīvatsa* symbol. Projecting disk in the palms of the hands and on the soles of the feet. Find-place unknown.

*B 21.—Statuette (ht. 1′ 7″ or 0 m. 48) of the first Jina, Ādinātha or Vṛishabhanātha, seated on a cushion in meditation. Head missing with top portion of the slab. The figure was originally placed in a chapel, the pillars of which are broken off above the base. The Jina's seat is supported by two lions couchant placed between two broken pillars. A piece of cloth with garlands hangs down from the seat, so that its border touches the wheel beneath. Below it is a miniature bull couchant, the cognizance of the Jina Vṛishabhanātha. The lower portion of the sculpture is divided by four pilasters into three compartments. In the proper right and central one are two, in that to the left, three standing figures of Jinas. Immediately beneath the outer pilasters are two kneeling figurines of human worshippers. On both sides of the projecting portion of the stone is a vertical row of five figures of which four are Jinas, seated in meditation. The missing top portion of the slab, probably contained eight more Tīrthaṁkara figurines making a total of twenty-four, the traditional number of Jaina patriarchs. The lowermost figures of both rows are a male and female probably a Yaksha and Yakshī; the latter holds a flower in each hand. A Nāgarī inscription in one line runs along the raised rim over the lions. It reads:—

Oṁ Paṁḍita Śrī-Gaṇavara-devāya.

---

1 Cf. *Ep. Ind.*, Vol. II, p. 202, No. XIII.

*B 22—Statuette (ht. 2′ 3″ or 0 m. 68) of the 22nd Jina Neminātha seated cross-legged in the attitude of meditation on a throne supported by two lions. On each side of the main figure stands a male attendant waving a fly-wisk. Under these two attendants are two crouching figurines, male and female, with a staff in each hand. They probably represent Yakshas. The male wears a diadem on the top of his head, the female a high tiara. Over the *chaurī* bearers are two flying figures, apparently carrying garlands, and over these two elephants standing on both sides of the parasol which surmounts the Jina's head. On the top of the parasol there are traces of a miniature figure beating a hand-drum. On the raised rim beneath the pedestal is an inscription, 1′ in length, of which the greater part is destroyed. It reads:—*Saṁvat* 1104 *Śrī Bho-dh-ā-aya-gachchha Mahila*. . . . . . The year, if referred to the Vikrama era, would correspond to A.D. 1047. Under the inscription is a conch, the cognizance of the Jina Neminātha.

The sculpture was preserved at the Allahabad Public Library till December 1907; it is uncertain whether it originates from Mathurā.

* B 23.—Statuette (ht. 1′ 4½″ or 0 m. 407) of a Jina seated crosslegged in meditation (Skr. *dhyāna-mudrā*) on a cushion placed on a throne, which is supported by a pair of lions couchant. The sculpture is much demaged and the head is missing. An attendant with a fly-fan to the left. The corresponding figure to the right is lost. A kneeling figure of a human worshipper on each end of the pedestal. There runs an inscription in one line along the lower rim of the pedestal, but only a few letters are preserved.

* B 24.—Fragment (ht. 6½″ or 0 m. 165) consisting of the lower portion of a Jina figure seated cross-legged in the attitude of meditation (Skr. *dhyāna-mudrā*) on a triangular cushion ornamentally carved along the front. It bears an indistinct Nāgarī inscription dated *saṁvat* 1234 corresponding to A.D. 1177.

This sculpture was found at the Kaṅkālī Ṭīlā according to Growse. (*Mathurā* 2nd. ed., p. 110, with plate; *Ind. Ant.* Vol. VI, p. 219, No. 10.)

* B 25.—Statuette (ht. 1′ 2″ or 0 m. 356) of white marble, representing a Jina seated cross-legged in the attitude of meditation. Head lost. In the palms of the hands is a four-petalled flower. On the soles of the feet is another symbol. On the front face of the cushion is an inscription in three lines, composed in a mixture of Sanskrit and Hindī and written in the Nāgarī character. The date is the Vikrama year 1826, Māgha *va. di.* 7 Thursday, corresponding to the 18th January A.D. 1870. It reads:—

1. *Saṁvat* 1826 *varshe mitī Māgha va. di.* 7 *Guravāsara Ḍiganagare Mahā*[*rā*]*je Kehari Si*[*ṁ*]*gha rājā vijaya*[*rajye*].

2. *mahābhaṭṭāraka śrī-pūjya-Śrī-Mahānaṁda-sāgara-suribhis tad upadat (—deśāt)* || *Pallī-vālavaṁśamagihāgai.*

3. *tre* [*Ha*] *rasāṇā-nagara-vāsinā Chaudharī Jodharājena patiṭṭā (pratishṭhā?) karāpiteya (kāriteyaṁ).*

"In the year 1826, [the month] Māgha, the 7th day of the dark fortnight, on Thursday, in the victorious [reign] of Mahārājā, Rājā Kehar Siṅgh at the Town of Dīg, by order of the great master the worshipful Śrī Mahānand Sāgar [1] Suri, this consecration (?) was caused to be made by Chaudharī Jōdh Rāj of the Pallivāl clan and of the Magihā family, and a resident of the town of Harasāṇā."

For part of the above reading I am indebted to Mr. Ajit Prasada, Vakil, High Court, Lucknow. Mahārājā Kēharī or Kōsarī Singh was a grandson of Mahārājā Sūraj Mall, the founder of the Bharatpur Gaddi. Mahārājā Jawāhar Singh was his father. On Jawāhar Singh's death his brother Ratan Singh became the ruler and Kēharī or Kōsarī succeeded Ratan Singh. He ruled from Chēt *sudi* 6th, *Sambat* 1826 (A.D. 1769) to Chet *badi* 15, *Sambat* 1834 (A. D. 1777).

B 26.—Statuette (ht. 1′ 8″ or 0 m. 51) of a Jina, either Supārśva or Pārśvanātha [2], wearing a Nāga-hood and seated cross-legged in meditation on a cushion, supported by sitting lions. The figure is placed in a miniature chapel, the pillars of which are broken. The projecting portions of the architrave are supported by lions rampant which stand on the heads of elephants couchant. This sculpture seems to be identical with that found by Growse at a depth of six feet in a field between the Kaṅkalī Ṭīlā and the Chaubārā mounds. He describes it as "a small pediment containing in a niche, flanked by fabulous monsters and surmounted by the mystic wheel, a figure of Buddha, canopied by a many-headed serpent and seated on a lion throne." (*Mathurā* p. 124.)

B 27. Fragment (ht. 1′ 5½″ or 0 m. 445) consisting of the lower portion of a Jina (?) image seated cross-legged in meditation, as expressed by the position of the hands which rest in the lap, with the palms turned upward. In each palm is the sign of the wheel (Skr. *chakra*). On the sole of the feet is the same emblem besides the symbol of the three jewels (Skr. *triratna*). The sculpture is said to originate from the Kaṅkālī Ṭīlā.

B 28.—Fragment (ht. 1′ 7″ or 0 m. 483) consisting of the lower portion of a Jina (?) image seated cross-legged in meditation. Left knee

[1] Sūri Ānanda is mentioned in *Ep. Ind.*, Vol. I, p. 377.

[2] *Cf.* above, p. 43.

missing; pedestal defaced. Symbol of the wheel in the palms of the hands and on the soles of the feet. Find-place unknown.

* B. 29.—Fragment (ht. 1′ or 0 m. 305) consisting of the legs and upper part of the pedestal of a Jina (?) seated cross-legged in meditation. The relief on the front face of the pedestal evidently represented a wheel with four worshipping figures who are holding bunches of flowers as offerings. Only the heads are partly preserved. On the raised rim over the front relief runs an inscription in two lines 1′ 4″ in length; the last portion of the first line and almost the entire second line are destroyed. It reads:—
(1) *Mahārājasya Devaputrasya Huvishkasya r*[*ā*]*jya-sa*(*ṁ*) 50 *he.* 3 *di.* [2] . . . . (2) *vaha* . . . . . . *boṭha sa gha ne.*
"In the reign of the king, His Majesty Huvishka, in the year 50, in the third month of winter, on the second day............................"
This inscription shows the image to belong to the Kushaṇa period.

The stone which had been set up by a subordinate in the Public Works Department to protect a culvert on the high road through cantonments was rescued by Mr. Growse (*Mathurā*, p. 165, and *Ind. Ant.* Vol. VI, pp. 217 and 291, No. 11.)

B 30.—Fragment (ht. 1′ 6½″ or 0 m. 47) of a Jina figure seated cross-legged on a throne much defaced. Find-place unknown.

* B 31.—Fragment (ht. 10¼″ or 0 m. 26) of the pedestal of a seated Jina image. To the proper right is a wheel placed on a throne which must have occupied the centre of the front relief. On the proper left side is a lion facing, part of whose body is carved on the side of the stone. Between the wheel and the lion are two figures, male and female, standing to front with folded hands in the attitude of adoration. There is an inscription in two lines, 13″ and 16″ long, of which the lower line is mostly destroyed, on the raised rims over and beneath the relief. For the following reading I am indebted to Professor H. Lüders:—

1. [*Saṁ*] *vva* [*t**] [97] *varsha-mā* 1 *Koṭeya-gaṇa-Vaira-śākhi*
2. *ddha* [*ma-ttadeshi*] . . . . *vi* [*bu ?*] *pratishṭh*[*ā*]*pita.*

In Professor Lüders' opinion the date refers to the Gupta era, in which case the inscription would be dated in A.D. 416.

The sculpture was preserved in the Delhi Municipal Museum till October 1907, when it was transferred to the Mathurā Museum. Judging from its style and the kind of stone used, it originates from Mathurā, but the exact find-place is unknown.

B 32.—Image (ht. 3′ 3½″ or 1 m.) of a standing Jina. Head and feet lost; hands injured. Male attendant with fly-wisk standing on each side. Lower portion of back square. Vertically along the back project three sides of an octagonal shaft. The image is said to come from the Kaṅkālī Ṭīlā.

B 33.—Fragment (ht. 1′ 11″ or 0 m. 584) of a slab containing the torso of a standing Jina figure. Head lost. Portion of an ornamental halo; straight locks on shoulders. On both sides an attendant standing on a lotus and holding a fly-whisk. Find-place unknown.

B 34.—Torso (ht. 2′ 4″ or 0 m. 71) of a standing Jina figure. Find-place unknown.

B 35.—Torso (ht. 2′ 8″ or 0 m. 81) of a standing Jina. Symbol in centre of chest. It was brought to the Museum from the bungalow no. 14.

B 36.—Torso (ht. 2′ 3½″ or 0 m. 686) of a Jina figure, standing against a slightly projecting pillar. Remnants of a circular halo visible on the back of the stone. Long straight locks falling on shoulders. Find-place unknown.

B 37.—Torso and head (ht. 1′ 8½″ or 0 m. 52) of the figure of a Jina. Arms missing, nose broken, lips slightly injured. No halo. Hair arranged in conventional short curls. Ear-lobes elongated. *Śrīvatsa* symbol in centre of chest. Find-place unknown.

B 38.—Torso (ht. 1′ 6″ or 0 m. 457) of a Jina (?) figure. *Śrīvatsa* symbol in centre of chest. Find-place Kaṅkālī Ṭīlā (?).

B 39.—Torso (ht. 1′ 3″ or 0 m. 38) of a Jina (?) figure. *Śrīvatsa* symbol in centre of chest. Find-place unknown.

B 40.—Torso (ht. 10″ or 0 m. 254) of a Jina figure. *Śrīvatsa* symbol in centre of chest. Find-place unknown.

B 41.—Torso (ht. 8½″ or 0 m. 216) of a Jina figure. *Śrīvatsa* symbol in centre of chest. Attendant holding fly-whisk to proper right. Find-place unknown.

B 42.—Torso (ht. 8″ or 0 m. 20) of a Jina figure. *Śrīvatsa* symbol in centre of chest. Find-place unknown.

B 43.—Fragment (ht. 8″ or 0 m. 20) consisting of thighs of standing Jina figure. Find-place unknown.

B 44.—Mask (ht. 1′ 9″ or 0 m. 53) of the head of a Jina (?) figure of colossal size. Left cheek and nose missing; lips and chin damaged. Hair in short conventional curls. Face round and full; eyes large and protruding; pupils not indicated. Neither *ushṇīsha* nor *ūrṇā*. Find-place Kaṅkālī Ṭīlā (?).

B 45.—Mask (ht. 1′ 3½″ or 0 m. 35) of the head of a Jina (?) image of colossal size. Nose and chin broken. Hair arranged in short conventional curls. The head seems to have an *ushṇīsha* and there is a small *ūrṇā* above the nose. Find-place unknown.

B 46.—Head (ht. 1′ 1″ or 0 m. 33) of a Jina (?) image, of buff-coloured sandstone. Nose, chin and ears slightly damaged. Hair in short schematic curls. Face round and full. Eyes large, pupils not marked. Eye-brows in two curves almost touching each other. Find-place Kaṅkālī Ṭīlā (?).

B 47.—Head (ht. 1′ 1″ or 0 m. 278) of a Jina (?) figure. Top of the head and nose broken. Ears and chin injured. Deep, round hole on place of left ear. Hair treated in schematic waves. Face round and full; eyes large. Pupils not indicated. No *ūrṇā*. Find-place unknown.

B 48.—Head (ht. 1′ or 0 m. 305) of a Jina (?) image. Nose broken; ear-lobes injured. Hair in short conventional curls. Face round and full, eyes large. Pupils not indicated. No *ūrṇā*. At back traces of pillar. Find-place Kaṅkālī Ṭīlā (?).

B 49.—Head (ht. 1′ or 0 m. 305) of a Jina (?) figure. Nose broken; chin injured. Back of head, including ears, missing. Hair arranged in short conventional curls. It was brought to the Museum from the Joint Magistrate's bungalow.

B 50.—Head (ht. 10″ or 0 m. 255) of a Jina figure, much defaced. Hair in wavy rows. Find-place Kaṅkālī Ṭīlā (?).

B 51.—Head (ht. 8½″ or 0 m. 215) of a Jina figure, well preserved Nose and ears slightly injured. Hair in rows of schematic waves. Face broad and flat. *Ūrṇā* between eye-brows. Find-place unknown.

B 52.—Head (ht. 11½″ or 0 m. 29) with portion of left shoulder and halo of Jina (?) figure. Hair arranged in wavy rows. Forehead, nose and lips damaged. Find-place unknown.

B 53.—Head (ht. 10″ or 0 m. 255) of a Jina figure. Nose broken; face much injured. Hair arranged in short schematic curls. Pupils indicated. Portions of ornamental halo. Find-place Kaṅkālī Ṭīlā (?).

B 54.—Head (ht. 10½″ or 0 m. 265) of a Jina figure. Much worn. Hair in short schematic curls. It was brought to the Museum from the Joint Magistrate's bungalow.

B 55.—Head (ht. 8½″ or 0 m. 215) of a Jina (?) figure. Nose, chin and right cheek broken. Hair plain. Find-place Kaṅkālī Ṭīlā (?).

B 56.—Head (ht. 8½″ or 0 m. 215) of a Jina (?) figure. Forehead and nose broken. Hair plain. Traces of *ushṇisha*. Find-place unknown.

B 57.—Head (ht. 7″ or 0 m. 179) of a Jina (?) figurine. Nose broken; lips, chin and left ear injured. Hair plain. No *ushṇisha* or *ūrṇā*. Pupils not indicated. Find-place unknown.

B 58.—Head (ht. 8" or 0 m. 205) of a Jina figure. Much defaced; nose broken. Hair arranged in short schematic curls. Face round and full; eyes large. Find-place Kaṅkālī Ṭīlā (?).

B 59.—Fragment (ht. 3¾" or 0 m. 95) consisting of the lower portion of the head of Jina (?) figure. Find-place unknown.

B 60.—Fragment (ht. 10" or 0 m. 25) of the head of a Jina (?) figure with hair arranged in conventional curls. Find-place unknown.

B 61.—Head (ht. 2′ 4" or 0 m. 71) of a Jina image of colossal size. The surface has peeled off in places. The hair is arranged in schematic curls. The sculpture was kept at the Allahabad Public Library till December 1907.

B 62.—Head (ht. 1′ 4" or 0 m. 40) with portion of a Nāga-hood, presumably belonging to a figure of the Jina Pārśvanātha. The hood must have consisted of seven snake-heads, one on the proper right side missing. Over each snake-hood is a sacred symbol. That over the central head is the *triratna* symbol and that over the outermost head on the proper left end the *svastika*. The head of the Jina, of which the nose and chin are missing, has short schematic curls and elongated ears. The eye-brows are drawn in one line. The cheeks are full; the lips thick and protruding. Find-place unknown.

B 63.—Statuette (ht. 1′ 4" or 0 m. 419) of a Jina seated cross-legged in the attitude of meditation between two attending figures, standing with folded hands. The central figure has a symbol in the middle of his chest and remnants of a circular halo with scolloped border on both sides of his head. On the pedestal is a relief, flanked by two lions, which represents four human figures worshipping a wheel. The carving is partly defaced and the workmanship poor.

B 64.—Fragment (length 8½" or 0 m. 216) consisting of two hands of a Buddha or Jina figure seated in the attitude of meditation. Find-place unknown.

B 65.—Stele (ht. 2′ 10" or 0 m. 862) with a nude Jina figure seated cross-legged in meditation on each of the four sides[1]. One wears a seven-headed Nāga hood; and another of the four figures has straight hair falling on both shoulders. Two are seated on a throne supported by a pair of lions between which stands a wheel, the narrow side facing. A

---

[1] Quadruple *Tīrthaṅkara* images like B 65—74 are designated in the inscriptions as *pratimā sarvato bhadrikā* "an image auspicious on all sides." (Cf. *Ep. Ind.* Vol. I, p. 382, No. 11) Growse (*Mathurā* p, 118) mentions two such sculptures found in the Kaṅkālī Ṭīlā under the name of *chaumukhī*. For similar images cf. V. A. Smith, *Jaina Stūpa*, plate XC.

similar wheel in the same position is found on the two remaining sides, but here it is placed between two squatting figurines, one a corpulent male figure holding a cup in his right and a money bag in his left hand; the other a female holding an infant in her left arm, and in her right an indistinct object. These figurines probably represent Kubera, the god of wealth and Hāritī, the goddess of abundance. Cf. beneath C 2 and 4-5. Each Jina has on both sides of his head a flying figure carrying a garland. Find-place unknown.

B 66.—Stele (ht. 2′ 4″ or 0 m. 709) carved on the four sides with a nude Jina figure seated cross-legged in meditation on a cushion placed on a throne (Skr. *siṁhāsana*) supported by a pair of lions, turned outward with one forepaw raised. Between each pair of lions, in the centre of each of the four sides, is a wheel. In one instance there are two kneeling human figures on both sides of the wheel. Along the four faces of the pedestal are miniature figurines in various attitudes. Most of them are male figures, probably Yakshas, squatting and holding a money bag in the left hand. On one side there is a kneeling female figure and on another side a grotesque head, perhaps Rāhu. The upper portion of the stone with the four heads is missing. One of the four figures is distinguished by long straight locks falling on the shoulders. Each Jina figure has symbols in the shape of conventional flowers, in the palms of the hands and on the feet. The sculpture is said to originate from the Kaṅkālī Ṭīlā.

B 67.—Stele (ht. 2′ 10″ or 0 m. 859, including tenon) with a nude Jina standing on each side. One is distinguished by a seven-headed Nāga hood; another by straight hair falling on both shoulders. Each figure has a *śrīvatsa* symbol in the centre of the chest. On each side of the pedestal is a bas-relief representing a devotional scene. In the top of the stone is a square mortice for the reception of a tenon; there is a square tenon in the bottom. Find-place unknown.

* B 68.—Stele (ht. 3′ 3″ or 0 m. 99) with a nude Jina figure standing on each of the four sides. The four figures are all defaced and otherwise injured. Three have ornamental haloes and one a seven-headed Nāga hood. One of the three haloed figures has straight locks falling on the shoulders. Each figure has the *śrīvatsa* symbol in the centre of the chest. There is a square mortice in the top of the stone. The pedestal is broken, on one side are traces of an inscription, which I read :...*ka bhaginīye Gho*..." [of] Gho...the sister of..." The character is that of the Kushaṇa period.

The sculpture is said to have been found in the Kaṅkālī Ṭīlā.

* B 69.—Stele (ht. 1′ 11″ or 0 m. 582) with a nude Jina figure standing on each of the four sides. Three of these figures have haloes and one a seven-fold Nāga hood. One of the haloed figures has long straight hair falling down on both shoulders. All four figures have a symbol in the centre of the chest. On the four corners of the pedestal are human worshippers, facing both sides. Round mortice in the top of the stone. On one face of the base is an inscription in one line.

The sculpture is said to originate from the Kaṅkālī Ṭīlā.

* B 70.—Stele (ht. 1′ 10½″ or 0 m. 57) carved with a nude Jina figure standing on each of the four sides. Three of these figures have a halo and the fourth has a seven-headed Nāga-hood. All four figures have a symbol in the centre of the breast. On the four corners of the pedestal are figurines of devotees facing both ways. There is a round mortice in the top of the stone. The base is broken. Along the three entire sides runs an inscription in two lines. The lettering on side *b* is partly, and that on *c* wholly, lost.

The inscription which was first brought to notice by General Cunningham and re-edited by Professors Bühler and Lüders, runs as follows:—

a 1. *Siddhaṁ* [*saṁ*] 35[1] *he* 1 *di* 12 *asya purvvāye Ko—*
2. *ṭāto Brahmadāsikāto Uchenakarito*
b 1. *Śr*[*i*]*grihāto* . . . . .
2. . . . . [*sha*]*ni*[*bha*] . . . . .
d 1. . . . *bodhi-labhāe Vish*[**ṇ*]*udeva prati—*
2. . . . *sarvu-sat*[*tvā*]*naṁ hita-sukha*[*ya*].

"Success! [In the year] 35, the first month of winter, the 12th day on this [date specified as] above, [at the request of] . . . . . out of the Koṭṭiya [*gaṇa*], the Brahmadāsika [*kula*], the Uchchānāgari [*śākhā*] the Śrīgṛiha [*saṁbhoga*] . . . . for the welfare and happiness of all creatures."

The sculpture was found in the Kaṅkālī Ṭīlā and preserved in the Delhi Municipal Museum till October 1907 when it was transferred to the Mathurā collection. (Cunningham, *A. S. R.*, Vol. III, p. 20, no. 2 and plate. Bühler, *Almanach der Wiener Akademie der Wissenschaften*, Vol. XXXVII, p. 266; *Vienna Oriental Journal*, Vol. I, p. 176, no. 5 and Vol. IV, p. 171 and Lüders, *Ind. Ant.*, Vol. XXXIII, p. 36, no. 5).

* B 71.—Stele (ht. 1′ 10″ or 0 m. 558) carved with a nude Jina figure standing on each of its four sides. Three of these figures have haloes and the fourth has a broken Nāga hood. All four figures have a

[1] Professor Lüders reads *sa* 5.

symbol in the centre of the chest. On the four corners of the pedestal are figurines of human devotees, facing both ways. Their hands are missing. There is a square mortice in the top of the stone. On the lower rim of the base along the four sides runs an inscription in one line, which was first published by General Cunningham and re-edited by M. Boyer.

(a) [*Saṁ*] 5 *he* 4 *di* 20 [*asya purvāyāṁ K*[*oṭiya*]

(b) [*gaṇā*]*to Uchenagarito śākhāto Baṁ*[*h*]*adā*[*sikāto*] [*kulāto*]

(c) M[*i*]*hila tasya śishyo aryyo* . . . . .

"[In the year] 5, the 4th month of winter, the 20th day, on that [date specified as] above . . . . . out of the [Koṭiya] *gaṇa*, the Uchenagara *śākhā*, the Brahmadāsika *kula* . . . . . Mihila—his disciple, the reverend . . . . ."

The sculpture was found in the Kaṅkālī Ṭīlā and preserved in the Delhi Municipal Museum till October 1907 when it was transferred to the Mathurā Museum. (Cunningham, *A. S. R.*, Vol. III, p. 31, plate XIII, no. 3; Boyer, *J. A.*, series IX, Vol. XV, p. 574.)

B 72.—Stele (ht. 1′ 3″ or 0 m. 393) carved with a nude Jina figurine standing on each of the four sides. Each of the figures has a *śrīvatsa* symbol in the centre of the chest. One is distinguished by a snake-hood and the other three by haloes with scolloped borders. The sculpture was found let into the wall of a small *liṅga* shrine near a well at the junction of the Circular Road and the cart-tract leading to Mahōlī and was being worshipped as Vīrabhadra, a *gaṇa* of Śiva. Possibly the image came originally from the Kaṅkālī Ṭīlā.

B 73.—Stele (ht. 1′ or 0 m. 314) carved with a nude Jina figurine standing on each of the four sides. The carving is much defaced. Pandit Radha Krishna purchased it from a Brahmin resident in Mathurā city, who worshipped it as Brahmā and at the same time explained it to the ignorant as a representation of the four Yugas, all but the Kaliyuga being obliterated! On loan from the Government of India.

B 74.—Fragment (ht. 10⅞″ or 0 m. 275) of a stele similar to Nos. B 65—73. Of the four images only the halo and remnants of the heads are preserved on three sides. One of them probably wore a Nāga hood. Over each Jina are two flying figures, much worn, which carry garlands, flowers, &c. On the top of the stone is a raised disk, with two concentric circles. The fragment is said to originate from the Kaṅkālī Ṭīlā.

B 75.—Sculpture (ht. 3′ or 0 m. 915) of buff-coloured sandstone representing a Tirthaṁkara seated cross-legged in the attitude of meditation (Skr. *dhyāna-mudrā*) on a lotus-throne supported by two lions couchant. The main figure is headless and all the attending figures as well as the proper left lion are defaced. Between the lions we notice a wheel and two deer, which in Budhist iconography denotes the Buddha's first sermon in the Deer-park near Benares. On the receding ends of the pedestal there are figurines of Kubera, the god of wealth, with his money-bag, and of the goddess of fertility, who holds a child on her left knee. Above them are two attendants, standing, who are broken and must have held fly-whisks, Each of these is surmounted by four figurines, arranged in groups of two placed one over the other, and seated on lotuses, so that four are placed to the right and four to the left of the ornamental halo of the Tīrthaṁkara. These eight figurines evidently represent the sun, the moon and the five planets (which have given their names to the seven week-days), the last of the number being Rāhu, the Eclipse demon who is shown as only a bust.

The main figure was evidently canopied by a parasol, on both sides of which there is a group of two flying celestials, male and female, probably meant for a Gandharva and an Apsaras. These figures are all defaced.

The sculpture forms a transition between the Tīrthaṁkara figures of the Gupta period like No. B 6, 7 and 33 and those of the late Middle Ages like No. B 77. It was obtained by Pandit Radha Krishna from Pōtrā Kuṇḍ. On loan from the Government of India.

B 76.—Sculpture (ht. 2′ 2″ or 0 m. 66) in buff-coloured sandstone representing the first Tīrthaṁkara Ādinātha or Vṛishabhanātha seated cross-legged in the attitude of meditation (Skr. *dhyāna-mudrā*) on a lotus-throne supported by two lions couchant. Between the lions there is an effigy of a bull, the cognizance of the first Tīrthaṁkara. We notice two kneeling figurines on both ends of the pedestal. They probably represent the donors of the sculpture. The back-slab is lost together with the head and arms of the Tīrthaṁkara figure. The knees also are broken. Note the lock of hair on the left shoulder. Obtained from Pōtrā Kuṇḍ. On loan from the Government of India.

B 77.—Image (ht. 4′ 5½″ or 1 m. 356) of the 22nd Tīrthaṁkara Neminātha seated cross-legged in the attitude of meditation (*dhyāna-mudrā*) on a throne which is supported on two dwarf pillars and a pair of lions seated with one forepaw raised. Half concealed behind the pillars are two figurines, male and female, standing with hands folded; they probably represent the donors of the statue. From the throne an ornamental clot hangs down between the two lions. Under it there appears to be a wheel and on the plain rim of the pedestal beneath we notice a conch, the cognizance of the Tīrthaṁkara Neminātha. To the right and left of the main figure there is an attendant standing with a fly-whisk in one hand, and on both sides of the halo, a couple of flying celestials—probably a

Gandharva and an Apsaras, of which the male figure carries a garland as an offering, whilst the female seems to shower flowers. Over each of these two groups there must have been an elephant standing on a lotus-flower. The feet of that on the proper left are still traceable. The head of the Tīrthaṁkara is provided with an ornamental halo and is surmounted by a triple parasol, on the top of which there is a prostrate figurine beating a hand-drum.

The sculpture is of the mediaeval type. It was presented by Captain F. B. Barrett, 15th Hussars, in the compound of whose bungalow (No. 23 in Cantonments) it stood for many years. It is said to have been found in the course of construction of one of the barracks about the time of the Mutiny. On loan from the Government of India.

B 78.—Head (ht. 1′ or 0 m. 304) of a Jina (?) figure. Hair only indicated by a line above the forehead. Nose broken, ears slightly damaged. From a *bāghīcha* near the Bhūtēsar mound. On loan from the Government of India.

B 79.—Statuette (ht. 8½″ or 0 m. 216) in black marble representing a Jina seated cross-legged in the attitude of meditation on a plain base. Head lost. Symbols on chest and on the palm of the hand. It was obtained with No. B 80 from the Sarasvatī Kuṇḍ, 1 mile from Mathurā on the Delhi road. On loan from the Government of India.

B 80.—Statuette (ht. 3¾″ or 0 m. 095) in white marble representing a Jina seated cross-legged in the attitude of meditation on a plain base. Head lost. Symbols on chest and in the palm of the hand. It was obtained with No. B 79 from the Sarasvatī Kuṇḍ, 1 mile from Mathurā on the Delhi road. On loan from the Government of India.

No. C. 1 ; Ht. 8' 8".

YAKSHA (?) STATUE FROM PARKHAM ; MAURYA PERIOD.

C. Yaksha and Nāgā Images.

C1.—PARKHAM IMAGE.—Statue of colossal size (ht. including pedestal, 8′ 8″ or 2 m. 62; width across the shoulders 2′ 8″ or 0 m. 812) representing a corpulent male figure, standing with the left knee slightly bent. The head is detached and both arms are lost. The head is provided with heavy ear-rings, but further details are obliterated. The figure wears a *dhōtī* held round the loins by means of a flat girdle tied in a knot in front. A second flat girdle is laid round the chest, which is decorated with a necklace and a torque. The latter is provided with four dependent tassels at the back. Near the break of the left arm traces of an ornamental bracelet are still visible. It is impossible to decide what the position of the arms was. But on the left side of the image there is a break which seems to indicate that the left hand was placed on the hip. The right arm was evidently free from the body, as on this side no break is visible. Possibly the right hand was raised towards the shoulder and the attitude of the image the same as that of standing Buddha and Bodhisattva images.

The statue was discovered by General Cunningham in the village of Parkham 14 miles south of Mathurā on the Grand Trunk Road. The villagers worshipped it under the name of *Dēvatā* (" Deity "). Cunningham conjectures that it represents " a *yaksha* or attendant demi-god who carried a *chauri* over the right shoulder." It does not however seem very probable that an image of this size should have served the purpose of a simple attendant. Besides, there is no indication that it held any object over its shoulder. On account of the corpulence of the figure, I feel inclined to identify it with Kubera, the god of wealth.

The Parkham statue is of particular interest, as it is the only image yet found in India which can be assigned to the second century B.C. It has an inscription in Maurya Brāhmī cut in three lines on the top of the pedestal on both sides of and between the feet. The first portion on the proper right side and that in the centre are partly destroyed, and in the third line several letters are uncertain.

I read it: . . . [*ni*] *Bhadapugarinā* [*ka*] . . [*ga*] *aṭha* . . . . . *pi* . . . . *Kuni*[*ka*]*tevāsinā* [*Gomitakena*] *katā*. " Made by Bhadapugarin . . . . Gomitaka the pupil of Kunika." (Plate XII. Cf. Cunningham, *A.S.R.* Vol. XX, p. 41 and plate VI; Konow, *Ind. Ant*).

C2.—" BACCHANALIAN GROUP."—Sculpture (ht. including tenon 5′ ½″ or 0 m. 538; width at base 3′ 5″ or 1 m. 04; thickness 1′ 6″ or 0 m. 458), carved on both sides with a so-called " Bacchanalian group." It was discovered by Mr. F. S. Growse in the winter of 1873-4 in a mound near the village of Pālī-Khōṛā (*khēṛā*-mound) belonging to the ancient site of Madhupurī 2 miles south-west from the ruined temple of Kēsab Dēv. "On one side," Growse says, "it represented a group of six persons, the principal figure being a man of much abdominal development who is seated in complete nudity on a rock or low stool." His right leg, which is somewhat injured, rests on the ground and his left, the foot of which is missing, is drawn up. The head is defaced, but enough remains to show that it was bearded and had long curly locks kept together by a fillet. His left hand rests on his calf; his right holds a cup, the curious shape and design of which deserve special attention. At his right knee stands a child, entirely defaced,[1] behind which is a female figure clad in a long-sleeved jacket and a skirt falling down on the feet which are shod with plump shoes. Her head-dress is that found on the Graeco-Budhist sculptures of Gandhāra. She has long curly locks falling on the shoulders, heavy ear-pendants, a necklace consisting of several rows of pearls or round beads, which hangs down between the breasts, and a bracelet. In her right hand she holds a cup of the same shape and design as that of the main personage of the group.

Another female figure, somewhat smaller in size, occupies the proper right side of the relief. Her dress is the same as that of the female just described. But she wears a flat torque round her neck and holds a bunch of grapes in her right hand.

In the back-ground between the two cup-bearers a defaced figure is partly visible —evidently a bearded man wearing a mantle or scarf over his left shoulder. On the other side of the chief figure stands a boy, clad in a long-sleeved tunic reaching down to his knees, long trousers (?) and plump boots. In his right hand he holds what appears to be a bunch of grapes. His head is missing. The dress of this figure is that of the Kushaṇa period. Above the figures we notice the foliage of an *aśoka* tree.

On the opposite side of the block we find the fat man again "in a state of helpless intoxication." He occupies the centre and is seated on what appears to be a low rock. A loose sheet covers the lower part of his body. His left leg is drawn up and his right is hanging down. His right arm is held by a female figure dressed in Greek costume and his left by a male person, who wears a mantle, "fastened at the neck by a fibula and hanging from the shoulders in vandyked folds, which are very suggestive of late Greek design." (Growse). On each side of the seated man we find

---

[1] On the photograph published by Growse (*Mathurā*, p. 168) this figure is still extant. Since writing the above, part of the figure has been recovered and refixed

PLATE XIII.

(*a*) OBVERSE.

(*b*) REVERSE.

No. C, 2; Ht. 5' ½".

BACCHANALIAN GROUP FROM PĀL KHĒṚĀ.

the figure of a little boy standing, apparently nude. That to the proper left has his right hand raised. All the figures of this group are defaced.

It is of interest that a sculptured stone, somewhat smaller in size (ht. 3′ 8″) and similar in subject, had been found in Mathurā by Colonel L. R. Stacy about 1836. The exact find-spot is not known. It is now in the Calcutta Museum. The Calcutta "Silenus" is tersely described by James Prinsep in the following terms: "His portly carcass, drunken lassitude, and vine-wreathed forehead, stamp the individual, while the drapery of his attendants pronounces them at least to be foreign to India, whatever may be thought of Silenus' own costume, which is certainly highly orthodox and Brahmanical. If the sculptor were a Greek, his taste had been somewhat tainted by the Indian *beau-idéal* of female beauty. In other respects his proportions and attitudes are good; nay, superior to any specimen of pure Hindu sculpture we possess; and, considering the object of the group, to support a sacrificial vase (probably of the juice of the grape), it is excellent." Colonel Stacy's idea was that the principal figure represents Silenus, that the sculptors were Bactrian Greeks, and that their work was meant to be a *tazza*, or rather a pedestal for the purpose of a *tazza*, or large sacrificial vase. These opinions were endorsed by James Prinsep. Mr. Growse conjectured that, more likely, they are the bases of pillars (probably octagonal), the socket being clearly visible on the top of the Mathurā Museum specimen. On the top of the Calcutta Silenus also Cunningham notes "a circular bason 16″ in diameter and 8″ deep." We may assume that they stood at the entrance of some Buddhist building.

That these sculptures are reproductions of classical Bacchanalian scenes has been recognized from the beginning. But the subject must have been adapted to an Indian conception. The main figure is a copy of Silenus, but not Silenus himself. Both the position and appearance of the figure suggest Kubera or Jambhala, the Buddhist god of wealth. Images which are supposed to represent this deity have been found in the Peshāwar district, the ancient Gandhāra. They are regularly accompanied by two or more nude figures—Cupids turned into Yakshas. The attitude of the boy to the proper left side of our second group singularly reminds us of similar figures on Gandhāra reliefs. The rock on which the main figure is seated I suppose to be meant for Mount Kailāsa, the abode of Kubera. Moreover, the explanation would well agree with the assumption that the stones stood at the entrance of some Buddhist building, as we know that this was the place where images of the king and queen of the Yakshas were commonly found.

We may compare two statuettes in the Mathurā Museum (Nos. C 4 and 5) which represent a corpulent deity who holds a cup in his left hand into which a female attendant is pouring some liquid. There can be little doubt that these two statuettes represent the same person as the principal figure in the so-called Bacchanalian-group, and I am inclined to identify them with Kubera on account of the pouch in their left hand, which is the typical attribute of the god of wealth.

(Plate XIII. Cf. Cunningham, *A.S.R.*, Vol. I, pp. 242—244; Growse, *Mathurā*, pp. 124 and 166-169, with two plates; and *J.A.S.B.*, Vol. XLIV (1875), Part I, pp. 212-215, with two plates. On Colonel Stacy's Silenus cf. also *J. A. S. B.*, Vol. V. (1838) pp. 567-570, with plate; and Burgess, *A. M. I.*, plates 60(2) and 61.)

C 3.—Image (ht. 3′ 8″ or 1 m. 115) of a crouching, corpulent male figure, presumably a Yaksha or goblin. His left knee is fastened to the body by means of a scarf. Round his neck is a wreath. Both the scarf and the wreath are also shown on the back of the image. From his left ear a heavy ear-ring hangs down. The broad flat face has a small moustache, a characteristic of demonical beings. The hair is arranged in short curls, turned alternately to the right and left. The arms are missing, but must have reached upwards, which indicates that the figure served the purpose of an Atlant. Crouching supporting figures are very common in the sculptures of Gandhāra.

There can be little doubt that this sculpture is the "strange squat figure of a dwarf, 3′ 9″ high and 2′ broad" which Growse obtained from "a mound immediately adjoining the pillar that marks the boundary of the township of Mathurā and the villages of Maholi and Pālī-khēṛā lying due south of the Kaṅkālī Ṭīlā and east of the Girdharpur mound."

(Plate XIV. Cf. Growse, *Mathurā*, p. 124.)

C 4.—Statuette (ht. 1′7½″ or 0 m. 49) of a corpulent squatting figure holding a cup in his right and a money-bag in his left hand. Hair arranged in short curls. Two female attendants, partly defaced, are standing to his right and left behind his shoulders. The one to his right seems to hold a pitcher (cf. no. C 5). The figure may have served the purpose of an Atlant at the foot of a pillar or pilaster, as indicated by the hemispherical projection over its head (cf. C.3.) and probably represents Kubera or Jambhala, the Budhist god of wealth.

C 5.—Statuette (ht. 1′ 2″ or 0 m. 355) of a corpulent male figure squatting and holding in his left hand a bag and in his right hand a cup into which a female attendant, standing at his right side, pours some

No. C, 3; Ht. 3'8".

YAKSHA FIGURE FROM MAHOLI MOUND.

liquid from a pitcher which she holds with both hands. Both figures wear the usual ornaments. Over the left shoulder of the seated figure is the leaf of a tree. On account of the bag in his left hand I am inclined to identify the male figure with Kubera of Jambhala, the god of wealth. The subject is evidently the same as that of the Bacchanalian group no. C 2; but the present sculpture must belong to a later date and is purely Indian in its style. It was preserved at the Allahabad Library till December 1907, and perhaps originates from the Jamālpur site. (*B. E. F. E. O.*, Vol. VIII (1908), p. 490 f., fig. 2.)

C 6.—Image (ht. 2′ 8″ or 0 m. 812) of a corpulent male figure. Legs, arms, nose and part of the halo broken. Hair arranged in schematic curls. Flat knot on top of the head. Large, slightly protruding eyes, thin moustache, teeth visible between lips. Pendants in ears, necklace and arm-rings. The figure shows the same type as the goblin No. C 3. The position of the legs was probably similar. It is said to originate from the Kaṅkālī Ṭīlā.

It is the image referred to by Mr. Growse as "a rudely executed figure of a fat little fellow, who has both his hands raised above his head, and holds in one a cup, in the other a bunch of grapes." Mr. Growse conjectured the figure to represent Buddha in the days of his youth or to be "a caricature of Buddhism as regarded from the point of view of a Brahmanical ascetic;" but there is nothing to support this supposition. From the plate published by Growse it appears that the two arms of the figure were broken since its discovery. (*Mathurā*, p. 169, and *J. A. S. B.* Vol. XLIV (1875), Part I, p. 215; plate XIV).

C 7.—Statuette (ht. 1′ 1½″ or 0 m. 353) of a corpulent male figure, perhaps a Yaksha, carved in the round. Head and arms missing. Like C 3 he has a flat band fastened round his belly and one of his legs. The attitude of the two figures is the same. The sculpture was obtained by Pandit Radha Krishna from a suburb of the village Naugāvā, 4 miles from Mathurā city on the Dīg road. On loan from the Government of India.

C 8.—Relief (ht. 8″ or 0 m. 203), much defaced, representing two squatting figures facing; the right one a pot-bellied male, wears an elaborate head-dress and ornaments. His right arm is raised to the shoulder. The hand is broken, but does not seem to have held any object. The left arm rests against the knee. To his left is a female figure in a similar attitude. On both sides four smaller figures are standing with folded hands in the attitude of adoration, one to the right and three to the left. The sitting persons possibly represent Kubera, the god of wealth, and his consort. We may compare the figurines occurring on the bases of the Jaina stele No. B 65. The sculpture seems to belong to the Kushaṇa period and is said to originate from the Kaṅkālī Ṭīlā.

C 9.—Fragment (ht. 5½" or 0 m. 132) carved with a corpulent male figure squatting and holding a cup (?) in his right and a bag in his left hand. At his side is another figure standing of which the upper portion is lost. The fragment was brought here from the Joint Magistrate's bungalow. Cf above No. C 5.

C 10.—Fragment (ht. 7½" or 0 m. 18) of a corpulent male figure, squatting and holding a cup in his right and a bag in his left hand. Cf. above Nos. C 4 and 5.

C 11.—Sculpture (ht. 9" or 0 m. 228) representing a corpulent male deity, probably Kubera, seated to front between two rudely carved dwarf pilasters, of which that to the proper right is broken. He holds a cup in his left hand. The right, holding an indistinct object, is raised to the shoulder. Provenance unknown.

C 12.—Sculpture (ht. 9" or 0 m. 228) representing two corpulent figures, male and female, seated side by side, the latter with a child on her left knee. Carving defaced. Provenance unknown.

*C 13.—Life-size statue (ht. 7′ 8" or 2 m. 407, including snake-hood and tenon; ht. of figure proper 5′ or 1 m. 57) of a Nāga standing in a spirited attitude with his right hand raised above the head. The left hand must have held a cup, as may be inferred from No. C 15, which is similar in attitude. Both arms are broken and the right leg damaged. The head is surmounted by a hood of seven serpent heads, that to the proper left being lost and the central one broken. The head of the image is defaced. It is clad in a *dhōtī* and a scarf tied round the loins. A necklace can be traced on the breast. It deserves notice that the coils of the snake are also indicated on the back of the stone.

The sculpture belongs to the Kushaṇa period, as appears from the following inscription cut in six lines on the back :—

1. *Maharajasya rajātirajasya Huviskasya savatsara chat[u]risa* 40
2. *Hematta-mase* 2 *divase* 23 *etta purvāyyā*
3. *Senahasti [cha] Piṇḍapayya-putro Bhoṇuke* (or *Bhoṇḍake* ?) *cha*
4. *Viravṛiddhi-putro etti vayyasyā ubhayye*
5. *Nāgā* (or *Nāgaṁ* ?) *prattistāp[e]tti pushkaraṇiyy[āṁ]*
6. *svakayyāṁ. Priyyatti Bhagavā Nāgo.*

Rendered into pure Sanskrit, this legend would run :—

1. *Mahārājasya rājātirājasya Huvishkasya saṁvatsare chatvāriṁse* 40

2. *Hemanta-māse 2 divase 23 atra pūrvāyām*
3. *Senahastī cha Piṇḍapayya-putro Bhoṇukaścha*
4. *Vīravṛiddhi-putra etau vayasyau ubhayau*
5. *Nāgaṁ pratishṭhāpayataḥ pushkariṇyāṁ*
6. *svakāyāṁ. Prīyatāṁ Bhagavān Nāgaḥ.*

Translation.

" In the fortieth year (40) of the king, the king of kings, Huvishka, in the 2nd month of winter, the 23rd day. On this [date specified as] above Senahasti[n] the son of Piṇḍapayya and Bhoṅuka the son of Vīravṛiddhi, these two comrades, erect[ed] both [this] Nāga at their own tank. May the Lord Nāga be pleased[1]."

The image, together with the inscribed slab O4, was discovered by Pandit Radha Krishna in March 1908 near the village of Chhaṛgaon 5 miles map-measurement almost due south of Mathurā City and one mile south-south-west of Bhaṁsā, the first railway station south of Mathurā on the narrow gauge line. The villagers used to worship the image as Dāujī, i.e., Baladeva or Balarāma, the elder brother of Kṛishṇa. It is not a little curious that ancient Nāga images found in the Mathurā district are nowadays regularly worshipped as idols of Baladeva; e.g., in the villages of Baldeo near Mahāban and Sakhana on the Delhi road and also at the Dhruv Ṭīlā just outside the City. Moreover, modern idols of Baladeva manufactured here are exact copies of the ancient Nāga figures. This will be evident from a comparison of the Chhaṛgaon Nāga of the reign of Huvishka with the white marble statuette of Baladeva made at Brindāban (No. D 36.) In the case of Baladeva the Nāga hood is explained as referring to his being an incarnation of the world-snake Śesha-nāga and the cup in his left hand is believed to refer to his drinking propensities.

On loan from the Government of India.

C 14.—Statue (ht. 5′ 7″ or 1 m. 758) of a Nāga standing in the same attitude as Nos. C 13 and C 15. The lower portion of the figure beneath the feet is missing and the sculpture much defaced. Both arms are broken. On the left shoulder and arm are traces of ornaments. The snake coils are also indicated on the back of the stone.

The sculpture was obtained by Pandit Radha Krishna from the village of Khāmnī 6 miles from Mathurā City on the road to Govardhan where

---

[1] Compare the formula found at the end of an inscription of the 10th year of Kanishka preserved in the British Museum: *Priyatāṁ devi grāmasya* " May the goddess of the village be pleased!" *Ep. Ind.*, Vol. IX p. 240 Cf. also *Ep. Ind.*, Vol. I, p. 386, no. VIII and beneath p. 94, no. C 28. My first reading was: *Svakaryyā priyatti Bhagavā Nāgo* " May the Lord Nāga delight in his own work!"

it was being worshipped as Dāujī or Balarāma, the elder brother of Kṛishṇa. On loan from the Government of India.

C 15.—Figure (ht. 3′ 1″ or 0 m. 935) of a Nāga surmounted by a hood of a seven-headed snake, the coils of which are visible on both sides. The right hand of the figure is raised above the head; the left holds a cup. He wears elaborate headgear and ornaments. A wreath is slung round his shoulders. The lower portion of the figure is missing. It was erroneously identified by Mr. Growse with Balarāma, the elder brother of Kṛishṇa.

The sculpture was obtained by Mr. Growse from the village of Kukargāṛh in the Sa'adābād *parganā*. (*Mathurā*, p. 169 and *J.A.S.B.* Vol. XLIV (1875). Part I, p. 815; plate XIV.)

* C 16. Fragment (ht. 1 ′5″ or 0 m. 445) consisting of the hind portion of a a coiled-up snake carved in the round. Possibly the sculpture represented a Nāga, the missing upper half being a human bust with snake-hood. Nāga figures of this type are said to exist in Bihār. On the front face of the roughly dressed base is the following Sanskrit inscription in two lines, the second line being continued on the proper left face of the base:

Śr[*ī*]*-Aśvadevasya* (2)*Bhuvana-tripravaraka-puttrasya.*

"[The gift] of Śrī Aśvadeva, the son of Bhuvana the Tripravaraka."

From the designation *tripravaraka* meaning "a descendant of three prominent *ṛishis*" it follows that the donor of the sculpture was a Brahmin. Judging from the character of the inscription, the sculpture must belong to the later Kushaṇa or early Gupta period. It was obtained by Pandit Radha Krishna from a place on the perambulation road between the villages of Mahōlī and Usphār. The owner had made a mud figure on the top of the sculpture which he explained to the ignorant pilgrims as a representation of Kṛishṇa subduing the Kaliya Nāga. On loan from the Goverαment of India.

C 17.—Head (ht. 1′ 4″ or 0 m 40) with a five-headed Nāga hood, much damaged. The head is presumably that of a Nāgī or female Nāga. It is very flat at the top, the hair being indicated by parallel straight lines, passing backward. In front is an ornament in the shape of a conventional flower. On the forehead over the nose is a circular mark. The ears and eyes are large. The nose is broken, the lips and chin are injured. Find-place unknown.

C 18.—Sculpture (ht. 3′ 2½″ or 0 m. 975) representing a male figure, perhaps a Yaksha, standing under a tree. He wears an elaborate head-dress, ear-rings, a torque and bracelets. His dress consists of a thin

PLATE XV.

a. No. A, 4; Ht. 2' 8".
BUDDHA STATUETTE; KUSHAṆA PERIOD.

b. No. A, 43; Ht. 1' 5".
BODHISATTVA STATUETTE; KUSHAṆA PERIOD.

scarf laid over the left shoulder and breast, and a *dhōtī* tied round the loins by means of a girdle. He holds a bag in his left hand; his right arm which is slightly injured is raised to the breast. Outside the feet are two crouching figurines much defaced. The sculpture is carved in the round. At the back the trunk of the tree is shown against which the figure is leaning. Find-place unknown.

C 19.—Figure (ht. 1′ 10″ or 0 m. 558) of a hooded Nāga standing with right hand raised. Lower portion of sculpture missing. Obtained from the Dīrgha-Vishṇu temple near the Bharatpur Gate, Mathurā City.

On loan from the Government of India.

C 20.—Sculpture (ht. 7½″ or 0 m. 19) representing two figures of a Nāga and a Nāgī standing, each with the right hand raised to the shoulder and holding a water-vessel in the left hand. The coils of the snake are visible behind their bodies. Obtained from Dhruv Ṭīlā on the bank of the Jamnā, south of Mathurā City. On loan from the Government of India.

*C 21.—Statuette (ht. 9¼″ or 0 m. 235) of a Nāga standing with his right hand raised to the shoulder, whilst the left holds a vessel. He is canopied by a hood of seven snake-heads, the coils of the snake-bodies being shown on both sides of the figure. In attitude and dress the figure is similar to the Bodhisattvas of the Kushaṇa period. At the same time it shows a close relationship to the Nāga statue of Chhargaon (no C 13), though the latter is superior in style. The Chhargaon image is only twelve years anterior in date. It is noteworthy that the statuette here described has a moustache.

On the base is an inscription in one line, 5″ long, which I read : *Saṁ* 52 *va* 3 *di* 25 *bhagava*[*ta*]. "In the year 52, in the 3rd month of the rainy season, on the 25th day. [Image] of the lord."

The statuette was worshipped as Baladeva in a shrine near the Jama' Mosque in the City and is said to have been found in the Bhūtēsar mound. On loan from the Government of India.

C 22.—Statuette (ht. 10¼″ or 0 m. 26) of a Nāga, canopied by a serpent-hood, standing between two smaller figures, male and female, kneeling with hands folded in the attitude of adoration. These two probably represent human devotees. It was obtained from a *sādhu*. On loan from the Government of India.

C 23.—Two fragments, one (ht. 4′ 2″ or 1 m. 27) consisting of the head and bust with part of the left arm, and the other (ht. 2′ 5″ or 1 m. 347) consisting of the feet and pedestal of a statue of colossal size. The carving is much obliterated, but the heavy earrings, the necklace with four tassels at the back, and the flat girdle suggest a close relationship between this figure and the Parkham image (no. C 1) which it surpasses in size. The present statue, when entire, must have been about 12′ in height, which would be about double life-size.

Pandit Radha Krishna obtained these fragments from the village of Barōdā 4 miles from Parkham and 2 miles from Chhaṛgaon. It was being worshipped under the name of Jakheya. On loan from the Government of India.

C 24.—Image (ht. 3′ 3″ or 0 m. 99 including tenon) of a crouching dwarf, probably a Yaksha, with large head and protruding belly. He is nude and wears a garland round his neck; the left is tied to the body by means of a scarf. The arms are broken, but were evidently stretched upwards. We may assume that the figure served the purpose of an Atlant and carried the shaft of a pillar on its head. It is similar to no. C 3, but not so well preserved. Pandit Radha Krishna found this sculpture let in the wall of a house at the village of Pālī Khēṛā 2½ miles west of the City. On loan from the Government of India.

C 25.—Double figure (ht. 1′ 7″ or 0 m. 482) of a Yaksha crouching and holding a cup in each hand. He has a disproportionately large head with moustache, a protruding belly and small legs. He is nude, but wears a garland round his neck and two bracelets on each arm. There is a tenon on the top of the head. Said to have been found in the river Jamnā near the Vināyak Ṭīlā. On loan from the Government of India.

C 26.—Sculpture (ht. 8″ or 0 m. 206) representing a corpulent male and female figure seated to front side by side. The male holds a money-bag in his right and a cup in his left hand. The female has a flower in her left hand, the right being raised to the shoulder. They probably represent the god of wealth and the goddess of fertility. Obtained from Pōtrā Kuṇḍ. On loan from the Government of India.

C 27.—Sculpture (ht. 10″ or 0 m. 254) representing a corpulent male and female figure seated side by side, the latter holding a child on her left knee. The male figure seems to hold a money-bag and a cup. They may be identified with Kuvera and Hāritī. On loan from the Government of India.

*C 28.—Sculpture (ht. 9″ or 0 m. 228) representing a corpulent male and female figure seated to front side by side. They are similar to nos. C 8 and 12, but the hands are broken with the objects which they held. On the base is an inscription consisting of two words, written one over the other, which I read: *Priyati Sidha*[*ḥ*]. "May the Siddha be pleased!"[1] The character is Brāhmī of the Kushaṇa period. The proper right side of

[1] For this formula cf. above p. 91, footnote.

No. A. 21 ; Ht. 1' 5½".

BUDDHA STATUETTE FROM SITALĀ GHĀṬI.

No. A, 21 ; Ht. 1' 5½".

BUDDHA STATUETTE FROM SITALĀ GHĀṬI.

the base is defaced. The sculpture was obtained from the ancient side of Rāl-Bhadar, 9 miles north-west of Mathurā. On loan from the Government of India.

C 29.—Sculpture (ht. 8¾" or 0 m. 222) representing a corpulent male and female figure crouching to front, side by side. The male holds a cup, the female a child and a flower (?). They probably represent Kubera and his consort. Obtained from the village Keravi, 2 miles off Mathurā opposite the Visrānt Ghāṭ on the left bank of the river Jamnā. On loan from the Government of India.

C 30.—Sculpture (ht. 6½" or 0 m. 165) representing one corpulent male and two female figures seated to front side by side. The male holds a cup in his left hand, the females a flower and a cup in their left hands, while all have the right hand raised to the shoulder. The male figure probably represents Kubera the god of wealth. The female figures are distinguished by hoods. The sculpture contains, moreover, four figurines probably human worshippers, standing with hands joined. The sculpture, which must belong to the Kushaṇa period, came from the Manōharpur mound in the City. On loan from the Government of India.

C 31.—Sculpture (ht. 12½" or 0 m. 317) representing a corpulent male figure, perhaps Kubera, crouching to front. He holds a cup in his right and a bag (?) in the left hand. Both hands are raised to the shoulders. The sculpture, apparently of the Kushaṇa period, was obtained from Bahādurpur near the Rajputana Malwa Railway station of Mathurā City. On loan from the Government of India.

C 32.—Sculpture (ht. 9¼" or 0 m. 235) representing a Nāga, standing, canopied by a seven-headed snake-hood; face and arms broken. Obtained from a *sādhu*. On loan from the Government of India.

D. Images of Brahmanical Deities.

D 1.—Torso and head (ht. 1′ 6½″ or 0 m. 469) of an image of Sūrya (?) the Sun-god. Remnants of a circular halo. Face considerably injured. He wears a helmet, fastened under the chin by means of a strap. Long curly locks falling down on both shoulders. Thin moustache (?). He is clad in a cuirass over which appears a very elaborate necklace. A scarf thrown over both shoulders is fastened in a knot on the left breast. A double-cord girdle is tied round the loins and fastened in front. Find-place unknown.

D 2.—Statuette (ht. 9″ or 0 m. 229) of Vishṇu standing. He wears a high mitre, a halo, various ornaments and a brahmanical cord. The face is injured and two of the four arms are broken. Of the two remaining hands the right holds the mace (*gadā*), the upper part of which is broken, the left the conch (*śaṅkha*). The others either held the lotus (*padma*) and the wheel (*chakra*) or were placed on the heads of the male and female attendant *chaurī* bearers, standing at his right and left side. The two figures seated at the sides of the halo must represent Brahmā and Śiva. Brahmā, with a pointed beard, sits to the proper right and Śiva, with a trident (*triśūla*), to the left. Possibly there was a Garuda projecting from the pedestal beneath the feet of the main figure.

D 3.—Statuette (ht. 11″ or 0 m. 279) of Sūrya the Sun-god, standing. The head which is broken, has a mitre and a halo. He holds in each hand a lotus-stalk with a full-blown flower raised over his shoulders. The flower to the left is defaced. The figure wears a cuirass (?) and high boots. On either side stands an attendant (Brahmā and Śiva ?). The one to the right has a pointed beard and holds an indefinite object in his right hand. Find-place unknown.

D 4.—Statuette (ht. 6″ or 0 m. 155) of Vishṇu erect, wearing a high mitre and halo, various ornaments and a brahmanical cord. In his four hands are the usual attributes, mace, lotus, wheel and conch. The right lower hand which held the conch is broken. Probably there was a kneeling figure under that hand, similar to the one to the left under the wheel. They represent human worshippers. At either side of the halo is a very indistinct miniature figure, apparently seated. These are probably Brahmā and Śiva, the two other members of the Brahmanical Trinity (Sanskrit *tri-mūrti* lit. three-form). Find-place unknown.

D 5.—Statuette (ht. 1′ 5″ or 0 m. 43) of a corpulent male (?) deity seated on an elephant, the trunk of which is broken. His head and arms are missing. The left hand evidently rested on the knee which is also injured. On each side of the central figure stands an attendant; upper portion of both missing. Beneath these are two human devotees, a man and a woman, kneeling with folded hands. They possibly represent the donors of the sculpture. Judging from the vehicle, the main figure seems to represent either Indra, the Indian thunder-god, on his elephant Airāvaṭa, or the Bodhisattva Samantabhadra—more probably the former as the sculpture is Brahmanical rather than Buddhist. (Cf. Foucher, *Iconographie bouddhique*, pp. 120-126; pl. VI. 2). Find-place unknown.

D 6.—Statuette (ht. 2′ 5½″ or 0 m. 745) of a goddess, perhaps Vaishṇavī the female counterpart (Skr. *śakti*) of Vishṇu, standing on a cushion supported by a Garuḍa. Originally the image must have had ten arms, each of which held a wheel (*chakra*). The head which is broken is surrounded by an elaborate halo in the shape of an expanded lotus-flower. On each side stands a female attendant, that to the right holding a fly-whisk (Skr. *chāmara*) and that to the left a wreath. Both are defaced. In the centre of the top of the slab is a cross-legged figure of a Jina (?) considerably injured, seated in meditation (Skr. *dhyāna-mudrā*). On both sides of it is a flying figure carrying a garland.

The sculpture seems to be the same as the "brahmanical female figure with ten arms" mentioned by Cunningham, as having been discovered in the Kaṅkālī Ṭīlā. If so, the sculpture is probably Jaina.
(Plate XVII. Cf. *A.S.R.* Vol. III p. 19).

D 7.—Statuette (ht. 1′ 9″ or 0 m. 549) of a female deity, perhaps Pārvatī, with ornamental halo, seated on a lotus cushion supported by a couchant lion, her left leg drawn up, her right foot placed on the ground. In her right hand she holds a bunch of flowers, partly broken, and with her left clasps a male child which sits on her thigh playing with the lower necklace on her left breast. Both these figures are defaced. The female figure is clad in a garment which covers the lower part of the body. A shawl thrown over the shoulders and passing behind the neck falls over the upper arms. She wears an elaborate head-dress, a double necklace, bracelets, anklets and an ornamental girdle. The child is nude, has a necklace, rings round its upper arm and wrist and a narrow band round its loins. To the left of the central figure stands another child, also mutilated, with similar ornaments and the right hand resting on the right knee of the goddess.

At the other side of the standing child is a miniature Gaṇeśa seated on a low cushion and holding in his left hand a vessel of sweetmeats to which he applies his trunk. On the corresponding side, to the right, is another seated figure, the face of which is broken. It holds a bowl in its right and a bag (?) in its left hand. It probably represents Kubera the god of wealth. This and the Gaṇeśa figure have oblong haloes. On both sides of the central group stands an attendant waving a fly-whisk. On the panel beneath are eight dancing female figures, probably Śaktis. From the upper portion of the relief projects a canopy of flowers. In the centre is a defaced figure of a Jina (?) seated cross-legged on a lotus in the attitude of meditation. On both sides is a four-armed figure standing on a flower. Next to these are two flying figures, one with folded hands and the other holding a fruit of some kind. Another pair of flying figures, carrying garlands, occupies the upper corners of the relief. All the figures are defaced except the Gaṇeśa. Find-place unknown. (Plate XVIIb).

D 8.—Sculpture (ht. 1′ 9″ or 0 m. 533) representing a chapel in which the defaced figure of a four-armed goddess, perhaps Pārvatī, is seated with a child on her left knee. On the roof squats a male figure (Sūrya?), wearing a high tiara, a cuirass (?) and high boots, and holding in each hand an expanded lotus, that to the left being defaced. Outside the chapel to the proper right is a two-armed female figure seated on a lotus-cushion, supported by a lion facing. She holds a mirror in her left hand. The right hand and head are missing. The corresponding figure to the proper left is lost. Find-place unknown.

D 9.—Image (ht. 1′ or 0 m. 305) of Lakshmī (?), the goddess of Fortune, holding in each hand a lotus on which stands an elephant. The sculpture, which is much defaced, is said to come from the Kaṅkālī Ṭīlā (Cf. Grünwedel—Burgess, *Buddhist art* p. 39, figs. 14 and 15.)

D 10.—Statuette (ht. 1′ 6½″ or 0 m. 47) of a squatting female deity with a circular halo, holding in her left arm a child, which is seated on her knee and touches her left breast. In her left hand she holds a cup (?) over her shoulder. Both figures are defaced. Behind the child rise two stalks, issuing from the pedestal and carrying each a lotus flower, naturalistically treated and projecting from the halo over the head of the child. Find-place unknown.

D 11.—Statuette (ht. 8¼″ or 0 m. 21) representing a squatting female figure holding on her left hip a child, which touches her breast with its left hand. In her right hand she holds an indefinite object. The idol was evidently until lately worshipped, as the faces of both figures are besmeared with redlead. The carving is rude and much defaced. It is said to originate from the Kaṅkālī Ṭīlā.

D 12.—Image (ht. 2′ 9″ or 0 m. 83) of the eight-armed goddess Durgā slaying the Buffalo demon (Skr. *Mahishāsura*). She wears a double necklace and flat ear-rings. The right arms which are provided with bracelets

PLATE XVII.

No. D, 6; Ht. 2' 5½".
STATUETTE OF VAISHṆAVĪ.

No. D, 7; Ht. 1' 9".
STATUETTE OF PĀRVATĪ.

are partly broken. Two hold a snake (?) over her head; the second and third arm are broken; the fourth holds a sword (?). With one left hand she clasps the tail of the buffalo-shaped demon whom she is piercing with a trident. The arm holding the weapon is broken. The sculpture which is of very inferior workmanship is said to originate from the Kaṅkālī Ṭīlā. I found it broken in two pieces, which have now been re-fixed.

D 13.—Fragment (ht. 1′ 4″ or 0 m. 405) consisting of the left leg of a seated male image of natural size wearing a loin cloth and a ring round its ankle. On his thigh a female figure is seated of which only the lower half remains. The sculpture probably represents Śiva holding Pārvatī. It is said to originate from the Kaṅkālī Ṭīlā.

D 14.—Statuette (ht. 7¼″ or 0 m. 183) representing Śiva and Pārvatī seated on the bull Nandi. Śiva is four-armed and holds in one of his right arms a trident and in one of his left arms a cobra. Pārvatī holds in her left hand a mirror; her right arm is laid round Śiva's neck. On both sides of the main group is a squatting figurine. That to the proper right is Gaṇeśa; that to the left is probably the god of war, Skanda, holding a lance in his left hand.

The statuette was presented to the Museum by Mahant Saligram from Cawnpore who had found it in digging the foundations of his house at Brindāban.

D 15.—Statuette (ht. 8½″ or 0 m. 216) of Sūrya, the Sun-god, standing between two attending male figures and holding in each hand a full-blown lotus-flower raised over his shoulders. It was obtained from a Kolī who is said to have found it in the Jamnā.

D 16.—Statuette (ht. 7¾″ or 0 m. 197) of Sūrya standing and holding a lotus-flower in each hand.

D 17.—Statuette (ht. 8½″ or 0 m. 216) of Śrī or Lakshmī, the goddess of luck, standing with her right hand raised to the shoulder and holding in her left hand a flower. On both sides of her head are the usual figurines of elephants pouring out water over her. It was presented by Mahant Saligram of Cawnpore who had found it in digging the foundations of his house at Brindāban.

D 18.—Figurine (ht. 5″ or 0 m. 127), rudely carved, of a male person sitting to front and holding both hands before his breast. It was presented by Mahant Saligram of Cawnpore who had found it in digging the foundations of his house at Brindāban.

D 19.—Figurine (ht. 5″ or 0 m. 127) of a woman seated to front and holding a child in her left arm. It was presented by Mahant Saligram of

Cawnpore who had found it in digging the foundations of his house at Brindāban.

D20.—Figure (ht. 4′ 1″ or 1 m. 289) of a three-faced, four-armed male deity, standing on a lotus. The arms with the attributes are broken. To the proper left are traces of a miniature attendant figure. The material is buff-coloured sandstone and the style modern. It probably belongs to the Muhammadan period. The sculpture is said to represent Dattatreya one of the twenty-four incarnations of Vishṇu. It was obtained by Pandit Radha Krishna from the Sarasvatī Kuṇḍ on the Delhi road outside Mathurā City. On loan from the Government of India.

D 21.—Figure (ht. 3′ 9″ or 1 m. 178) of Vishṇu standing on a lotus. The head and four arms with the attributes are broken. On each side of the main figure are three attendants. Two, apparently a male and a female, are kneeling in front; possibly they represent the donors of the sculpture. Behind them two male figures are standing which hold two of Vishṇu's attributes, the conch (Skr. *śaṅkha*) and the wheel (Skr. *chakra*). The two remaining figurines are a male and a female occupying the two recessed ends of the front face and each holding a lotus-stalk. Over the two last-mentioned figures we notice the decorative device of the leogryph on the elephant, originally meant as a bracket supporting the projecting ends of the back of the throne. The leogryphs are surmounted by *makara* heads, over which are figurines of Brahmā to the proper right and Śiva to the left, each accompanied by a female attendant. It should be remembered that Brahmā and Śiva form with Vishṇu the Trimūrti or Hindū Trinity.

The top of the slab is carved with a row of miniature figures, of which the two seated on each end seem to be Brahmanical ascetics, whereas the others represent the ten *avatāras* of Vishṇu. Beginning from the proper right we notice :—1. The fish, 2. the tortoise with two figures churning the ocean, 3. the boar, 4. the man-lion disemboweling the demon Hiraṇyakaśipu, 5. the dwarf, 6. Paraśurāma, 7. Rāma, 8. Kṛishṇa, 9. Buddha and 10. Kalki (the future incarnation) on horseback.

The sculpture was obtained by Pandit Radha Krishna from the village Gaṇṭyauli 1 mile east of Govardhan. On loan from the Government of India.

D 22.—Sculpture (ht. 1′ 10″ or 0 m. 576) in buff-coloured sandstone representing Brahmā, the Creator, and Sarasvatī, the goddess of Wisdom, seated on a lotus-flower, his right and her left foot being placed on small lotuses which spring from a common stalk. Between these two lotuses we notice a pair of geese, of which the one to the proper left is broken Of Brahmā's four faces only three are visible, as the fourth is supposed to be at the back; the god is four-armed. The two right hands hold a staff and a waterpot which is broken. The two left arms are slung round the neck and waist of Sarasvatī; one of the left hands holds a manuscript of the Veda. Sarasvatī has a mirror in her left hand, her right arm is laid round the neck of her consort. The two lower corners of the carved surface are occupied by two male devotees, standing in the attitude of adoration. In each of the two upper corners is a Gandharva carrying a garland and accompanied by an Apsaras, both figures projecting from a cloud. The sculpture, judging from its style, is of comparatively recent date. It is well-preserved, except for the breakage of the right leg of the male figure. Pandit Radha Krishna purchased the sculpture at Mahāban. On loan from the Government of India.

D 23.—Sculpture (ht. 1′ 10½″ or 0 m. 59) in buff-coloured sandstone representing Vishṇu standing on a lotus. He wears the usual ornaments and a high tiara. Behind his head is a halo shaped like a conventional lotus. His four arms with the emblems are broken. On each side of the god are three figurines of attendants. Two of these, a male and a female, which are kneeling in front possibly represent human devotees. Two male figures standing behind them carry a conch and a wheel, two of Vishṇu's emblems. The two remaining figurines, male and female, occupy the recessed ends of the slab, and seem each to carry a lotus flower. The male figure is perhaps a Nāga. Over the last-mentioned pair of figures we notice two leogryphs of the usual type and over these two seated deities: Brahmā to the proper right and Śiva to the proper left. These two gods, as remarked above, form with Vishṇu the Hindū Trinity or Trimūrti. The sculpture is well preserved. It was obtained by Pandit Radha Krishna from the Askuṇḍa Ghāṭ in Mathurā City. On loan from the Government of India.

D 24.—Sculpture (ht. 2′ 7″ or 0 m. 812) representing Agni (?), the god of fire with a halo of flames, standing between two miniature attendants of which the one to the right has a goat's head. The central figure has a pointed beard and holds a bag (?) in his left hand. On each side of his head is a flying figure carrying a garland. The sculpture was obtained from Nārad Kuṇḍ, a ruined tank between Rādhā Kuṇḍ and Gōvardhan, where it was being worshipped as Nārad. On loan from the Government of India.

D 25.—Statuette (ht. 1′ 2½″ or 0 m. 38) of the goddess Durgā with her infant son Kārttikeya seated on her left knee. Her vehicle, the lion, is sitting in front. Behind the head of the goddess is a halo in the shape of a conventional flower, to the proper right of which we notice an animal-headed female figure crouching on a lotus-flower. The upper left corn of the slab is broken. The sculpture was obtained by Pandit Radha Krishna from Mahāban. On loan from the Government of India.

D 26.—Slab (ht. 4′ 9½″ or 1 m. 50) carved with a figure of Kṛishṇa standing to front and lifting with his left hand Mount Gōvardhaṇ on which two parrots and four peacocks are walking. At his feet are a cow and a human figurine standing with both hands in front of the breast. The two raised vertical borders on both sides of the deity are carved with a series of fourteen small panels, containing various figurines and symbols. The upper four show the attributes of Vishṇu: the lotus, the conch, the mace and the wheel. On the remaining panels we notice to the proper right: Balarāma, Kṛishṇa's elder brother carrying a plough, a Brahmin with a rosary and a staff, two female figures (perhaps milk-maids) and the Kadamba (?) tree. The lowermost panel on the proper left side represents the milk-churn of Yaśodhā, the foster-mother of Kṛishṇa. The figures above I am unable to identify with certainty.

Judging from the freshness of the stone and from the style of the carving, the sculpture is not earlier than the Mughal period. Note particularly the cusped arch above the main figure. It was obtained by Pandit Radha Krishna from the village of Hans Ganj on the left bank of the Jamnā opposite the City. On loan from the Government of India.

D 27.—Statue (ht. 6′ 7″ or 2 m. 07; width 1′ 6″ or 0 m. 471) of colossal size representing Hanumān (?), the monkey hero. He is standing with his left foot on a prostrate female figure, the head of which is lost. The left leg of the god and his right arm which is raised above the head are broken with the top of the slab. A flying figure carrying a garland is shown above.

The statue was obtained by Pandit Radha Krishna from the village of Parkham, 14 miles south of Mathurā on the Grand Trunk Road, which also yielded the inscribed colossal figure No. C 1. On loan from the Government of India.

D 28.—Statuette (ht. 11½″ or 0 m. 202) of Vishṇu standing. He is three-headed, the side ones being those of a boar and lion, evidently symbolic of the Boar (Skr. *Varāha*) and Man-lion (Skr. *Narasiṁha*) incarnations. Two of the usual four arms of the god are broken. The remaining two hold a conch and a wheel, placed on the heads of two miniature male attendants. The sculpture was acquired by Pandit Radha Krishna from the same spot as C 14. On loan from the Government of India.

D 29.—Sculpture (ht. 10″ or 0 m. 268) apparently representing Vishṇu standing with three attendants on each side. The sculpture which is much defaced was obtained by Pandit Radha Krishna from a weaver (*Kōlī*) in the City. On loan from the Government of India.

No. D. 35 ; Ht. 2' 4½"

STATUETTE OF VISHNU.

D 30—31.—Two figurines (ht. 8" or 0 m. 21) of Hindū ascetics seated cross-legged and holding a rosary with both hands in front of the breast. The two figures which are apparently modern were obtained by Pandit Radha Krishna from Mahāban. One of them is defaced. On loan from the Government of India.

*D 32.—Stele (ht. 3′ or 0 m. 942), broken in two, with a rudely carved figure of the eight-armed goddess Durgā standing with her right foot on her vehicle, the lion, and with the left on the prostrate Buffalo demon (Skr. *Mahishāsura*). The figurine of a warrior between these two animals probably represents the same demon in human shape. The stone bears a Nāgarī inscription: *Pudyā Gosāiṁ-jī* over which there are traces of a line in characters of an earlier period. The stone was obtained from the village of Midhauli, Sa'adābād *parganā*. On loan from the Government of India.

D 33.—Statuette (ht. 7½" or 0 m. 197) of Sūrya standing with a lotus-flower in each hand. Purchased in Mathurā City. On loan from the Government of India.

D 34.—Statuette (ht. 6½" or 0 m. 164) of Vishṇu standing between two attendants. The sculpture is water-worn. Purchased at Mathurā. On loan from the Government of India.

D 35.—Sculpture (ht. 2′ 4½" or 0 m. 745) in blue schist representing Vishṇu between two female attendants, each standing on a conventional lotus. The god wears a high conical diadem (Skr. *mukuṭa, kirīṭa*), a breast-jewel (Skr. *kaustubha*) attached to an elaborate necklace, a sacred thread, an elaborate girdle and a long garland reaching down beneath the knees. The folds of the drapery of his two garments are only slightly indicated on the chest and the thighs. He is four-armed and holds his usual emblems: the mace (*gadā*) and the lotus flower (*padma*) in his right hands and the wheel (*chakra*) and the conch-shell (*śaṅkha*) in his left hands. Of the two female attendants, that to the right of the central figure raises her right hand and holds the stalk of a lotus (*padma*) in her left. The other plays the lute (*vīṇā*). In front of the lotus-flower on which Vishṇu stands are three figurines: Garuḍa between two kneeling devotees, apparently male and female, who carry vases of offerings. The Garuḍa is defaced; for the rest the sculpture is in excellent preservation. It is a fine specimen of mediaeval Brahmanical art. It was purchased from a resident of Brindāban in December 1908 and is said to have been found in the vicinity of that town. On loan from the Government of India. (Plate XVIII),

D 36.—White marble statuette (ht. 1′ 5½″ or 0 m. 458) of Balarāma the elder brother of Kṛishṇa. He is standing with his right hand raised and with a cup in the left. Over his head is a serpent-hood of seven snake-heads which is believed to refer to the circumstance of his being an incarnation of the world-snake Śesha-nāga. A comparison with Nos. C 13—15 will, however, make it quite clear that the modern representations of Balarāma are copied from ancient Nāga figures. The statuette, which is modern, was purchased at Brindāban in December 1908. On loan from the Government of India.

D 37.—Sculpture (ht. 2′ 10″ or 0 m. 862) of buff coloured sandstone, representing the four-armed Vishṇu apparently in the Buddha *avatāra* seated cross-legged on a lotus-seat. He holds the mace (*gadā*) and the wheel (*chakra*), whilst the two remaining hands are resting on his lap in the attitude of meditation. He has long locks and wears a high, elaborately carved tiara, ear pendants, a double necklace, a breast jewel (*kaustubha*), bracelets round his arms and wrists, a brahmanical thread and a long garland hanging down on his lotus-seat. Beneath the lotus-seat is a group of miniature figures: in the centre a female figurine seated cross-legged to front with hands joined in adoration, on each side of it two Nāgas with serpent tail and triple snakehood, which likewise join their hands in the attitude of worship, and at the ends two kneeling figures, male and female, which probably represent the donors of the sculpture.

Next we notice four attendant figures of somewhat larger size standing on both sides of Vishṇu's lotus-throne, two to the right and two to the left. That on the extreme proper right is a female, the others are male. They hold Vishṇu's attributes: the lotus-flower (*padma*), the conch (*śaṅkha*), the wheel (*chakra*), whilst the fourth holds a cobra. The projecting ends of the bar of Vishṇu's throne are supported by rampant leogryphs standing on elephants, whilst they are surmounted by *makara* heads on which female musicians are standing.

Behind Vishṇu's headdress we notice a decorative halo shaped like a full-blown lotus-flower. On both sides of it and above it are three projecting chapels supported on a pair of dwarf pillars with leogryphs rampant. They contain seated figures of the three great gods: Brahmā, Vishṇu and Śiva who form the Hindu Trinity (*trimūrti*). Vishṇu occupies the centre, Brahmā the proper right and Śiva the proper left side. Each of these figures is four-armed and holds the usual attributes. On both sides of the central chapel there is a group of flying and garland-carrying celestials.

The sculpture was found in a mound near the Gatasram Temple in Mathurā City together with nos. D 38-42. Evidently they belonged to a Vishṇu temple which was destroyed by the Muhammadans. On loan from the Government of India.

D 38.—Sculpture (ht. 1′ 4¾″ or 0 m. 425) of buff sandstone representing Vishṇu standing on a lotus. The head is lost and two of the fore-arms are broken. In the remaining two hands he holds a mace and a wheel. To his left stand three miniature male figures, of which two hold a conch and a cobra respectively. The corresponding figurines on the proper right are lost. On both sides of the slab we notice the usual leogryph (proper right broken) and *makara*, whereas the top is occupied by seated figurines of Brahmā and Śiva, forming with the main figure the Hindū Trinity (Skr. *trimūrti*). Cf. above sub no. D 37. On loan from the Government of India.

D 39.—Sculpture (ht. 1′ 1½″ or 0 m. 343) of buff sandstone, evidently a counterpart of no. D 38. The main figure is four-armed, but its two right hands are lost with the attributes. The left hands hold an ornamental wheel and a mace. There can, therefore, be little doubt that the image represents Vishṇu, but from its corpulence I infer that it is meant for Vishṇu, in the Dwarf incarnation. The head of the figure is lost and likewise the feet with the lower portion of the slab. On both sides we notice the leogryph and *makara* ornament, and in the top portion seated figurines of Brahmā and Śiva similar to those found on no. D 38. On loan from the Government of India.

D 40.—Fragment (1′ 6½″ or 0 m. 469) forming the lower portion of a large image slab which probably represented Vishṇu standing on a lotus surrounded by the usual attendants. Of the main figure only the feet now remain. To his left there were three standing figures, of which only one is preserved, who holds a lotus-flower, one of Vishṇu's four attributes. The second holds a cobra in both hands. In front of the first attendant a female figurine is seated with hands joined in adoration. Of a corresponding figure to the proper right only the legs are extant. *Cf.* above sub no. D 37. On loan from the Government of India.

D 41.—Two fragments (ht. 1′ or 0 m. 304) containing a head with lotus-shaped halo and high head-dress which probably belonged to a figure of Śiva. This may be inferred from the frontal eye and from the trident which is partly preserved. Behind it there is a figurine of Brahmā three-faced (the fourth face is supposed is to be at the back) and four-armed. He is seated on a goose and holds his usual attributes—a staff, a rosary, a book and a water vessel. To his right we notice a skeleton (?) figure standing on a *makara* head. *Cf.* above sub no. D 37. On loan from the Government of India.

D 42.—Fragment (ht. 7½" or 0 m. 19) of an image slab containing three attendant figures standing, of which the second, a female, holds a lotus-flower in her left hand. *Cf.* above sub no. D 37. On loan from the Government of India.

D 43.—Image (ht. 3′ 2″ or 0 m. 864) of buff-coloured sandstone, representing Śiva seated. He is four-armed and holds a trident (*triśūla*), a tabor (*ḍamaru*), a wheel (*chakra*) and a rosary (*akshamālā*). He wears his hair tied up in a top-knot (*jaṭā*) and has cobras serving as ear-rings, diadem, necklace and bracelets. Small cobras support his knees. His forehead is marked with the frontal eye, a crescent and a sect mark (*tilaka*). He wears a necklace of human heads.

The sculpture is of inferior workmanship and evidently of a late date. It came from a *bāghīcha* near the Bhūtēsar mound. On loan from the Government of India.

D 44.—Image (ht. 2′ 1″ or 0 m. 636) of Śiva seated with his right knee raised. He is four-armed and holds a trident, a rosary, a wheel and a tabor. His forehead is marked with the crescent and the frontal eye. He wears his hair tied up in a top-knot and has cobras serving him as a necklace, ear-rings and bracelets. Round his neck is also a string of human heads. The sculpture is very similar to No. D 43 and evidently belongs to a late date. On loan from the Government of India.

D 45.—Sculpture (ht. 2′ 9″ or 0 m. 838) of buff-coloured sandstone, much defaced, representing Sūrya, the Sun-god, seated on his chariot drawn by seven horses. Between his feet the figure of Aruṇa, the charioteer, is still traceable and at the sides two other figures too much worn to be identified. Two female attendants, one of which holds a lotus-flower, stand on both sides of the chariot.

The sculpture which is of the mediaeval type was obtained from the village of Dhangaon, 7 miles west of the City south of the Bharatpur road. On loan from the Government of India.

D 46.—Slab (ht. 2′ 9″ or 0 m. 834) with a corpulent figure of Sūrya, the Sun-god, seated squatting on a chariot drawn by four horses. He holds in each hand an indistinct object, probably a lotus-flower. He has long locks and wears a torque round his neck. It is deserving of note that his shoulders are provided with small wings, as we find in Garuḍa figures. Another point of interest is the number of horses which corresponds with that found on a railing-pillar at Bōdh-Gayā [1], whereas in mediaeval sculptures the chariot of Sūrya is invariably drawn by seven horses. The present sculpture belongs to the Kushaṇa period. It was extracted from the Saptasamudrī well, ¾ mile south of the City and was presented to the Museum by Pandit Ram Chand, Head Clerk, Collector's office. On loan from the Government of India.

D 47.—Sculpture (ht. 1′ 8½″ or 0 m. 52) representing Kṛishṇa standing and balancing Mount Gōvardhaṇ on the palm of his left hand. He wears a long garland and heavy ear-pendants. On each side is a dwarf-life figure standing with both hands resting on a club and surmounted by two cows one placed over the other. The sculpture is interesting as the earliest representation of Kṛishṇa hitherto found at Mathurā. Obtained from a mound near the temple of Gataśram Nārāyaṇ in the heart of Mathūra city, when the foundations of a new building were laid. On loan from the Government of India.

D 48.—Statuette (ht. 7¾″ or 0 m. 197) of the Sun-god Sūrya seated on his chariot drawn by seven horses. Obtained from a boatman who is said to have found it in the river Jamnā. On loan from the Government of India.

D 49.—Figurine (ht. 2½″ or 0 m. 063) of black marble representing Jagannātha, *viz.*, Kṛishṇa, Subhadrā and Balabhadra. Obtained together with previous number. On loan from the Government of India.

D 50.—Group (ht. 4¼″ or 0 m. 107) consisting of Kṛishṇa uplifting Mount Gōvardhan on his left hand, a cow and a calf. Found in the river Jamnā. On loan from the Government of India.

D 51.—Statuette (ht. 10″ or 0 m. 253), much defaced, of Pārvatī, standing between a *liṅga* and a miniature figure of Gaṇeśa. The goddess is four-armed and holds a conch (?) with two hands in front of her breast. In the second right hand she holds what appears to be a ram's head. On both sides of her head are flying garland-carrying celestials. Obtained from a *sādhu*, resident in a *bāghīcha* near Pōtrā Kuṇḍ, Mathurā City. On loan from the Government of India.

• D 52.—Sculpture (ht. 1′ 8½″ or 0 m. 52) with sunk panel containing a three-headed male figure (Brahmā ?) seated cross-legged. Under it there is a Nāgarī inscription in two lines : *Śrī-Gan* [*e*] *śāya nama* [*ḥ*] 167[3] *Śa* [*ka*] 153[8]. The date corresponds to A.D.1616. The sculpture came from the Arjunpura Ṭīlā in the City. On loan from the Government of India.

[1] Foucher, *L'art gréco-bouddhique du Gandhâra*, pages 206 f figs. 82 and 83; also *J. R. A. S.* for 1908, pages 1096 f, plate IV and *Si-yu-ki* (transl. Beal), vol. I, p. 89.

D 53.—Fragment (ht. 10½″ or 0 m. 266) containing two standing figurines—a corpulent male figure holding a conch and a female with a lotus-flower in her left hand. The fragment perhaps belonged to a Vishṇu image. From Manōharpur Maḥalla in the City. On loan from the Government of India.

D 54.—Sculpture (ht. 1′ 3″ or 0 m. 38; length 1′ 10½″ or 0 m. 572) probably the top portion of a large Vishṇu image containing three chapels with figurines of Brahmā, Vishṇu and Śiva. On both sides of the central chapel we notice a female attendant carrying a fly-whisk and one or two flying celestials. Beneath the chapels there is a row of figures representing the nine *Grahas* and the ten *Avatāras*, but on both sides several figures are missing. Of the *Grahas*, which occupy the proper right side, the following are preserved: Śukra, Saniśchara, Rāhu and Ketu. The *Avatāras* which are preserved are the fish, the tortoise, the boar, the man-lion and the dwarf. Most of the figures are defaced. The sculpture was obtained by Pandit Radha Krishna from the Manōharpur Maḥalla in the City. On loan from the Government of India.

D 55.—Figurine (ht. 4¾″ or 0 m. 12) of a cow with a calf and Kṛishṇa uplifting Mount Gōvardhan. From Hakīmpur 6 miles south-west from Mathurā. On loan from the Government of India.

E.—Miscellaneous Images.

E 1.—Statuette (ht. 1′ 3½″ or 0 m. 393) of the goat-headed god Nemesa or Naigamesa who presides over child-birth. Right arm and legs beneath knee missing. In his left hand he holds two children hanging down along his thigh. Besides, there was on each of his shoulders a figure of which only the legs are still traceable. Judging from the style, the statuette belongs to the Kushaṇa period. It is said to originate from the Kankālī Ṭīlā (Cf. *A. S. R.* Vol. XX, plate IV, 5; Bühler. *Ep. Ind.* Vol. II, p. 314, plate II; and V. A. Smith, *Jain Stūpa*, plate XVIII. Cf. *J. R. A. S.*, for 1895 p. 153).

E 2.—Figure (ht. 1′ 4″ or 0 m. 405) of a goat-headed goddess with prominent breasts holding with her left hand a pillow (?) on which a male child (defaced) is lying with hands joined on its breast. The right hand of the goat-headed figure is broken, but seems to have been raised to the shoulder. (Cf. *A. S. R.* Vol. XX, plate IV, 2).

E 3.—Fragment (ht. 1′ ¾″ or 0 m. 315) of a goat-headed goddess with prominent breasts over which is a necklace. The figure is evidently a replica of no. E2. It is said to originate from the Kankālī Ṭīlā.

E 4.—Fragment (ht. 1′ 1″ or 0 m. 333) of a female figure holding with her left hand a pillow (?) placed in her lap. On it a male infant is lying, which she seems to fan with her right hand, which is broken. The sculpture was obtained by Mr. Growse from the Manōharpur Quarter of the City (*J. A. S. B.* Vol. XLVII (1878), Part I, p. 120; plate XX. Cf. *A. S. R.* Vol. XX, plate IV, 3).

E 5.—Fragment (ht. 11½″ or 0 m. 292) of a seated female figure of which only the left leg and left hand remain. She holds a cradle (?) on which an infant is lying. On both sides of her feet is a crouching figure. Pedestal defaced. The fragment was obtained from Arjunpura Maḥalla in Mathurā City.

E 6.—Image (ht. 3′ 7″ or 1 m. 09) of a standing male deity, perhaps a Bodhisattva, wearing an elaborate diadem and profuse ornaments. The lower portion of the figure is missing. The upper portion of the body is nude, the lower half is clad in a *dhōtī* tied to the loins by means of a girdle. A garland hangs down along the arms, which are broken off at the elbows. From the left shoulder a double cord interlaced with *aśoka* (?) flowers runs down along the breast towards the knee. The figure was originally provided with a circular halo, the lower portion of which is still visible at the back. Judging from its style, the figure belongs to the Kushaṇa period. Its find-place is unknown.

E 7.—Image (ht. 3′ 7″ or 1 m. 09) of a standing male figure. It has an elaborate head-dress, heavy ear-rings, a double necklace and a bracelet and wears a *dhōti* and a scarf, thrown over the left shoulder. The lower portion of the image beneath the knees and the right arm are missing. The left hand holds an ornamental staff, considerably injured, resting against the left shoulder. Possibly it belonged to an umbrella. The figure is carved in the round, from which it appears that it had neither a halo nor a snake hood. Judging from its style, it belongs to the Kushaṇa period. Its find-place is unknown.

E 8.—Fragment (ht. 2′ 5″ or 0 m. 735) of a standing male figure holding a bunch of lotuses in his right hand and a garland under his left arm. The figure is clad in a *dhōti* tied round the waist with a flat girdle over which a scarf is bound. Judging from the style, the figure belongs to the Kushaṇa period. Find-place unknown.

E 9.—Bust (ht. 2′ 4″ or 0 m. 711) of a male figure wearing a turban and heavy earrings. Carving much defaced. Pandit Radha Krishna found this sculpture let into the wall of the house of a Chamār inside the Bharatpur Gate and secured it for the Museum.

E 10.—Fragment (ht. 1′ 8″ or 0 m. 523) consisting of the right shoulder of a colossal image, with a necklace, a garland and a double bracelet round the upper part of the arm. It was standing in the compound of the Collector's bungalow and was made over to the Museum by Mrs. Last in January 1908.

E 11.—Fragment (ht. 8¾″ or 0 m. 222) of a male figure standing to front with a garland in his right and a flower-offering in his left hand. Find-place unknown.

E 12.—Statue (ht. 3′ 10″ or 0 m. 204) of a male deity standing with his left hand resting on his hip. Both arms are broken and the figure is otherwise damaged. The feet and pedestal are missing. It had evidently three heads, but that to the proper right is lost. Judging from the style, the image seems to belong to the Kushaṇa period. It is of interest as the only polycephalic image which can be attributed to that epoch. It was found by Pandit Radha Krishna at the village of Bhadār 9 miles north-west of Mathurā City, but, according to local tradition, it came from Chaumuhā where it was worshipped as the four-faced Brahmā. On loan from the Government of India.

E 13.—Statuette (ht. 1′ 6″ or 0 m. 471), carved in the round, of a male standing with his right hand raised in front of his shoulder and holding a staff or spear in his left hand. He wears the usual ornaments, a *dhōti* fastened to the loins by means of a flat girdle, and a scarf thrown over the left shoulder and arm. The head is mutilated and the feet are missing. This sculpture belongs to the Kushaṇa period. It was purchased by Pandit Radha Krishna in Mathurā City. On loan from the Government of India.

E 14.—Torso (ht. 1′ 7½″ or 0 m. 511), carved in the round, of a male figure standing. He wears a *dhōti* fastened to the loins by means of a flat girdle tied in a knot above the left thigh. His necklace is fastened on the back with a pair of flat bands. Part of a garland is visible on the back. The sculpture was acquired by Pandit Radha Krishna from the village of Khāmnī 6 miles west of Mathurā on the Gōvardhan road. On loan from the Government of India.

E 15.—Sculpture (ht. 5½″ or 0 m. 144) with a square panel containing two half-figures, male and female, the former holding a cup in his right hand. Obtained from the village Gaṛhī between Gaṇēsrā and Sitōhā. The sculpture was placed over a buried double-headed hatchet. On loan from the Government of India.

E 16.—Sculpture (ht. 2′ 5″ or 0 m. 736) with two seated figures, male to proper right and female to proper left, both defaced. The male figure is seated on a rectangular block with his left leg drawn up and holds an indistinct object in his left hand. The female is crouching with her right hand raised to the shoulder. Obtained from the village of Usphahār. On loan from the Government of India.

E 17.—Figurine (ht. 10⅜″ or 0 m. 265) of a bird probably meant for Garuḍa, the bird of Vishṇu. Very clumsily carved. It was brought to the Museum from the Joint Magistrate's bungalow.

E 18.—Figurine (ht. 4½″ or 0 m. 115) of a bird probably meant for Garuḍa.

E 19.—Figurine (ht. 1′ 3½″ or 0 m. 395) of a Garuḍa holding a cobra in its beak.

• E 20.—Two fragments (ht. 3′ 1″ or 0 m. 94) making the lower half of a female figure, carved in the round, standing with her left hand placed on her hip. She wears a short petticoat and a loose garment hanging down from her left arm. On the pedestal there is a fragmentary inscription in three lines which I read:—

(1) . . . . . . *sya* [*H*]*uv*[*ish*]*ka*[*sya*] . . . . . .
(2) . . . . . . *etasya purvaye Mathurikalavadap* . . . .
(3) . . . . . . *ye Tośāye patimā* . . . . . .

The sculpture, together with nos. E 21—23, was obtained from an ancient site 1 mile west of the village of Mōrā (*cf. sub* Q 7). These fragments were found lying near the remains of a brick temple, in which evidently they were originally enshrined. On loan from the Government of India.

E 21.—Torso (ht. 3′ or 0 m. 914) of a corpulent male figure, standing, carved in the round. Head, arms and feet lost. He wears a heavy necklace tied in a knot at the back, a flat girdle and a shawl tied round the legs. From the Mōrā site. Cf. above *sub* No. E 20. On loan from the Government of India.

E 22.—Torso (ht. 2′ 3″ or 0 m. 686) of a male figure, standing, carved in the round. Head, arms and feet lost. He wears a double necklace fastened in front by means of a clasp, a *dhōtī* held to the loins with a girdle and a shawl tied round the legs. From the Mōrā site. Cf. above *sub* No. E 20. On loan from the Government of India.

E 23.—Pedestal (ht. 2′ or 0 m. 61) of a standing statue, of which only the feet now remain. From the site of Mōrā. Cf. above *sub* E 20. On loan from the Government of India.

E 24.—Torso (ht. 1′ 9″ or 0 m. 533) of a male figure, carved in the round but very flat, wearing a torque, a necklace and a long garland and holding in his left hand a thunderbolt (*vajra*) with triple prong on both sides. The sculpture appears to belong to the Kushaṇa period. It was acquired at the village of Tārsi six miles from Mathurā on the road to Bharatpur. On loan from the Government of India.

• E 25.—Figure (ht. 2′ 5″ or 0 m. 737) of a male, standing, clad in Indo-Scythian dress: tunic, trousers and boots. He holds a bunch of lotus-flowers in his right hand and an indistinct object in his left hand. Head lost.

On the base is an inscription, in two lines, too much obliterated to be deciphered. It appears to be dated *saṁvatsare 42*; the sculpture would therefore belong to the reign of Huvishka. It was found in a *bāghīcha* on the Brindāban road about 1½ miles from Mathurā. On loan from the Government of India.

E 26.—Figurine (ht. 6″ or 0 m. 153) of a ram standing. From Bharatpur Gate of Mathurā City. On loan from the Government of India.

E 27. Sculpture (ht. 12½″ or 0 m. 32) carved on the front and back face with two figures, male and female, standing. In one instance the female is looking in a mirror and the male seems to assist her in her toilet. On the reverse the female is dressing her hair and the male seems to hold a bunch of flowers and a garland. Tenons in top and bottom of stone. On loan from the Government of India.

E 28.—Figurine (ht. 6½″ or 0 m. 165) of a male standing with hands folded. On loan from the Government of India.

PLATE XIX.

(a) OBVERSE.

(b) REVERSE.

No. F. 2; Ht. 2' 5".

SCULPTURE REPR., THE QUEEN OF THE NĀGAS.

F.—Female Images[1].

F 1.—Sculpture (ht. 8′ 8″ or 0 m. 51) carved on both faces with the figure of a galloping female centaur ridden by a male with floating garments who holds a dagger (?) in his left hand. The centauress wears round her neck a garland, which she holds by one hand, besides bracelets and a flat girdle. Her horse-shaped body is disproportionately elongated. Below is a palm-leaf which is continued on one of the narrow sides of the stone. The sculpture was preserved at the Allahabad Public Library till December 1907 and probably came from the Jamālpur site.

M. Foucher has drawn attention to two medallions on the railing of the small *stūpa* of Sānchi. One represents a centaur and the other a centauress which carry a woman and a man respectively. With these he compares the Mathurā sculpture just described, which seems to be derived from such Old-Indian examples. (Foucher, *L'art gréco-bouddhique*, p. 211).

F 2.—Fragment (ht. 2′ 5″ or 0 m. 734) of a sculpture carved on both faces. On one face is the nearly life-size figure of a female deity, identified by Cunningham as "Queen of the Nāgas." Over the head, now defaced, is the remnant of a Nāga-hood, which once must have consisted of nine snake heads. Both arms are broken off near the elbow and over the left arm a scarf is thrown. The right hand is raised towards the head, but there is nothing to show what was her attitude. The head is surrounded by a large circular halo, of which only the lower half is extant. From it radiate five female figures, presumably snake-maidens (Skr. *nāga-kanyā*). The lower portion of their bodies is hidden by the main figure, according to Cunningham, "to avoid the representation of the snaky lower extremities." It will, however, be noticed that the figure to the proper left side, the head of which is preserved, has no snake-hood.

The central and two adjoining figures are almost entirely destroyed. Evidently they were nude to the waist, and wore a broad girdle to which a loin-cloth was attached. Their dress is the same as that of the figures on the railing-pillars. Of the figure to the proper right side the head and hands are missing. That to the proper left is well preserved. The forehead, nose, chin and right breast are slightly damaged. This figure has a very elaborate hair dress. The hair is drawn flat over the top of the head where it is kept down by a narrow band, and collected at the back in three heavy chignons. On the palms of the hands which are raised tothe height of the shoulders she carries two bowls, from each of which rises a cobra (?). The bowl to the left is defaced, and that to the right slightly damaged.

[1] Other female images are included in section D.

On the reverse is an *aśoka* tree, carved in very shallow relief. On its trunk is a striped squirrel ascending. Cunningham remarks that " the style of the tree is similar to that of the back of a group from Kota " (No. F 11). Find-place unknown.

(Plate XIX. Cf. *A.S.R.*, Vol. XX, pp. 34—35 and 38 ; plate III.)

F 3.—Slab (ht. 3′10″ or 1 m. 165) showing three standing figures in relief, much worn. The central one is a female, evidently a Nāgī with a hood of five snake-heads. The upper portion of her body is nude and the lower broken. Her left hand, draped with a scarf, rests on her hip and holds a vessel. Her right hand is raised to the shoulder. She stands between two somewhat larger figures of warriors, each holding a spear in his left hand and raising his right hand to his shoulder. Find-place unknown.

With this relief should be compared a fragmentary sculpture, from the Kaṅkālī Ṭīlā, now preserved in the Lucknow Museum, which contains a female figure and to her left a male, somewhat larger in size, holding a staff. The right arm of the female and the head of the male are lost, but their attitude and dress are exactly the same as on our sculpture. It is noteworthy that over the left shoulder of the woman two figurines are visible occupying the same position as on the group of the " Queen of the Nāgas " (No. F 2 of the Mathurā Museum). This leads us to assume that the central figure of the present sculpture and that of the Lucknow fragment also represent a Nāga Queen, guarded by two soldiers. (The Lucknow fragment is reproduced by V. A. Smith, *The Jain Stūpa*, plate LXXXVI.)

F 4.—Statuette (ht. 1′ 1½″ or 0 m. 354) of a female (Nāgī ?) standing with her right hand raised in front of her shoulder and holding a vessel (?) in her left hand. Besides the usual ornaments, she wears a short petticoat and a scarf thrown over the left shoulder. The mutilated canopy over her head is probably a snake-hood. The right hand is damaged and the feet are missing. The style of the sculpture is that of the Kushaṇa period. With this statuette may be compared the central figure of the group No. F 3.

F 5.—Image (ht. 5′ or 1 m. 57) of a female standing with her left hand resting on her hip. Right arm and feet broken. The figure wears a scarf round her left arm and shoulders, a girdle and the usual ornaments. It is broken in two pieces. It was pointed out to me by Pandit Radha Krishna in the Arjunpura Maḥallā of Mathurā City, where it was being worshipped as Kubjā, and obtained for the Museum in January 1908. On loan from the Government of India.

F 6.—Figure (ht. 1′ 11½″ or 0 m. 615), carved in the round, of a female standing with her right hand raised to the shoulder and the left resting on her hip. She wears a scarf round her back and falling down from her shoulders, a broad zone round her loins and the usual ornaments. The elaborate head-dress shown on the back deserves special notice. Judging from the style, the figure belongs to the Kushaṇa period. It was obtained from a cowherd who is said to have found it near the village of Akrūr, 4 miles north of Mathurā City on the Brindāban Road. On loan from the Government of India.

F 7.—Figure (ht. 1′ 5″ 1 or 0 m. 445), carved in the round, of a female standing with her right hand raised in front of her shoulder and her left hand resting on her hip. The carving is much defaced. She wears a torque and a necklace hanging down between her breasts. A scarf is thrown over her left shoulder. The lower portion beneath the knees is missing. Judging from the style, the sculpture belongs to the Kushaṇa period.

F 8.—Fragment (ht. 1′ 10″ or 0 m. 576) consisting of the lower portion of a female figure. She is seated in the European fashion on a bench and apparently is playing with a child lying on its back in her lap. The carving is much defaced, but it seems that the woman holds with her left hand the left hand of the child and puts the forefinger of her right hand in its mouth. It was found by Pandit Radha Krishna in a *bāghīcha* near the Bhūtēsar Temple. On loan from the Government of India.

F 9.—Bust (ht. 1′ 11″ or 0 m. 603) of a female figure of which the right arm and halo are partly preserved. She wears a double necklace hanging down between the breasts, heavy earrings and a garland (?) attached to her head-dress. The nose of the figure is broken.

It was found together with No. F 8 in a *bāghīcha* near the Bhūtēsar Temple. On loan from the Government of India.

F 10.—Fragment (ht. 2′ or 0 m. 628) consisting of the upper half of a female (?) figure wearing the usual ornaments and standing under a tree (?). The carving is much defaced. It was purchased by Pandit Radha Krishna together with the inscribed pedestal No. G42 from a Koli who is said to have obtained it from a Brahmin's house in the village of Gaṇēsrā, 5 miles north-west of the City. On loan from the Government of India.

F 11.—Sculpture (ht. 1′ 8″ or 0 m. 505) carved in the round. On one face are two female figures, whose feet are lost with the lower portion of the stone. They are clad in a *dhōtī* held round the loins by means of a broad ornamental girdle, and have a scarf tied round the waist. They seem to carry offerings and are standing under an *aśoka* tree, the foliage of which is also shown on the reverse of the sculpture. The top of the stone is carved in the shape of a calice which makes it probable that it served the purpose of a pillar base. The sculpture was found by General Cunningham at the village of Kōṭā, three miles to the north-west of Mathurā and sent to the Lahore Museum. It was made over to the Mathurā Museum by the Panjāb Government in July 1905. (Cf. *A. S. R.*, Vol. XX, plate III.)

F 12.—Bust (ht. 1′ 8½″ or 0 m. 55) of a female figure. Arms broken, scarf over the left shoulder. Ear-pendants. Hair falling on breasts, Kushaṇa period. Find-place unknown.

F 13.—Torso (ht. 1′ 2½″ or 0 m. 368) of a female figure clad in a close-fitting bodice, as is still worn round Delhi, covering the waist and the shoulders. She wears a double necklace over her breasts. Over her left shoulder are traces of a scarf. Her right arm, decorated with numerous bracelets and raised towards the shoulder, holds a defaced object, perhaps a flower or a fly-whisk. Find-place unknown.

F 14.—Fragment (ht. 1′ 11″ or 0 m. 582) consisting of the central portion of a standing female figure with highly ornamental bead girdle over which a broad flat belt is passed tied in a double bow, and apparently made of some costly material, which was worth embroidering. One of the ends is placed towards the right, while the other hangs down midway between the thighs. The sculpture must be identical with the fragment of a colossal female statue wearing a curious bead girdle, which, according to Cunningham, was found in the Kaṅkālī Ṭīlā before 1871. (*A. S. R.*, Vol. III, p. 19, plate XI, A.)

F 15.—Fragment (ht. 1′ 7″ or 0 m. 48) consisting of the middle portion of a female figure wearing a triple bead girdle round the loins and holding in her left hand the handle of a fly-whisk (?). Drapery slightly indicated. It is said to originate from the Kaṅkālī Ṭīlā.

F 16.—Fragment (ht. 1′ ½″ or 0 m. 318) containing the bust of a female with elaborate head-dress and profuse ornaments, who stands under an *aśoka* tree, and holds on her left hip a child which with its left hand touches her breast and with its right grasps a lock of her hair. In her right hand she holds a fan (?). Tenon on the top of the stone. Find-place unknown.

F 17.—Fragment (ht. 9″ or 0 m. 227) containing the upper half of a female figure playing on a flute. She wears a flat cap and a scarf thrown over the left shoulder. Over her is a cluster of conventional flowers. Tenon in top of stone. Find-place unknown.

F 18.—Fragment (ht. 5⅝" or 0 m. 145) consisting of the bust of a female figure playing on a flute and wearing the usual ornaments. The figure is similar to No. F 17. Its find-place is unknown.

F 19.—Fragment (ht. 8½" or 0 m. 215) consisting of the head of a female figure, with elaborate head-dress, standing under a tree. Tenon in top of stone. Find-place unknown.

F 20.—Stele (ht. 1' 5½" or 0 m. 443) carved on two sides with a female figure standing under a tree of which she grasps a branch. Find-place Kaṅkālī Ṭīlā (?).

F 21.—Fragment (ht. 1' 4" or 0 m. 44) containing the lower portion of a female figure standing in front of a cluster of lotus-flowers and holding her girdle with her left hand. There are traces of a bird perched on her arm. Find-place Kaṅkālī Ṭīlā (?).

F 22.—Fragment (ht. 11" or 0 m. 28) carved with the bust of a female figure, with elaborate head-dress, standing under a tree and playing a flute. Tenon in top of the stone. It was preserved at the Allahabad Library till December 1907 and perhaps originates from the Jamālpur site.

F 23.—Fragment (ht. 10' or 0 m. 252) carved with the bust of a female figure standing under an *aśoka* tree, a branch of which she holds with her left hand. Tenon above. It was preserved at the Allahabad Library till December 1907 and perhaps originates from the Jamālpur site.

F 24.—Fragment (ht. 6" or 0 m. 154) consisting of the bust of a female figure. The right hand is raised to the shoulder. She wears a torque round her neck. It was preserved at the Allahabad Library till December 1907 and perhaps originates from the Jamālpur site.

F 25.—Fragment (ht. 9" or 0 m. 227) carved on both sides with the bust of a female figure standing (?) with her left arm raised. On background foliage and flowers of a tree. The figure presumably grasped a branch of this tree with her left hand. Find place unknown.

F 26.—Statuette (ht. 9" or 0 m. 235), broken in two, representing a female, crouching, with a child in her lap. Her right hand is raised to the right shoulder. Over the left shoulder is a lotus-flower. The sculpture probably represents Hārītī or some other goddess of abundance and fertility.

F 27.—Relief (ht. 1' 3" or 0 m. 38) carved with a female figure, wearing Greek dress and standing to the right with hands folded. Foliage above head. From Mahōlīpur Ghāṭī. On loan from the Government of India.

F 28.—Figurine (ht. 6″ or 0 m. 152) of a female seated on a wicker stool to the left with her right foot placed on a foot stool. With her right hand she holds a goblet which rests on her right knee. From Mahōlīpur Ghāṭi. On loan from the Government of India.

F 29.—Figure (ht. 1′ 1″ or 0 m. 33) of a female standing under a tree, of which she seems to clasp a branch with her right hand. She is nude, but for the usual ornaments, and holds an indistinct object in her left hand. Obtained from Manōharpur Maḥalla in Mathurā City. On loan from the Government of India.

F 30.—Image (ht. 2′ 8″ or 0 m. 812) of a female deity. Head and right arm broken; knees damaged. She probably represents the goddess of fertility, seated to front with an infant in her lap and four children between her feet. By her right foot is a corpulent figure of which the head is lost. It seems to represent Kubera, the god of wealth. The pedestal is carved with a group of playing children, much defaced. The sculpture is interesting on account of its close relationship with images of Hāritī, the queen of Yakshas, found in Gandhāra. We may compare particularly the Hāritī group of the British Museum.[1] Pandit Radha Krishna obtained this sculpture from the village Tayapur two miles from Mathurā City on the road to Rāyā, where it was being worshipped as Gāndhārī the mother of the Kauravas. It was said to have been extracted from a well. On loan from the Government of India.

F 31.—Relief (ht. 1′ 6½″ or 0 m. 47) showing a row of four female figures seated to front with their feet placed on foot-stools. Each holds a child in the left arm. Over these figures there is a row of arches supported on brackets. The proper right lower corner of the stone is missing with a considerable portion of two of the figures. Obtained from a *bāghīcha* near the Kaṅkālī Ṭīlā not far from the City. On loan from the Government of India.

F 32.—Relief (ht. 1′ 6½″ or 0 m. 476) containing a female figure, apparently a Nāgī, standing between two warriors armed with spears. All three figures have their right hand raised to the shoulder. Lower portion of the sculpture with the feet of the three figures defaced. The subject is evidently the same as that of no. F 3. The sculpture was obtained from a *bāgīcha* near the village of Girdharpur beyond the Bhūtēsar Mound. On loan from the Government of India.

F 33.—Head (ht. 1′ 2″ or 0 m. 354) of a life-size female figure, with elaborate head-dress and a large earring on the proper right side. From

1 Cf. *Journal of Indian Art*, Vol. VIII, no. 62; pl IV, fig. 2.

Chāmuṇḍā Maṭh at 'Āzampur Sarāi three miles from Mathurā on the road to Delhi. On loan from the Government of India.

F 34.—Sculpture (ht. 3′ 1″ or 0 m. 94) representing three female figures seated to front, side by side, with their feet placed on footstools and each holding a child in various attitudes. The figures are all more or less damaged and the carving is generally worn. They are surmounted by a projecting cornice, supported on brackets, and decorated with ogee-arches corresponding with the female figures beneath. Each arch contains a corpulent male half-figure holding a garland. The sculpture is evidently broken off on the proper right side. It was acquired by Pandit Radha Krishna from the village of Rāl, 8 miles north-west of the City. On loan from the Government of India.

F 35.—Figurine (ht. 8″ or 0 m. 204) of a female seated with a child in her lap with her right hand raised to the shoulder. Two figures of attendants standing on both sides can be traced. From the Bhūtēsar temple near the Kaṅkālī Ṭīlā. On loan from the Government of India.

F 36.—Sculpture (ht. 8″ or 0 m. 202) with a female figure seated to front with right hand raised to the shoulder and holding a lotus-flower in her left hand. Two miniature figures on both sides of the base. From the city. On loan from the Government of India.

F 37.—Sculpture (ht. 8″ or 0 m. 202) with a female figure seated to front with right hand raised to shoulder and holding an infant in her lap. Two attendant female (?) figures standing on both sides, partly preserved. From Manōharpur Maḥalla. On loan from the Government of India.

F 38.—Sculpture (ht. 1′ 3½″ or 0 m. 395; length 3′ 3″ or 1 m. 258) containing a row of eight figures standing with their right hand raised to the shoulder. The one on the proper right end is a male, holding a staff or lance in his left hand, the others are females. From Dhangaon, a village 6 miles south of Mathurā, east of the road to Bharatpur. On loan from the Government of India.

F 39.—Sculpture (ht. 1′ 3½″ or 0 m. 395; length 2′ 7″ or 0 m. 787) containing a row of five seated female figures and one male figure standing with a lance in his left hand. All have the right hand raised to the shoulder. The sculpture belongs to the Kushaṇa period. It was found on the Jamālpur site and presented to the Museum by Pandit Ram Chand, Head Clerk, Collector's office.

F 40.—Fragment (ht. 7½″ or 0 m. 19) of a goddess seated with a child on her left knee, between two standing figures. On loan from the Government of India.

F 41.—Figurine (ht. 7" or 0 m. 18) of a two-armed goddess standing with her right hand raised to shoulder and an indistinct object in her left hand. On loan from the Government of India.

F 42.—Image (ht. 4′ 5" or 1 m. 347; width 1′ 11" or 0 m. 585) probably representing Hāritī, the goddess of abundance and fertility. She is clad in a well-draped robe and wears a flat torque and a necklace hanging down between the breasts. She has bracelets round the upper arms and a wreath on her head. The feet, arms below the elbows and nose are broken. This sculpture is of particular interest as it is made of the blue schist of Gandhāra and exhibits the style of the Graeco-Buddhist school. It was evidently imported from the North-West to serve as an example for the sculptures of Mathurā.

The image was found by Bhagawan Lal Indraji in the Saptarshi Ṭīlā on the right bank of the Jamnā immediately below the City. It was first preserved in the Municipal Museum at Delhi, then transferred to Lahore with other Gandhāra sculptures and finally returned to Mathurā. (Cf. *J. R. A. S.* 1894, pp. 542 f; Burgess, ***Ancient Monuments***, plates 56 and 57.) Presented by the Government of the Punjab.

G.—Miscellaneous fragmentary figures.

G 1.—Torso (ht. 1′ 7″ or 0 m. 481) of a male figure wearing a double necklace and a breast jewel. Both arms are broken. The left hand rested on the hip. The sculpture is said to originate from the Kankālī Ṭīlā.

G 2.—Torso (ht. 8½″ or 0 m. 215) of a male figure nude to the waist, and decorated with two necklaces and a bracelet round the upper arm. Find-place unknown.

G 3.—Sculpture (ht. 1′ 8″ or 0 m. 506) carved with a male figure standing on a *makara* and holding a staff in his right hand. Head and right arm lost. Tenon beneath. Kushaṇa period. It was preserved at the Allahabad Library till December 1907 and perhaps originates from the Jamālpur site.

G 4.—Fragment (ht. 10½″ or 0 m. 267) consisting of the legs of a squatting male (?) figure. The left hand rests on the knee. On the front of the pedestal is the kneeling figurine of a devotee.

The fragment possibly belongs to a statuette of Jambhala. (See above no. C 5.) It was preserved at the Allahabad Library till December 1907 and probably originates from the Jamālpur site.

G 5.—Fragment (ht. 7″ or 0 m. 18) consisting of the right foot and left leg of a male (?) figure seated on a pedestal carved in front with a railing, in the centre of which stands a figurine holding a tabor under his left arm. The fragment possibly is a portion of a Jambhala image. (See above no. C 5.) It was preserved in the Allahabad Library up to December 1907 and probably originates from the Jamālpur site.

G 6.—Torso (ht. 1′ or 0 m. 305) of a male figure standing and holding his right hand raised towards the shoulder. He wears a flat torque and ear-pendants. It was found in clearing a well at Jamālpur and rescued for the Museum by Lieutenant-Colonel W. Vost, I.M.S.

G 7.—Torso (ht. 1′ 3″ or 0 m. 38) of a male figure carved in the round. It has a necklace, and a garland hanging down from its shoulders. The figure is four-armed, but the arms are broken off at the elbows. It was found in clearing a well at the village of Jamālpur and made over to the Museum by Lieutenant-Colonel W. Vost, I.M.S.

G 8.—Bust (ht. 1′ or 0 m. 305) of a female figure with long locks falling down on the breasts. She wears ear-pendants, a torque round her neck and a necklace hanging down between the breasts. It was found in clearing a well at the village of Jamālpur and made over to the Museum by Lieutenant-Colonel W. Vost, I.M.S.

G 9.—Fragment (ht. 7″ or 0 m. 18) consisting of the feet, ornamented with bangles, of a female figure standing on a conventional lotus. It was found in clearing a well at the village of Jamālpur and made over to the Museum by Lieutenant-Colonel W. Vost, I.M.S.

*G 10.—Fragment (ht. 7½" or 0 m. 19) consisting of the lower portion of a corpulent male (?) figure seated to front and supported by another corpulent male figure of smaller size squatting between its feet. On the base is an inscription in one line of Kushaṇa characters. It reads : [*Su*]-*gatapara Buddhadarśava.* These two words I take to be the names of the donors. It was found in clearing a well at the village of Jamālpur and made over to the Museum by Lieutenant-Colonel W. Vost, I.M.S.

G 11.—Statuette (ht. 7" or 0 m. 178) of a male figure standing to front in the attitude of adoration (Skr. *namaskāra*), the hands folded before the breast. Rudely carved. Find-place unknown.

G 12.—Statuette (ht. 8⅛" or 0 m. 205) of a female figure standing under a canopy and holding a water-vessel or flower-vase in her right hand raised at the level of her shoulder. Indefinite object in left hand. Carving indistinct. Find-place unknown.

G 13.—Sculpture (ht. 2' 8½" or 0 m. 825) carved on both faces with a male figure clad in a tunic and trousers and holding a garland in both hands. Feet missing, carving much worn. Find-place unknown.

G 14.—Fragment (ht. 8½" or 0 m. 21) with crouching female figure facing. Find-place unknown.

G 15.—Head (ht. 7" or 0 m 178) of a female figure with elaborate head-dress. From Arjunpura Maḥalla, Mathurā City.

G 16.—Fragment (ht. 3½" or 0 m. 09) containing the busts of two female figurines, each carrying a bunch of lotus-flowers. Find-place unknown.

G 17.—Fragment (ht. 5½" or 0 m. 14) with the lower portion of a male figure dressed in a long, ample robe. Find-place unknown.

G 18.—Fragment (ht. 6" or 0 m. 152) with a seated Buddha (?) figurine wearing a halo. Rudely carved. Find-place unknown.

G 19.—Fragment (ht. 7" or 0 m. 178) with two seated figurines in monk's dress, partly destroyed.

G 20.—Fragment (ht. 8" or 0 m. 203) showing the feet of a standing image over a lion-faced dragon.

G 21.—Head (ht. 1' 3" or 0 m. 38) of a male (?) figure with elaborate head-dress, with foliage behind and portion of foliated calice over it. Nose broken, face otherwise injured. Find-place unknown.

G 22.—Head (ht. 1' 1" or 0 m. 33) of a female figure, defaced. Nose broken. The hair is fastened on the top of the head by means of a wheelshaped buckle. Circular mark, probably *tilaka*, between the eyebrows. Find-place unknown.

G 23.—Head (ht. 1′ or 0 m. 305) of a male figure wearing an elaborate diadem. Find-place unknown.

G 24.—Head (ht. 7½″ or 0 m. 19) of a male figure with moustache. Found in clearing a well at the village of Jamālpur and made over to the Museum by Lieutenant-Colonel W. Vost, I.M.S.

G 25.—Figurine (ht. 9″ or 0 m. 23) of a male, facing, with his hands folded in front of his breast. Find-place unknown.

G 26.—Fragment (ht. 8½″ or 0 m. 215) consisting of central portion of a male figure clad in a *dhōti* and shawl and holding an offering in his left hand.

G 27.—Bust (ht. 9½″ or 0 m. 24) of a male figure carrying a bird in his left hand. Find-place unknown.

G 28.—Bust (ht. 5″ or 0 m. 127) of a male figure resting his chin on his hand. Find-place unknown.

G 29.—Fragment (ht. 7″ or 0 m. 177) of a standing figure of which the feet remain. Pedestal carved with a couchant bull and a fish inserted between the stalks of the lotus on which the figure is standing. Find-place unknown.

G 30.—Fragment (ht. 10½″ or 0 m. 267) showing a lion's head, presumably portion of pedestal. Find-place unknown.

G 31.—Head (ht. 1′ 4½″ or 0 m. 42) of a life-size Bodhisattva (?) statue with elaborate head-dress. Kushaṇa period. Find-place unknown.

G 32.—Head (ht. 1′ 6″ or 0 m. 455) of a life-size statue with high conical hat. Kushaṇa period. *Cf.* Kōṭā railing pillar no. J 56. Find-place unknown.

G 33.—Head (ht. 9″ or 0 m. 23) of a male (?) figure with elaborate head-dress. Lower portion of face destroyed. Find-place unknown.

G 34.—Head (ht. 10″ or 0 m. 262) of a male figure wearing a close-fitting cap with raised rim. The hair is indicated by straight parallel lines. The nose and lips are damaged.

G 35.—Fragment (ht. 2′ 2″ or 0 m. 66) of a halo carved with concentric decorative borders of various design. Those borders are partly similar to those on the haloes of the images nos. A 4 and B 1. The fragment must have belonged to a statue of colossal size. It was preserved at the Allahabad Public Library till December 1907 and perhaps originates from the Jamālpur site.

G 36.—Fragment (length 9¾″ or 0 m. 248) of an ornamental halo Find-place unknown.

G 37.—Fragment (length 8½" or 0 m. 216) of an ornamental halo. Find-place unknown.

*G 38.—Fragment (ht. 9¼" or 0 m. 235) of pedestal with rampant lion to proper right and upper portions of two standing figures, perhaps Buddhist friars, one carrying a garland and a bunch of flowers. On the raised rim over these figures is a fragmentary inscription in two lines. [l.1.] *Mahārājasya Vā*[*su*] . . . [l.2.] *sya vadhuyā Sena*[*sya*] . . . .

The sculpture which belongs to the Kushaṇa period (reign of Vāsudeva ?) came from the ancient site of Lakhanū near Hathras, Aligarh district.

* G.39.—Fragment (ht. 6½" or 0 m. 165) of the upper proper right corner of a pedestal with lion's head and portions of a fragmentary inscription in four lines. The first line is incised on the raised border over the lion's head. The inscription reads: [l.1.] [*Si*]*ddha*[*m*] *Mahārājā* . . . . [l.2.] *ya* . . . . . . [l.3.] *paṭimā* [*te*] . . . . [l.4.] *va* . . . .

Find-place unknown.

G 40.—Fragment (ht. 9½" or 0 m. 249) of a halo with scalloped border surrounded by foliage from which a flying *Deva* figure projects. Kushaṇa period. Find-place unknown.

G 41.—Fragment (ht. 6¾" or 0 m. 177) with a female figure seated on a tortoise between two mermaids.

* G 42.—Pedestal (ht. including tenon 1' 7" or 0 m. 497) of a standing figure of which only the feet, apparently shod, remain. On the top of the pedestal between the feet is a partly effaced inscription in two lines of 10" and 12½" in length which I read: [l.1.] . . *Maha*[*hi*]*na*[*yanasya*] *yamasha* [l.2.] [*heka*]*sya* [*Vi*]*sā*[*ya*]*sya Ulanāsya paṭimā*. "The image (*paṭimā*=Skr. *pratimā*) of Ulanā" (rest illegible). The pedestal was acquired by Pandit Radha Krishna together with the fragment No. F10 from a Koli who is said to have obtained it from a Brahmin's house in the village of Gaṇēsrā, three miles north-west of the City.

* G 43.—Fragment (ht. 6" or 0 m. 157) of a pedestal carved with three figurines of devotees standing, two with garlands and the third with his hands folded in adoration. A headless lion, standing, must have occupied the proper right side of the stone, when complete. On the raised rim beneath these figures is a fragmentary inscription in one line *Jayadeva-putreṇa Ghoshena* . . . . "By Ghosha the son of Jayadeva . . ." The character is Brāhmī of the Kushaṇa period. The sculpture must be the same as the inscribed base of a statue found by General Cunningham at Kōṭā, three miles north of Mathurā. He must have deposited it in

the Lahore Museum together with another sculpture from the same place. (F. 11.) In December 1908 it was, at my request, made over to the Mathurā Museum by the Panjāb Government. (Cf. Cunningham, *A. S. R.*, Vol. XX; plate V, no. 2.)

G 44.—Fragment (ht. 7½″ or 0 m. 19) representing two garland-carrying, flying figures, male and female, perhaps Gandharva and Apsaras. It must have formed the upper right corner of a large image slab. Found in the river Jamnā. On loan from the Government of India.

G 45.—Fragment (ht. 4″ or 0 m. 10) of a statuette, of which only the feet are preserved, standing on a lotus with three kneeling figurines, two male and one female. Of an attendant, standing on the proper left of the main figure, the feet are preserved. Obtained from a *Kōlī*. On loan from the Government of India.

G 46.—Fragment (ht. 9″ or 0 m. 229) showing a miniature Tīrthaṁkara figure seated in meditation on a lotus in a chapel supported on two dwarf pilasters. To the proper left of this chapel there is a nude Tīrthaṁkara figure standing and a female figurine seated with a child on her left knee. The fragment has evidently made part of an image slab. It was obtained from a garden at Mathurā. On loan from the Government of India.

*G 47.—Fragment (ht. 3¾″ or 0 m. 095) containing the feet of a female figure which rests on a footstool. On the base is a fragmentary inscription consisting of two lines in characters of the Kushaṇa period, which I read: . . . . *vashorishā māsa* . . . . . . (2) *tvanā hita-sukhā*[*rthaṁ*] Obtained from the village of Saknā, two miles west of Gaṇēsrā and five miles west of the City. On loan from the Government of India.

G 48.—Fragment (ht. 9″ or 0 m. 229) carved with a lotus-rosette which contains a female figure seated on a bench and playing on a harp under a palm-tree conventionally treated. The fragment appears to belong to a railing-pillar. Obtained from a *maṭh* in the Gōpālpur Quarter of Mathurā City. On loan from the Government of India.

G 49. Fragment (ht. 7″ or 0 m. 177) of a dressed stone carved on one face with a cobra. Found in a brick-kiln near the Mathurā Junction railway station. On loan from the Government of India.

G 50.—Fragment (ht. 6″ or 0 m. 152) carved on both sides with a scroll. From brick-kiln near the Mathurā Junction railway station. On loan from the Government of India.

G 51. Head (ht. 7½″ or 0 m. 19) of a lion with tenon above. From Jamālpur site. On loan from the Government of India.

G 52.—Relief (ht. 11" or 0 m. 28) carved with two figurines, male and female, standing with their right hands raised. From a mound near the Brindāban gate of Mathurā City. On loan from the Government of India.

G 53.—Fragment (ht. 9" or 0 m. 23) containing the foliage of a tree with the upper half of a male figure and the capital of a Persepolitan pillar. Find-place unknown. On loan from the Government of India.

G 54.—Head (ht. 11" or 0 m. 28) of a male figure, perhaps a Bodhisattva, wearing elaborate head-dress. Obtained from Sarāi, Āzampur, two miles north of Mathurā on the road to Delhi. On loan from the Government of India.

G 55.—(ht. 8½" or 0 m. 215) consisting of a male figure standing with a garland in his right and a handful of flowers in his left hand. Head and feet missing. Find-spot unknown. On loan from the Government of India.

G 56.—Fragment (ht. 8½" or 0 m. 215) carved with three male figures walking to the proper left, of which one in front carries a garland and the other two a dish with some offering. Obtained from a *Kōṭi* at Mathurā. On loan from the Government of India.

G 57.—Fragment (ht. 6" or 0 m. 153) carved with a row of five female figures seated with their right hand raised to the shoulder and three male figures standing with hands joined. On loan from the Government of India.

G 58.—Fragment (ht. 7" or 0 m. 178) carved on the obverse with a standing female figure and on the reverse with three lotus-rosettes. It must have belonged to a solid miniature railing. From the village of Gaṇēsrā. On loan from the Government of India.

G 59.—Fragment (ht. 6½" or 0 m. 166) carved with a railing surmounted by a seated Buddha figure. From the village of Gaṇēsrā. On loan from the Government of India.

H—I.—BAS—RELIEFS.

H.—Scenes of Buddha's life.

H 1.—Bas-relief (ht. 2′ 2″ or 0 m. 66; with 3′ 5¾″ or 1 m. 06) containing five scenes of Gautama Buddha's life:

(*a*) (proper left) His birth in the Lumbinī garden near Kapilavastu His mother Māyā is shown standing in the usual attitude under the *sāl* tree, a branch of which she clasps with her right hand She is supported by her sister Prajāpatī standing to her left. On the other side is Indra who receives the child on a cloth Beneath the Nativity is the scene of the first bath. The infant Buddha (or more correctly Bodhisattva) stands in the centre, whilst the two Nāga kings Nanda and Upananda, their hands joined in the attitude of adoration, issue from masonry wells. Cf. nos. H 2 and N 2(*a*).

(*b*) Buddha's enlightenment (Skr. *bodhi*) at Bōdh-Gayā. Buddha is seated under the *bodhi* tree in the traditional pose of touching the earth with his right hand. The female figure to his right is probably one of Māra's daughters. Beneath is Māra in the act of shooting an arrow at the Śākya Sage. The other big-headed figure is probably a demon of Māra's host. Cf. nos. H 6 and N 2 (*b*).

(*c*) His descent from the "Heaven of the thirty-three gods" where he had preached the law to his mother reborn as a *deva*. Buddha, accompanied by the gods Indra (Śakra) and Brahmā, is shown in the act of descending by the triple ladder, at the foot of which we notice the kneeling figure of the nun Utpalavarṇā who was the first to receive him. Cf. no. N 2 (*f*).

(*d*) His first sermon in the Deerpark near Benares. It should be noted that Buddha is not shown here in the attitude of "turning the wheel of the law" which in Buddhist art is peculiar for this scene. He has his right hand raised towards his shoulder, a gesture which in Buddhist iconography denotes the imparting of protection. Beneath there is a wheel placed on a pillar with two worshipping figures at its sides. Cf. nos. H 7 and N 2(*c*).

(*e*) His death or *parinirvāṇa* at Kusinārā or Kuśanagara. Buddha is lying under the twin *sāl* trees. Three mourning figures are standing behind his couch and three are seated in front. Cf nos. H 7, 8, 9 and N 2 (*d*).

The sculpture was pointed out to me by Pandit Radha Krishna at the Rāj Ghāṭ in Mathurā City, where it was being worshipped by the Hindus.

It was purchased for the Museum in January 1908.—(Plate VI*a*). On loan from the Government of India.

H 2.—Sculpture (ht. 1′ 9½″ or 0 m. 542) carved on two faces in bas-relief. On the obverse is the nude figure of a male child standing on a platform, with his right hand raised towards his shoulder and his left resting on his hip. On each side of him a Snake-god (Skr. *Nāga*), canopied by a nine-headed snake-hood, issues from a round masonry well. Both are turned towards the central figure and have hands joined in adoration (Skr. *namaskāra*). The faces of the central figure and of one of the *Nāgas* are destroyed. Suspended in the air are six musical instruments, namely a conch (Skr. *śaṅkha*), flute, tabor, harp, bag-pipe (?) and drum. Cunningham believed the nude figure in the centre to be a Jina, but a comparison with the scene of Buddha's birth on H 1 (*a*), and on the bas-relief no. *a* of the *stūpa* drum no. N 2 makes it evident that the relief represents the infant Buddha and the two Nāga kings Nanda and Upananda who are mentioned in the *Lalitavistara* (ed. S. Lefmann. Halle 1902, pages 83, 84 and 93). I refer also to the following passage from Hiuen-Tsiang (*Si-yu-ki* transl. Beal, Vol. II, p. 24 f) "to the east of this *stūpa* are two fountains of pure water, by the side of which have been built two *stūpas*. This is the place where two dragons appeared from the earth. When Bodhisattva was born, the attendants and household relations hastened in every direction to find water for the use of the child. At this time two springs gurgled forth from the earth just before the queen, the one cold, the other warm, using which they bathed him."

It appears from Hiuen Tsiang's account that the *stūpas* which commemorated the Buddha's first bath by the Nāga kings Nanda and Upananda, stood not far from the famous Aśoka pillar of Rummindei which marks the spot where he was born.

The six musical instruments shown on our sculpture indicate the heavenly music which according to the Buddhist scriptures was heard on this joyous occasion.

On the reverse are a male and a female figure, both defaced, walking to the proper left. They are clad in a *dhōtī* and a shawl or scarf tied round the waist. The male figure carries in both hands a dish or basket containing a garland. The female has her right hand raised over head; in her left hand she holds an unrecognizable object. It seems that both figures were standing under trees.

Cunningham states that the sculpture was brought either from the Kaṅkālī Ṭīlā or from one of the mounds in that direction. (*A. S. R.*

Vol. XX, p. 35; plate IV, fig. I., cf. *B. E. F. E. O.*, Vol. VIII, p. 493 and *A. S. R.* for 1906-7 p. 152; plate LIII.)

H 3.—Fragment (ht. 1′ 6″ or 0 m. 457) containing a series of scenes placed one above the other. The only scene almost completely preserved represents the Bodhisattva (i.e., the future Buddha) in the act of leaving his royal abode in order to become a recluse. The technical designation of the subject is "the great Renunciation" (Skr. *Mahābhinishkramaṇa*). Siddhārtha (the Buddha's secular name) is rising from the couch on which his wife Yaśodharā is sleeping. In front of the couch are the figures of three female musicians, who have fallen asleep over their instruments. The sculpture is of great interest, as it is undoubtedly copied from Graeco-Buddhist examples. The panel immediately below may have contained the scene of Siddhārtha's leaving Kapilavastu which in Gandhāra is usually found combined with the *zenana* scene. If so, the head immediately above the break would be that of Siddhārtha. The sculpture formed evidently part of a doorjamb. To the right and left of the panels are vertical ornamental borders. The stone is also carved on the proper left side. (Cf. Grünwedel, *Buddhist art*, figs. 50—53 and 81. Foucher, *L'art gréco-bouddhique du Gandhāra*, pp. 349—361 ; figs. 178—183).

H 4.—Fragment (ht. 8½″ or 0 m. 216) carved with the figure of a man to front on horseback ; possibly the future Buddha riding out through the city gate of Kapilavastu. Cf. above No. H 3. It was found in clearing a well at Jamālpur and made over to the Museum by Lieutenant-Colonel W. Vost, I.M.S.

H 5.—Fragment (ht. 1′ 3″ or 0 m. 393) of a stele (*ūrdhvapaṭṭa*) carved with two panels, placed one over the other and separated by a Buddhist railing and by a band of *chaitya* windows. The lower panel, of which only the upper half is preserved, seems to represent the future Buddha leaving home. The head of the horse and part of the mounted figure are preserved. Among the remaining figures we notice in the centre the one holding a bow, which no doubt is Māra, the Evil Spirit, and at his side another with a fly-whisk (?) in his right and a thunderbolt in his left hand. It is not a little curious to see here the Thunderbolt-bearer (Vajrapāṇi), so common in Gandhāra sculpture, reappear on a Mathurā relief.

The upper panel seems to represent the future Buddha, after leaving home, in the act of laying off his royal ornaments and making them over to his groom Chanda kneeling in front of him. In the third figure above we may perhaps see either a repetition of Chanda or a Deva. At his side we discern the head of the horse Kanthaka which is always present at this scene. But it is curious to find an elephant also introduced here, perhaps meant to indicate the royal rank of the main person. The rest of the panel is occupied by five figures which are not so easy to identify. I conjecture that the female figure seated in front on a stool is Yaśodharā, the Buddha's spouse, who receives from a maid servant the news of her lord's departure. It will be noticed that her right hand is raised to the head in an attitude of grief which is common with the mourning figures of the Nirvāṇa scene. The other figures are too indistinct to be identified with any amount of certainty.

Pandit Radha Krishna obtained this sculpture from a *bāghicha* near the Sēṭh's Garden on the right bank of the Jamnā about 1½ mile south of the City. On loan from the Government of India.

H 6.—Stone (ht. 1′1″ or 0 m. 33) of curvilinear shape, probably from the top of some building. The front is carved with a bas-relief representing the Buddha seated cross-legged on a platform under the Bodhi tree. His right hand which is broken was probably raised towards the shoulder in the attitude of protection (Skr. *abhaya-mudrā*). On each side are three female figures, perhaps Māra's daughters Desire, Pining and Lust. (Cf. Cunningham, *Bharhut*, p. 28).

H 7.—Fragment (ht. 10½″ or 0 m. 265) of a bas-relief containing two scenes: (*a*) (Proper right) Buddha's first sermon at Benares. Buddha (defaced) is turning the wheel of the law, i.e., preaching. He has a halo with scolloped border. On each side are two figures in monk's dress, one seated, the other standing. Those to the proper right are only partly preserved.

(*b*). Buddha's death or *parinirvāṇa* (final extinction). The Buddha is lying on his right side with his head supported by his right hand and one foot resting on the other in close agreement with the Buddhist scriptures (*Mahāparinibbāṇa-sutta*, Ch. 5§ 1. *The Book of the Great Decease*, S. B. E. Vol. XI, pp. 85f). In front of his couch are three figures. The central one in monk's dress is Subhadra, the Buddha's last convert. The other two are laymen and possibly the Malla chieftains who witnessed the Master's last moments. Behind the couch three figures are standing with arms outstretched in the attitude of grief.

The sculpture, when complete, presumably contained the four principal events of the Buddha's life, namely :—(1) His birth near Kapilavastu in the Lumbinī garden (Padaria, Rummindei tappa, Nepal Tarai). (2) His attaining of enlightenment (*bodhi*) under the *bodhi* tree at Bōdh-gayā (Gayā District, Bihār). (3) His first sermon in the Deerpark, now Sārnāth near Benares, to the five mendicant friars. (4) His death at Kusinārā in the Malla country (locality not identified).

It is noteworthy that the antelopes in front of Buddha's seat, which elsewhere characterize plastic representations of the third event, are wanting here. But this may be due to inadvertence on the part of the sculptor. In the same way we do not find the two *sāl* trees which are typical of the death-scene.

The treatment of the two scenes pictured here shows distinctly the influence of the Gandhāra school of sculpture, which is also noticeable in the dwarf-pilaster with Indo-Corinthian capital on the proper left. Such pilasters are commonly found to divide the different scenes portrayed on Gandhāra bas-reliefs.

The sculpture must have belonged to the stone facing of the square basement of a *stūpa*. Its find-place is unknown.

H 8.—Fragment (ht. 3′ 4″ or 1 m. 03) of " a high slab " (Skr. *ūrdhva-paṭṭa*), the lower portion of which represents the *parinirvāṇa* or death of Buddha Śākyamuni between the twin *sāl* trees of Kusinārā. The Master is lying on his right side on a couch, his head supported on his right hand and one foot resting on the other. The head is provided with a halo. Behind the couch are three figures of mourners. That to the proper right, apparently a monk (Skr. *bhikshu*), holds in his left hand a square board on which four four-petalled flowers are visible; his right hand is applied to his head. The two others are evidently lay-members, possibly two Malla chieftains who witnessed the Master's last moments. One raises his two arms as in despair; the other stands weeping, his face concealed by a kerchief. To the proper right is one of the twin *sāl* trees; from its foliage issues a *dryad*, who showers flowers on the dying Buddha. Of the corresponding tree to the left only a portion of the trunk can still be traced. In front of the Buddha's couch are three figures. The one to the left, wrapt in meditation, must be Subhadra, the Tathāgata's last convert, who before his conversion was a Brahmanical mendicant. This we may infer from the three staffs placed at his side to indicate that he belonged to the sect of the Tedaṇḍikas (from Skr. *tridaṇḍa* " a triple staff"), though this is not expressly stated in the Buddhist books. The central figure is possibly one of the Malla chiefs and that to the proper right the Thunder-bolt-bearer (Vajrapāṇi) who dropped his diamond mace (Skr. *vajra*) on the occasion. The monk standing at the Buddha's feet must be Mahākāśyapa, one of his chief disciples, who hastened to pay reverence to the Master's feet. The figure at the head wears the dress of a layman. The scene is enclosed between Persepolitan pilasters with capitals containing winged animals (horses ?) The missing panel above perhaps represented the Illumination (Skr. *bodhi*), expressed by the scene of the presentation of the cups by the four guardian-gods (Skr. *lokapāla*); only two standing figures are partly preserved. It is separated from the lower panel by a row of two busts and a Buddha figurine placed in niches separated by dwarf-pilasters. Cf. H 11. The proper left side of the two panels is decorated with a lotus stalk rising from a vase. This border is much defaced. Find-place unknown. (Cf. Foucher, *L'art gréco-bouddhique*, p. 260, fig. 282).

H 9.—Fragment (ht. 9½" or 0 m. 24) of a bas-relief representing the *parinirvāṇa* or death of Buddha. He is shown lying on a couch in the usual attitude. At the side of his bed, two figures, apparently monks, are seated; and behind it a figure is standing which is only partly preserved. The stone probably belonged to the facing of the basement of a miniature *stūpa*. It was found in clearing a well at Jamālpur and made over to the Museum by Lieutenant-Colonel W. Vost, I.M.S.

H 10.—Fragment (ht. 1′ 4″ or 0 m. 395) of a slab, perhaps belonging to a doorway, carved on one side with two panels enclosed between vertical decorative borders and separated by an ogee arch and a railing. The upper panel represents Buddha receiving in his alms-bowl a handful of dust from the children Jaya (the future Aśoka) and Vijaya. The subject is often pictured in the Graeco-Buddhist art of Gandhāra. The lower panel shows Buddha standing and a small figure to his right offering flowers. This scene is perhaps an abridged rendering of the Dīpaṅkara-jātaka, as represented in Gandhāra reliefs. On one of the narrow sides of the stone are two figures placed one over the other and separated by an ogee arch and two railings. The upper one appears to be a Bodhisattva standing with a garland in his right hand. The lower one is a Buddha with a haloed head standing on a lotus in the attitude of imparting protection. The stone was found in clearing a well at Jamālpur and made over to the Museum by Lieutenant-Colonel W. Vost, I.M.S. (On the scenes represented in the two panels, cf. Foucher *L'art gréco-bouddhique*, pp. 517—520, figs. 255—256 and pp. 273—279, figs. 139—141).

H 11.—Bas-relief (ht. 1′ 6″ or 0 m. 457) representing Buddha visited by Indra in the Indraśaila cave near Rājagṛiha (the modern Rājgir in Bihār). To the proper left of the slab a piece of about 8″ in width is lost. The original centre of the bas-relief is occupied by Buddha seated in meditation inside the cave on which a peacock above and two lions at the sides should be noticed. Towards his right approaches Indra, the lord of the gods, clad in royal robes and carrying a bunch of flowers and a garland as an offering. He is preceded by the chief of the Gandharvas or heavenly musicians who is recognisable from a harp which he plays. Indra is followed by three female figures, each carrying a bunch of flowers and a garland. They may be identified as celestial nymphs (Skr. *apsaras*) of Indra's heaven. On the other side of the cave we notice Indra's elephant Airāvaṭa and three male figures crouching in front.

The upper portion of the sculpture is divided into a series of arches separated by dwarf pilasters. Under the central arch is Buddha's head-dress; the others enclose the upper halves of worshipping figures, probably Devas. Buddha's crest jewel (Skr. *chuḍāmaṇi*), according to the Buddhist scriptures, was worshipped in the heaven of the thirty-three gods, of which Śakra is the head. This explains why the sculptor has combined it with the representation of Indra's visit. The lower portion of the sculpture is carved with a Buddhist railing and some decorative borders. The stone was pointed out to me by Pandit Radha Krishna in front of a hut near the third milestone on the Mathurā-Delhi road. On loan from the Government of India.

The scene of Indra's visit to Buddha in the Indraśaila cave is a favourite subject of Buddhist art. It occurs first on a railing pillar at Bōdh-Gayā; here only the empty cave is shown and a figure with a harp standing at its side. On a bas-relief from Loriyān Tangai in the Svāt valley we have a very fine and full representation of this scene. The Buddha figure in the cave is remarkable for its expression of repose and serenity. Indra is attended by numerous celestials and above and below the cave are various plants and animals such as lions in caves, peacocks and also monkeys who are imitating the meditative attitude of Buddha. The Loriyān Tangai sculpture is preserved in the Calcutta Museum, which also possesses another Mathurā bas-relief of Indra's visit. Finally I draw attention to the fine rendering of this scene on the *toraṇa* architrave No. M 4 of the Mathurā Museum. There can be little doubt that here again Mathurā has copied Gandhāra. An innovation found on the Mathurā reliefs is the introduction of Indra's elephant Airāvaṭa[1]. (Plate VI b. Cf. Anderson, *Catalogue*, Part I, pp. 182 f. M 7; Burgess, *Ancient Monuments*, pl. 60; T. Bloch, *Buddha worshipped by Indra* in *Proc. A. S. B.* for 1898, pp. 186—189; Foucher, *L'art gréco-bouddhique*, Vol. I, pp. 492—497).

H 12.—Slab (ht. 1′ 7″ or 0 m. 482) carved with a figure of Buddha seated cross-legged with his right hand raised to the shoulder, on a throne

[1] It should, however, be remarked that the British Museum contains a bas-relief (ht. 8′) from Kāfir Kōṭ which represents the same scene and shows the elephant sitting in front of the cave. It was presented by Sir Harold Deane.

supported by a pair of lions. He is surmounted by four figures, of which two stand to the right and two to his left, each holding a cup. We may, therefore, assume that the scene refers to the presentation of the four bowls by the four guardian-gods (*lokapāla*), though the treatment is uncommon. Cf. beneath no. N 2*g*. The scene evidently belonged to a series of similar illustrative panels placed one over the other and separated by Buddhist railings. Pandit Radha Krishna acquired it from the village of Īsāpur on the left bank of the Jamnā opposite the City. On loan from the Government of India.

I. Decorative Bas-Reliefs.

I 1.—Fragment (ht. 3′ 1″ or 0 m. 94) of a slab carved on two faces, each divided by concentric arches into three lunulate areas. On one face the centres of the three compartments are occupied by an alms-bowl[1], apparently filled to the brim with offerings, a Buddha seated in the protecting attitude, and a Bodhisattva in royal attire seated in meditation under a tree. On the reverse we have in the upper compartment Buddha's head-dress (which, as we know, received the homage of the thirty-three gods) and in the central one a Bodhisattva—perhaps Maitreya, as may be inferred from the vessel in his left hand—who raises his right hand in the conventional attitude of protection. Of the figure occupying the centre of the lowermost division only a portion of the halo is preserved.

The worshipping figures are divine or semi-divine beings—flying, as indicated by their pose, and carrying cabbage-like nosegays from which they are showering flowers. The narrow end of each compartment is occupied by yawning crocodiles. The spandrils are decorated with conventionalized Garuḍas.

Among the Graeco-Buddhist sculptures of Gandhāra numerous pediments are found decorated in the same manner as this Mathurā relief, but in expression much more classical. We may also compare a sculpture from the Kaṅkālī Ṭīlā, now in the Lucknow Museum, which was published by Professor Bühler. It is a fragment of the same shape as the one in the Mathurā Museum, but more elaborately decorated. Bühler describes it as a *toraṇa*, both fragments evidently served the same purpose.

The present fragment was preserved at the Allahabad Public Library till December 1907 and was perhaps originally found on the Jamālpur site. (Cf. *A. S. R.*, 1906-07 p. 159; plate LVI. On the fragment from the Kaṅkālī Ṭīlā, cf. Bühler, *Ep. Ind.*, Vol. II, p. 319, plate III; and V. A. Smith, *Jain Stūpa*, plates XIX and XX.)

I 2.—Slab (ht. 2′ 5½″ or 0 m. 745, width 5′ 6⅜″ or 1 m. 685) containing a portion of an ornamental frieze in low relief. The subject, Cupids carrying a garland, was borrowed from Hellenistic sarcophagi and appears first in India in the Graeco-Buddhist school of Gandhāra (Peshāwar district). Here the pseudo-Cupid, the head of which is lost, walks to the proper right. He wears a torque and bracelet round the arms and a *dhōtī* fastened to the loins by means of a narrow girdle. This purely Indian costume is an

[1] Buddha's alms-bowl was worshipped at Peshāwar at the time of Fā-hien's visit (A.D. 400). But when Hiuen Tsiang came to Peshawar, it had gone to Persia Cf. Fā-hien, *Travels* (transl. Legge), pp. 34 f, *Si-yu-ki* (transl. Beal), Vol. I, p. 98.

innovation, not found in Gandhāra, where the garland-carrying figures are nude and wholly represent the well-known type of the Cupids of later classical art. The intervening spaces between the garland are filled by a palmette rising from a lotus rosette. The stone which is pierced by two round holes must have formed part of the facing of a *stūpa*. Its find-place is unknown.

I 3.—Slab (ht. 9′ or 0 m. 229; width 3′ 3½″ or 1 m.) carved in bas-relief with two male figures, walking to the proper right, who carry a triple garland, interlaced with flowers, the ends issuing from the mouths of a pair of crocodiles (Skr. *makara*). This device is also found on the Amarāvatī *Stūpa*. Cf. above sub. I 2. The stone must have belonged to the facing of a small *stūpa*. Its find-place is unknown.

I 4.—Fragment (ht. 11″ or 0 m. 278; width 3′ ½″ or 0 m. 926) of a slab decorated with two friezes separated by a horizontal raised rim. The upper frieze consists of an ornamental border of three male figures carrying a heavy garland, the curves of which are filled with various flowers. The lower frieze contains three scenes, evidently of some birth story (Skr. *jātaka*)—

(a) That to the proper right, of which a part is missing, shows a bearded man, seated on a grass cushion and recognisable as an ascetic (Skr. *tapasvin*) from his hair which is tied in a knot on the top of his head. He pets a bird of which only the head is preserved. Behind him a young ascetic clad with a loin cloth stands in front of a *bengi*, such as are used to carry holy Ganges-water (Skr. *Gaṅgā-jala*). At his side are a fire-altar and a water-pitcher.

(b) The ascetic's leaf hut (Skr. *parṇaśālā*) separates the scene from the central one, in which we find a male and a female antelope walking to the proper left over a rocky eminence between two trees.

(c) The same hut separates this scene from that to the proper left one, of which only the standing figure of a bearded hermit is partly preserved.

The sculpture probably decorated the square basement of a small *stūpa*. Its find-place is unknown.

I 5.—Fragment (ht. 7½″ or 0 m. 19) of a frieze decorated with two garland-carrying figures which have the appearance of dwarfs and wear turbans, ear-pendants and *dhōtīs*. In the curves of the garland are flowerpots each containing three buds. Above the frieze runs a decorative border in low relief; and along the top of the stone is a cornice supported by brackets. The fragment probably formed part of the facing of the square basement of a miniature *stūpa.* Cf. above *sub* no. I 2. It was kept at the Allahabad Library till December 1907 and is probably from the Jamālpur site.

I 6.—Fragment (ht. 9″ or 0 m. 228) carved with a frieze of garland carrying Cupids. In each interval are a lotus-flower and two lotus-buds. Over the frieze is a bracket. The sculpture probably made part of the facing of the basement of a small *stūpa.* It was found in clearing a well at Jamālpur and made over to the Museum by Lieutenant-Colonel W. Vost, I.M.S.

I 7.—Fragment (ht. 1′ 7½″ or 0 m. 492; width 3′ 2″ or 0 m. 963) of a frieze with a sunk panel on which are five Buddha figures seated cross-legged. Each has two attendants with fly-whisks standing at his sides. The figure to the proper left wearing royal dress must be the future Buddha or Bodhisattva Maitreya. In his left hand we recognise the vessel, which is his emblem in the Gracco-Buddhist sculptures of Gandhāra. The other five figures wear monk's dress; that next to Maitreya seated in meditation must be Śākyamuni, the Buddha of the present age, and the other three his immediate predecessors Krakuchchhanda, Kanakamuni and Kāśyapa. Probably three Buddha figures are lost to the proper right. The panel is enclosed within ornamental borders. The stone which is broken in two and has a dove-tail mortice on the top probably decorated the façade of some Buddhist shrine. Find-place unknown.

The bottom of the stone is carved with three flying Deva figures and a lotus-rosette which probably occupied the centre of the stone when entire. From this it appears that the front of the missing portion contained four more seated Buddha figures.

I 8.—Sculpture (ht: 1′ 10″ or 0 m. 558) carved on one side with a bas-relief containing four figures standing turned to the proper right. The first and third figures are males in royal head-dress standing with folded hands in the attitude of adoration. The figure between is that of a woman who holds a nosegay in her right hand. The last figure, somewhat smaller in size, appears also to be of a male. Over it the head of some animal is visible. The carving is much defaced. The sculpture was preserved at the Allahabad Public Library till December 1907 and probably originates from the Jamālpur site.

I 9.—Fragment (ht. 1′ 5″ or 0 m. 435; width 2′ or 0 m. 61) of a relief representing a *stūpa* worshipped by a pair of Nāgas. Of the *stūpa* only the top portion remains, surmounted by a parasol with two garlands attached to it. Of one of the Nāgas only the head remains with an ornamental head-dress and a hood of five snake-heads. Of the other only a portion of the hood can be traced. The scene is enclosed between two Persepolitan pilasters with a couchant winged lion on their capitals. These pilasters support a plain architrave on which two *chaitya* windows are carved in low relief. Find-place unknown.

I 10.—Fragment (ht. 10″ or 0 m. 252; width 2′ 1″ or 0 m. 631) of a frieze with a relief (defaced) representing a *stūpa* decorated with two parasols being worshipped by three male figures. One of these carries a long staff to which a streamer is attached and the second an umbrella. Find-place unknown.

I 11.—High slab (Skr. *ūrdhvapaṭṭa*; ht. 5′ 3½″ or 1 m. 66; width 11½″ or 0 m. 29) carved both on the front and sides which are divided into several compartments of varying height separated from each other by Buddhist railings. The front is in parts much defaced; the two uppermost panels are almost entirely destroyed. The lower-most panel, supported by four partly defaced Atlantes, shows a stately gateway provided with two balconies. This gateway is flanked by crenelated walls over which the heads of armed men and palm-trees are visible. On both sides rises a tower. In the next panel, the sides of which are occupied by standing Atlantes, we find a soldier guarding a covered road which slopes upwards to the next panel. In this and the two following panels we find some young men desporting themselves in the company of fair damsels. On the corresponding narrow sides of the stone there are female figures. In the two upper panels we distinguish portions of three figures, one of which carries a sword in his left hand, while the right is raised towards his shoulder. An elephant with elevated trunk can also be traced. The relief probably represents one of the lower heavens (Skr. *Kāmaloka*) in which the sensual element is prominent. The style of the sculpture with its crowded scenes bears a strong resemblance to that of the Amarāvatī school. Probably it formed the facing of a *toraṇa* pillar, the other three faces being decorated with similar slabs. Find-place unknown. (Plate XX.)

I 12.—Fragment (ht. 1′ 8½″ or 0 m. 52) carved with a relief which represents a male figure who wears a scarf round his loins and a heavy necklace and bracelets, and stands with his right foot placed on a stool of wickerwork. He touches with his left hand the shoulder of a female figure. She wears a scarf round her loins, the usual ornaments and a broad girdle which she is in the act of unloosing. The panel is enclosed between pilasters; that to the proper left is broken. The lower part of the sculpture contains the upper portion of another panel, likewise enclosed between

Plate XX.

No. I, 11 ; Ht. 3' 3½".

Sculptured Slab.

pilasters. The two panels are separated by a Buddhist railing and an architrave decorated with *chaitya* windows. Find-place unknown.

I 13.—Fragment (ht. 1′ 5½″ or 0 m. 443) carved with a rampant lion mounted by a nearly nude male figure, which holds the reins. Similar lions, often placed over or on elephants, are a decorative device commonly met with in Indian sculpture. Tenon on top of stone. Find-place unknown.

I 14.—Fragment (ht. 1′ 2″ or 0 m. 35) of a relief containing a group of figures turned to the proper left in the attitude of adoration (Skr. *namaskāra*). Two of them are males clad in a loin-cloth and a scarf or shawl leaving the upper part of the body nude. Between these two figures a third male (?) person is partly visible. In front are three figures of children; the one in front headless and the other two defaced. They are likewise turned to the left, with folded hands. The child in front is a girl, wearing a girdle round her loins. Find-place unknown.

I 15.—Fragment (ht. 1′ 4″ or 0 m. 405) of a relief containing the bust of a male figure, wearing an elaborate turban and various ornaments. Drapery over his left shoulder and breast slightly indicated by wavy line. With his right hand he clasps the handle of a fly-whisk, the upper portion of which is broken off. Left arm broken below the elbow. Find-place unknown. (Plate XXI b.)

I 16.—Fragment (ht. 1′ 2½″ or 0 m. 367) of a slab with flying, garland carrying figures in relief.

I 17. Fragment (ht. 6″ or 0 m. 152) of a sculpture with foliage in low relief and on a projecting piece two figurines flying to proper left, both headless and much injured. The one in front is a male wearing a loin-cloth and holding a garland in both hands before his breast. The second, slightly smaller, is a female, nude to the waist. It seems that her right arm was raised and that her left was stretched out over the head of her companion. Find-place unknown.

I 18.—Fragment (ht. 1′ 3″ or 0 m. 38) of a slab containing the upper portion of a male figure, wearing an elaborate turban and the usual ornaments and holding in his right hand a sword, partly broken, over his shoulder. A child, facing, is standing in his left hand, resting, as it were, against his shoulder and holding its hands folded before its breast. The figurine of the child is defaced. The corners of the slab have been out away square. Find-place unknown. (Plate XXI a).

I 19.—Bas-relief (ht. 11½″ or 0 m. 285), considerably injured, representing a fight between a four-armed figure, probably Vishṇu in one of his *avatāras* or incarnations (attributes irrecognizable) and a monster with enormous head and protruding eyes. Behind the figure supposed to represent Vishṇu, stands a female figure holding what seems to be a staff. In front four miniature figures are playing. Find-place unknown.

I 20.—Fragment (ht. 1′ 8½″ or 0 m. 515) of a slab, containing the head of a Buddha figure under a projecting arch which is decorated with a foliated design. Nose missing. Hair arranged in concentric rows of schematic waves surmounted by a high *ushṇīsha* of peculiar shape. Find-place unknown.

I 21.—Fragment (ht. 1′ 3″ or 0 m. 495) with portion of the hand of a colossal image.

I 22.—Fragment (ht. 4″ or 0 m. 10) consisting of the head and right hand of a female figurine with a cluster of flowers at the side of her head Find-place unknown.

I 23.—Fragment (ht. 11″ or 0 m. 277) with a winged flying figure carrying a garland. Find-place unknown.

I 24.—Fragment (ht. 9″ or 0 m. 23) with portions of two standing female figures. Find-place unknown.

I 25.—Fragment (ht. 5½″ or 0 m. 139) with the legs of a standing male figure.

I 26.—Fragment (ht. 7¾″ or 0 m. 997) of a bas-relief containing the heads of two figures.

I 27.—Fragment (ht. 10″ or 0 m. 248) of a bas-relief with a female figure standing facing under an ogee arch. Find-place unknown.

I 28.—Fragment (ht. 9″ or 0 m. 222; width 1′ 6″ or 0 m. 455) of a bas-relief decorated with a border of scroll-work over which one male figure seated to front and part of a second figure. Find-place unknown.

I 29.—Fragment (ht. 4½″ or 0 m. 115) of a bas-relief exhibiting a full-blown lotus and another flower. Find-place unknown.

I 30.—Fragment (ht. 1′ 1″ or 0 m. 232) carved with two bas-reliefs placed one over the other. The upper panel which contains a standing Buddha figure is defaced. The lower panel shows two male figures worshipping a *stūpa* decorated with three parasols and two streamers. The panel which is enclosed between pilasters, is broken below. The fragment was found let in a wall at the Sītalā Ghāṭī and obtained for the Museum by Pandit Radha Krishna. On loan from the Government of India.

I 31.—Fragment (ht. 1′ 7″ or 0 m. 49) of a railing, consisting of a railing-pillar, on which is a male figure holding a lotus in his right hand,

PLATE XXI.

No. I, 10; Ht. 1' 3".

No. I, 15; Ht. 1' 4".

FRAGMENTS OF BAS-RELIEFS.

of a coping stone carved with a head under an ogee arch and of three cross-bars decorated with lotus-rosettes. The fragment was found at a shrine at the Sītalā Ghāṭī and acquired for the Museum by Pandit Radha Krishna. On loan from the Government of India.

I 32.—Fragment (ht. 9″ or 0 m. 225) of a bas-relief carved with a railing consisting of a railing pillar with a male figure holding a garland, a coping stone carved with an ogee arch and two cross-bars on each side. The fragment was found in clearing a well at Jamālpur and made over to the Museum by Lieutenant-Colonel W. Vost, I.M.S.

I 33.—Fragment (ht. 7½″ or 0 m. 19) carved on one side with a flying Deva figure carrying an offering (?) in its left hand and on the reverse with flowers and leaves in low relief. The sculpture was preserved at the Allahabad Library till December 1907 and probably originates from the Jamālpur site.

I 34.—Fragment (ht. 1′ 6″ or 0 m. 457) with the figure of a Harpy (Skr. *suparṇa*) flying to the proper left and holding an offering. The figure has conventional wings and tail and wears a turban and *dhōtī*. The sculpture has perhaps made part of a tablet of homage like no. Q 2, representing a *stūpa* worshipped by *suparṇas*, A portion of the parasol surmounting the *stūpa* is still preserved. The fragment was presented to the Museum by Mr. Ingram in 1909 and came from the bungalow once occupied by Mr. Growse. Its original find-place is unknown.

I 35.—Fragment (ht. 1′ 3″ or 0 m. 38) with portion of a nimbus surrounded by foliage of the *pīpal* tree (*ficus religiosa*) and with the figure of a flower-showering celestial being, flying to the proper right. The fragment evidently formed the upper, proper left corner of a Buddha image. It was brought to the Museum in 1909 from Usphahār 6 miles south-west of Mathurā, east of the road to Sonk.

I 36.—Fragment (ht. 1′ 1″ or 0 m. 33) with portion of a circular halo surrounded by foliage of the *pīpal* tree (*ficus religiosa*) and with the figure of a flower-showering celestial, flying to the proper right. The fragment evidently is the upper, proper left corner of a Buddha image. It is said to have come from Ānand Ṭīlā at Uchhāgaon, 7 miles south-west of Mathurā on the road to Sonk. On loan from the Government of India.

I 37.—Fragment (ht. 10¾″ or 0 m. 273) of a frieze carved with three figures, a Bodhisattva and two Buddhas, seated cross-legged. The Bodhisattva raises his right hand in the attitude of imparting protection (*abhaya-mudrā*), the Buddhas are seated in meditation. Each of those figures appears to have been placed between two attendants standing and holding flowers and garlands, but only four of these attendant figures are preserved.

The upper part of the frieze is decorated with a foliated border in which animal heads appear to be introduced.

This sculpture may be compared with I 7. Similar rows of Buddhas with attendants are found in the Graeco-Buddhist art of Gandhāra. Obtained from a *bāghīchā* near the Bhūtēsar mound. On loan from the Government of India.

I 38.—Fragment (ht. 10½" or 0 m. 267; width 3′ 2⅓" or 0 m. 975) of a frieze carved with a row of six figures walking towards the right. The first figure of the row, who wears the dress of a wealthy lay-member, carries a garland. Of the remaining five, who all wear monks' robes, one holds a fly-whisk, one blows in a conch-shell and three are shown in the act of beating a drum. The proper right half of the relief is occupied by a city gate, from which presumably the procession just described was supposed to have issued. The gate is flanked by two square towers with conical roofs. Each tower has a window and over it a balcony with balustrade. The gate adjoins a crenelated wall, over which the slopping roofs of three buildings are visible. In front of the wall we notice a structure with a window (?) and curvilinear roof decorated with three pinnacles. This building is evidently shown in side elevation. It is possible that the group of edifices shown here represents not a town but a Buddhist convent. With the scene here portrayed may be compared that found on the *toraṇa* architrave from the Kaṭrā (no. M 1). Finally we notice a dragon rampant who occupies the proper right end of the carved surface.

Pandit Radha Krishna obtained this sculpture from the Galī Qānungōyān where he found it let into the wall of a house. On loan from the Government of India.

I 39.—Fragment (ht. 1′ 9" or 0 m. 53) of a frieze containing three male figures, perhaps Bodhisattvas, standing to front with the right hand raised to the shoulder and the left placed on the hip. The central figure holds a small vessel in his left hand. There are traces of a fourth figure on the proper right side. The sculpture, which belongs to the Kushaṇa period, was obtained from Kans-kā-Qilā' on the bank of the Jamnā in Mathurā City. On loan from the Government of India.

I 40.—Sculpture (ht. 1′ 6" or 0 m. 457) representing a male figure standing with a fly-whisk in his right hand. It belongs to the Kushaṇa period and came from the Sarasvatī Kuṇḍ, 1 mile from Mathurā on the Delhi road, where it was worshipped as Kṛishṇa. On loan from the Government of India.

J—P AND R—S—ARCHITECTURAL SCULPTURES.

J. RAILING PILLARS.

* J.1. Railing pillars (ht. 6′ 8½″ or 2 m. 04; section 1′ 6¼″ by 9¾″ carved with a female figure (defaced) wearing a scarf tied round her waist, a broad bead girdle, bracelets, anklets and other ornaments. She holds a bunch of flowers (?) in her right and a defaced umbrella of plaited sedge in her left hand. Over this figure is a rectangular panel representing two monkeys seated on stools. One is addressed by an ogre (Skr. *yaksha*) who applies his hands to his eyes. The other monkey seems to cure the eyes of an owl (?) perched on a similar stool of wickerwork. The scene, which is enclosed between a pair of Persepolitan pilasters, probably refers to some *Jātaka.*[1] On both sides of the stone are three mortices, 1′ 8″ long, for the reception of cross-bars. The back is plain. The pillar once stood on the Bhūtēsar mound in front of the entrance to the temple where it was discovered by General Cunningham and Mr. Growse "On the side of the rail," the former says, "is engraved the Arian letter *h*, which was the figure for 100 in use at Mathurā during the Indo-Scythian period. There must, therefore, have been no less than 100 of these large railing pillars, which, with their rails, would represent a length of not less than 300 feet." The figure in question, however, appears to be 30.

(*A. S. R.*, Vol. III, pp. 21 f.; Growse, *Mathurā* p. 120 and *J. A. S. B.*, Vol. XLVII (1878), part I, p. 118; plate XIX).

J 2. Railing pillar (ht. 6′ 5″ or 1 m. 952; section 10¾″ by 10″), the central portion of which is octagonal in section. It is carved on one face only with a female figure with elaborate headdress in the act of unloosing her girdle. She stands over a crouching, grotesque figure with protruding eyes and erect ears which is partly defaced. A medallion above the female figure represents a man with an umbrella in his left hand who apparently is addressing an assembly of people. On both sides of the pillar are three mortices (11¼″ long) for the reception of cross-bars.

J 3. Railing pillar (ht. 6′ 2½″ or 1 m. 89; section 11″ by 10″) The front is embellished with three lotus-rosettes, the central one containing a human face. On the top there are traces of a circular medallion. At the sides are four mortices, 1′ long, for the reception of cross-bars. Perhaps this pillar is identical with that which Mr. Growse recovered from a well near the Balbhadar Kuṇḍ, though the measurements do not quite agree (*Mathurā* p. 120.)

[1] Cunningham describes this bas-relief incorrectly as "a comic scene between two lions and two monkeys." Growse rightly calls the four actors of the scene "two monkeys, a bird, and a misshapen human dwarf." It is, of course, quite possible that the story depicted here is that of only one monkey shown twice in different attitudes on the panel.

J4. Railing pillar (ht. 4′ 8″ or 1 m. 42; section 11″ by 6½″) carved on one face with a nude female figure in the act of unloosing a scarf from around her waist. She is standing on a prostrate dwarf, his chin resting on his hands. Over her is a male figure (defaced) on a balcony, his right arm slung round the neck of a boy who holds a flute (?) in his right hand.

On the reverse are three panels carved in low relief which refer to the birth-story of Viśvantara (Pāli Vesantara) the paragon of generosity[1]. The scenes represented are the following:

Top panel: Viśvantara, who lives in exile as a hermit, gives his children away to a Brahmin.

Central panel: He makes the children over to the Brahmin, notwithstanding their supplications.

Lower panel: His wife returns to the hermitage carrying a watervessel and fruit. In the two upper panels the man with the little vessel in his left hand must be the Bodhisattva Viśvantara. The other with the topknot and the garment of bark (Skr. *valkala*) is the Brahmin.

On each side are three mortices (10½″ long) for the reception of the cross-bars. The sculpture was acquired by General Cunningham from the verandah of a *chaupāl* or *dharamsālā* near the temple of Bhūtēsar, together with no. J 5 and three other pillars all belonging to the same railing. Of the three remaining pillars one is now in the Lucknow Museum and two are in the Calcutta Museum, which also possesses a sixth pillar of this railing discovered previously by Colonel L. R. Stacy. Cunningham makes, moreover, mention of two fragments of pillars of this railing which in 1860 were in a museum at Agra. These may be nos. J 51 and 52 returned to Mathurā from Allahabad in December 1907. Professor Grünwedel, in referring to the Bhūtēsar pillars, maintains that they are not Buddhist. The occurrence, however, of the Viśvantara-jātaka on one of them can leave no doubt that they belonged to a Buddhist edifice, presumably a *stūpa* (Cunningham, *A. S. R.*, Vol. III, pp. 20ff, plates VI, VII and XI; Growse, *Mathurā*, pp. 120f. Grünwedel, *Buddhist Art*, p. 41; Burgess, *Ancient Monuments*, plates 58-59; Anderson, *Catalogue*, Pt. I., pp. 186-190, M. 15 a, b and c.)

J5. Railing pillar (ht. 4′ 7″ or 1 m. 393; section 10¾″ by 7½″) carved with a nude female figure in the act of adjusting a pendant to her right ear with the aid of a mirror in her right hand. She stands on a prostrate dwarf. Over her are two male figures on a balcony, one turning away from the other

---

[1] This birth-story is no. 547 of the Pali book (ed. Fausböll) vol. VI, pp. 479ff. transl. Rouse vol. VI, pp. 247ff. and is also found in the Sanskrit collection *Jātaka-mālā* (ed. Kern) no. 9, pp. 51ff.

(*a*) OBVERSE.

(*b*) REVERSE.

No. J. 7 ; Ht. 2' 7½".

RAILING PILLAR FROM CHAUBĀRĀ MOUND.

who seems to offer him a garland. On the reverse are three panels, much worn, with scenes which probably refer to the *jātaka* of the tigress[1].

Top panel: The Bodhisattva seated between two attendants.

Central panel: The Bodhisattva as ascetic, seated on a cushion of holy grass. In front of him his disciple and the hermit's hut behind are traceable.

Lowermost panel: The tigress devouring the Bodhisattva. On each side of the pillar three mortices (11″ long) for the reception of crossbars. It was acquired by General Cunningham, from a *dharamsālā* near the temple of Bhūtēsar and must have belonged to the same railing as no. J4.

J6. Railing pillar (ht. 3′ 5″ or 1 m. 04; section 11½″ by 5½″.) On the obverse is a female figure standing on a prostrate dwarf, of which alone part of the face is preserved, and under a tree, which she grasps with her right hand; while her left hand rests on the hip. She is nude, but wears an elaborate girdle round her loins, a torque and a necklace hanging between the breasts. On the reverse are three compartments containing scenes of adoration. In the upper panel there is an enclosure with a sacred tree which is being worshipped by two male persons with elaborate head-dress. One stands with folded hands; the other seems to offer lotus-flowers. The central panel has an almsbowl (?) worshipped by two male figures similar to those of the upper panel. In the lower panel we see a Buddha and another figure standing in the attitude of adoration. The lower portion of the pillar is missing. On the two sides are three mortices (9¼″ long) for the reception of cross-bars.

*J7. Fragment (ht. 2′ 7½″ or 0 m. 80; section 9½″ by 6″) of a railing pillar. On the obverse is a male figure of Faun-like appearance with elaborate turban, necklace of beads and other ornaments. He is standing under a mango tree in blossom with his right hand raised to his lips, and with his left placed against his thigh. He wears a sash round his waist and a curious necklace round his shoulders. Over the tree is a balcony without figures. On the reverse are three sunk panels carved in relief. The upper panel contains a sacred tree surrounded with a railing, and worshipped by two male figures who approach it with offerings of garlands and lotus-flowers. In the central panel are two seated male figures; in front of one stands a bench on which a couple of birds are perched. Two figures appear in the background. The lower relief is almost entirely destroyed. Each scene is enclosed between two Persepolitan pilasters with a single winged lion couchant in their capitals. On both sides are two mortices (9″ long) for the reception of cross-bars.

---

[1] The *jātaka* of the tigress is the first story of the *Jātakamālā* (ed. Kern) pp. 1ff.

Beneath the upper panel is an inscription in one line of 8½″ or 0 m. 22, which was first published by Mr. Growse and re-edited by Professor Lüders. It reads *Abhyaṁtaropastāyakasa Kaṭhikasa dānaṁ* "Gift of Kaṭhika the servant of the interior". On palæographical grounds the sculpture is to be assigned to the early Kushaṇa period. It was obtained from one of the Chaubārā mounds (namely *A*—the same which yielded the steatite relic-casket, now in the Calcutta Museum) by Mr. Growse, who erroneously described the figure on the obverse as a dancing girl. With it he found a copper-coin of Kanishka.

(Plate XXII. *Mathurā*, 2nd ed., p. 114, with plate, 3rd ed., p. 123; Cf also *Ind. Ant.* Vol. VI, p. 219, no. 6 and *J. A. S. B.* Vol., XLVII (1878) pt. I, p. 188, plates, XVIII and XX; and Lüders. *Ind. Ant.* Vol. XXXIII, p. 152, no. 29.

J 8. Railing pillar (ht. including tenon 3′ 8″ or 1 m. 115; section 7″ by 5″). On the obverse is a female figure with a scarf round her shoulders, a girdle and various ornaments. She holds a bunch of flowers in her right hand and stands under a tree on a dwarf who is lying on his back with his head resting on a cushion. The back of the pillar is ornamented with two full and two half lotus-rosettes. On both sides are three mortices, 10½″ long, for the reception of cross-bars. The top and bottom of this pillar are bevelled, from which Cunningham concludes that they belonged to a flight of steps.

J 9. Railing pillar (ht. including tenon 3′ 7″ or 1 m. 09; section 7½″ by 4¾″) carved on one side with a female figure wearing a scarf and a girdle round her loins and the usual ornaments. She is standing on the belly of a dwarf who is lying on his back with folded hands, his head resting on a cushion. With her left hand she grasps a branch of the tree under which she is standing. In her right is some indefinite object. The back of the pillar is ornamented with two full and two half lotus-rosettes. On both sides are three mortices, 8″ long, for the reception of cross-bars. The pillar has a bevelled top and must have formed part of the side-railing of a staircase (*A. S. R.*, Vol., XVII p. 110; plate XXXI *h*.)

J 10. Railing pillar (ht. 3′ 2½″ or 0 m. 949; section 7½″ by 4¼″) carved on one side with a female figure holding a flower in her right hand and standing under a balcony over which a defaced figure is partly visible. On the obverse is a medallion with a *stūpa* decorated with a parasol and streamers, and one full and two half lotus-rosettes. On each side are three mortices, 6½″ long, for the reception of cross-bars. The pillar, together with J 12, was obtained by Mr. Growse from the mound of Jaisinghpūra, a village on the road between Mathurā and Brindāban. (Plate XXIII, Cf.

J. A. S. B. Vol. XLVII (1878), pt. I, p. 118; plates XVIII and XX. Cf. *A. S. R.* Vol. XVII; plate XXXI *a*).

J 11. Railing pillar (ht. 3′ ½″ or 0 m. 91; section 7½″ by 3½″) carved on one side with a female figure wearing the usual ornaments, a bead girdle and a scarf which she holds with her left hand. In her right hand she has a bunch of lotus-flowers raised over her shoulder. Above is a balcony with the head of two figures looking over it. On the reverse is a medallion with a *stūpa* decorated with streamers, one full and two half lotus-rosettes. On both sides of the pillar are three mortices, 7″ long, for the reception of cross-bars. From Jaisinghpūra (Plate XXIII. Cf. *A. S. R.*, Vol. XVII plate XXXI *e*.)

J 12. Railing pillar (ht. 2′ 11″ or 0 m. 885; section 6½″ by 5″) carved on the obverse with a female figure wearing a girdle and ornaments and holding a flower stalk (?) in her right hand. The arms and feet are broken. Over her is a balcony with a male figure with short curly hair resting his head on his right hand. His left arm which is now broken reached down over the balustrade. The reverse is ornamented with two full and two half lotus-rosettes. On both sides are mortices, 7½″ long, for the reception of cross-bars. (*A. S. R.*, Vol. XVII, plate XXXI *f*.)

*J13. Fragment (ht. 3′ ½″ or 0 m. 95; section 9½″ by 6″) of a railing pillar. On the obverse is the lower portion of a female figure standing on a cushion. She wears a bead-girdle round her loins and the usual ornaments. The reverse has two compartments. In the upper one are two male figures wearing elaborate turbans. Each holds a bunch of lotus-flowers in his right hand. In the lower panel is a male figure in Indo-Scythian dress: a conical cap, a tunic, trousers and heavy boots. He rests his left hand on the grip of his sword bound to his left side, and holds in his right hand a bunch of flowers and a garland which he seems to have taken from a flat basket or dish carried on the head of a kneeling dwarf. Both scenes are enclosed between pilasters. On each side are two mortices, 9″ long, for the reception of cross-bars. There is an inscription beneath the lower panel consisting of five letters. I read it: *Sa[ṁ]ghadevasa* "Gift of Saṅghadeva." From the donor's name it may be inferred that he was a Buddhist and that the pillar belongs to a Buddhist railing. The character used in the inscription shows that it was erected during the Kushaṇa period. Find-place unknown.

J 14. Railing pillar (ht. 3′ or 0 m. 911; section 6″ by 3½″). On the obverse is a female figure standing on a cushion under a tree and wearing round her loins a bead-girdle and a scarf which she holds with her right hand. With her left hand she grasps a heavy necklace which she seems to be putting round her neck. On the reverse are two full and two half lotus-rosettes. At the sides of the pillar are three mortices, 5¾" long, for the reception of cross-bars. (*A. S. R.*, Vol. XVII, plate XXXI *g*.)

J 15 Railing pillar (ht. 2′ 8½" or 0 m. 825; section 6½" by 4½") carved on the obverse with a male figure standing under a tree. He wears a conical head-dress and holds in his right hand a bunch of lotus-flowers and in his left an indistinct object. On the reverse are two full and two half lotus-rosettes. On both sides are three mortices, 7½" long, partly filled with mortar. To the left of the head of the figure are three numerals read by Cunningham as 118. The numerical symbols used show that the railing to which this pillar belonged was constructed in the Kushaṇa period. It was found with five others of the same size in the excavation of the Jamālpur (or Jail) mound.

(Cunningham, *A. S. R.*, Vol. I, p. 241; Dowson, *J. R. A. S.*, N. S., Vol. V (1871), p. 194; plate XXX).

J 16. Fragment (ht. 2′ 2" or 0 m.66; section 7½" by 3¾") of a railing pillar carved on the obverse with a female figure nude but for ornaments, girdle and scarf round her loins. Stone broken at ankles. With her left hand she holds her scarf, and in her right some fruit which a dwarf, crouching at her feet, is stretching out both hands to receive. The female is distinguished by a curious head-dress of which the hair is tied together in a knot on the top of the head. Behind her head is a curtain fastened on both sides to pilasters, of which the capitals alone are visible. Over this curtain peeps a female (?) head. On the reverse are one half and two full lotus-rosettes in low relief, the bottom half one being missing. On both sides of the pillar are three mortices, 6¾" long, for the reception of cross-bars. Find-place unknown. (*A. S. R.*, Vol. XVII, plate XXXI *b*.)

J 17. Fragment (ht. 2′ 9" or 0 m. 835; section 8½" by 4¾") of a railing pillar carved on the obverse with a female figure standing under a tree, which she grasps with her left hand. The reverse has three compartments. In the upper one is a casket placed on a throne and surmounted by a parasol with streamers. The middle one has a male figure with an elaborate head-dress who takes fruit or flowers from a flat basket or dish placed on the head of a kneeling dwarf. The lower one contains a male figure standing in almost the same posture as on the central panel, but holding in his right hand a fly-whisk(?). The scenes are enclosed between Persepolitan pilasters. On both sides are three mortices, 8¾" long, for the reception of cross-bars. Find-place unknown.

J 18. Fragment (ht. 2′ 4" or 0 m. 71; section 8½" by 4½") of a railing pillar carved with a Bodhisattva figure, defaced, standing under a *pipal*

(*a*) OBVERSE.

(*b*) REVERSE.

No. J, 10; Ht. 3' 2½".

(*c*) OBVERSE.

(*d*) REVERSE

No. J, 11; Ht. 3' ½".

RAILING PILLARS.

tree (*ficus religiosa*). Circular halo with scalloped border. *Ushṇisha* broken. His right hand is destroyed, but was evidently raised towards the shoulder in the attitude of protection. A scarf hanging over his left arm which rests on his hip is thrown loosely round both legs. There is an indistinct object between his feet. The posture and drapery are similar to those of the inscribed Bodhisattva statues of Sārnāth and Sahēṭh-Mahēṭh. On the reverse are two full and a portion of one half lotus-rosette. On each side are three mortices, 6¾" long, for the reception of cross-bars. Find-place unknown. (Plate III b.)

J 19. Fragment (ht. 1′ 1½" or 0 m. 342; section 8½" by 4½") of a railing pillar. On one side are the legs of a female figure standing on some indistinct object, and on the other side portions of two panels, much defaced. The upper one shows a standing male (?) figure dressed in a tunic reaching down to the knees, trousers and stout boots. Another figure, apparently female, is kneeling at his side and holds a basket(?) between both hands. On each side are two broken mortices for cross-bars. Find-place unknown.

J 20. Fragment (ht. 1′ 7½" or 0 m. 595; section 7½" by 4½") of a railing pillar carved on one side with a portion of a female figure standing under an *aśoka* tree. Her face, right arm and breasts are broken. The reverse is decorated with one full and a portion of one half lotus-rosette. At each side are two mortices, 8½" long, for the reception of cross-bars. The top of the stone is bevelled. Find-place unknown.

•J 21. Fragment (ht. 1′ 9½" or 0 m. 545; section 9" by 5½") of a railing pillar, presenting on one side a prostrate dwarf on which a figure is standing of which only the feet remain. On the reverse is a panel with a dwarf-like figure with short petticoat carrying on his head a flat dish or basket filled with fruit or flowers from which another person whose head is broken seems to take something. The panel is enclosed between Persepolitan pilasters. Under this panel is an inscription of three letters which I read :—*Jodasa.* " [Gift] of Joda." The character shows that the sculpture belongs to the Kushaṇa period. Find-place unknown.

J 22. Fragment (ht. 11½" or 0 m. 294; section 9½" by 5½") of a railing pillar. On one face are the feet of a figure standing on a cushion. The reverse contains a panel with two women, seated on stools, one holding a bow and the other touching her ear-ring with her left hand. On each side of the stone is a mortice for a cross-bar. Find-place unknown.

J 23. Fragment (ht. 1′ 9" or 0 m. 503; section 8½" by 5½") of a railing pillar. On one face are traces of two feet with some drapery (?) between. On the obverse is a panel with a man, whose head and right arm are missing, seated on the head of a dwarf who holds his feet. Possibly this scene refers to the *Sutasōma-jātaka*[1] which occurs also on the Javanese *stūpa* of Borobudur. It is enclosed between pilasters. On both sides is a mortice for a cross-bar. Find-place unknown.

J 24. Fragment (ht. 1′ 7″ or 0 m. 745 ; section 8″ by 5½″) of a railing pillar. On one side are the legs of a female figure with heavy anklets. The reverse consists of two panels. The upper panel contains an ornamental building with high roof, presumably a temple. The carving is much defaced. In the lower panel, partly defaced, is seated under the Bodhi tree a Buddha figure with right hand raised ; and left on his knee. The right shoulder is bare. Each scene is enclosed between pilasters. On each side is a mortice, 9″ long, for the reception of a cross-bar. Find-place unknown. (Plate III *a*)

J 25. Fragment (ht. 1′ 6″ or 0 m. 445 ; section 7″ by 3″) of a railing pillar carved on one side with a male figure standing and holding a fly-whisk in his right hand over his shoulder. His left hand rests on his hip. He wears a *dhōtī* and a scarf tied round his loins. On the obverse are two lotus-rosettes ; the lower one is defaced. On each side are three mortices partly destroyed, 5½″ long, for the reception of cross-bars. Find-place unknown.

J 26. Fragment (ht. 1′ 2½″ or 0 m. 368 : section 5″ by 3½″) of a railing pillar in white sandstone carved with a female figure standing under an *aśoka* tree and unloosing a scarf from her left hip. The legs are missing below the knees. The reverse is decorated with one half and one full lotus-rosette. The fragment was evidently part of a solid railing, the cross-bars of which were not detachable.

(*A. S., R.*, Vol. XVII, p. 110, plate XXXI*d*. *J. A. S. B.*, Vol. XLVII (1878), pt. I., p. 119 ; plate XX, where it is erroneously described as a " pillar with the figure of Māyā Devi under the *sāl* tree. ")

J 27. Fragment (ht. 1′ 8½″ or 0 m. 52 ; section 8½″ by 5″) of a railing pillar. On one side are the feet of a female figure standing on a cushion. The obverse contains two panels enclosed between pilasters. In the upper panel are a male and female figure standing ; the lower has figure erect under a tree. On each side is a mortice, 9″ long, for the reception of cross-bars. Find-place unknown.

J 28. Fragment (ht. 1′ 10″ or 0 m. 557 ; section 6¾″ by 4½″) of a railing pillar carved on one side with two medallions containing fabulous animals. The upper one is broken ; in the lower one is a crocodile. Reverse either

[1] *Jātaka* (ed. Fausböll), Vol. V, p. 456 ; *Jātakamālā* no. 31 (ed. Kern) pp. 207ff transl. Speyer pp. 291ff.

plain or defaced. On each side are mortices, 9″ long, for cross-bars. Find-place unknown.

J 29. Fragment (ht. 1′ 7″ or 0 m. 477 ; section 6½″ by 4″) of a railing pillar. One side are two lotus-rosettes ; the other face is destroyed. On each side are mortices, 7″ long, for cross-bars.

J 30. Fragment (ht. 10½″ or 0 m. 267 , section 6½″ by 4½″) of a railing pillar. On one side are two lotus-rosettes ; the other face is destroyed.

J 31. Fragment (ht. 1′ ½″ or 0 m. 215; section 6″ by 4″ ?) of a railing pillar. On one side is a lotus rosette ; the other side is broken.

J 32. Fragment (ht. 8½″ or 0 m. 201 ; section 7½″ by 4½″ ?) of a railing pillar. On one side is a portion of a lotus-rosette ; the other side is defaced.

J 33. Fragment (ht. 1′ 6″ or 0 m. 445 : section 7″ by 3½″) of a railing pillar. On one side is the upper portion of a male figure, standing under a cluster of full-blown flowers (carved in very low relief) and holding a bunch of lotus flowers in his right hand. His left hand rests on his hip. The reverse is carved with one full and one half lotus-rosette.

On both sides are two mortices, 6½″ long, for the reception of cross-bars. The top of the stone is bevelled. Find-place unknown.

J 34. Fragment (ht. 10½″ or 0 m. 27 ; section 8¼″ 5½″) of a railing pillar. On the reverse is a portion of a panel with a male and a female figure enclosed between pilasters. Find-place unknown.

J 35. Fragment (ht. 11″ or 0 m. 275 ; section 7″ by 6″ ?) of a railing pillar. On one side is a demon with human head, but erect, pointed ears and wide mouth over which are traces of a moustache. He seems to support a railing, above which the feet of a standing figure are still extant. Traces of mortice holes on both sides. Find-place unknown.

*J 36. Fragment (ht. 1′ 3″ or 0 m. 38 ; section 8¼″ by 4¼″) of a railing pillar. On one side are the feet with stout boots of a figure standing on a cushion. On the reverse in a panel enclosed between two pilasters are two men in the act of killing a tortoise with sticks. This is the concluding scene of the birth story of the tortoise (Pali *Kachchhapa-jātaka*) which is a Buddhist adaptation of the fable of the loquacious tortoise and the two geese, which is found in the Indian fable books *Pañchatantra* and *Hitopadeśa* and is best known in the West from La Fontaine's *La Tortue et les deux Canards* (X 3).[1]

---

[1] A representation of the tortoise *jātaka* occurs also on a railing-pillar at Bōdh Gayā and on the Buddhist temple Chandi Mendut in Java (B. Kersjes and G. den Hamer, *De Tjandi Mendoet*, Batavia and The Hague, 1903, p. 9, plate 13).

Cf. *Jātaka* (ed. Fausböll) no. 215, Vol. II, pp. 175ff ; translation Rouse, Vol. II, pp. 123ff. *Pañchatantra* (ed. Kosegarten, Bonn, 1848) p. 76, 113 ; transl. Benfey, p. 90, *Hitopadeśa IV*, 2 ; L. von Schröder, *Indiens Literatur und Cultur* (Leipzig, 1887), pp. 535 f.

Under the panel are two letters which I read *Dasa.* On each side is a broken mortice, 9″ long, for the reception of a cross-bar. The fragment is reproduced by Cunningham (*A. S. R.*, Vol. XVII, plate XXXI*c*), but no reference is made to it in the text. Its find-place is unknown. (*A. S. R.*, 1906-7, p. 156f., fig. 1; *B. E. F. E. O.*, Vol. IX (1909), p.528*f.*).

J 37. Fragment (1′ 2½″ 0 m. 367, section 9″ by 5″) of a railing pillar. On one side is the lower portion of a standing male figure clad in a tunic and close-fitting trousers. Reverse defaced. On both sides traces of mortices. Find-place unknown.

J 38. Fragment (ht. 7½″ or 0 m. 19; section 7½″ by 3½″) of a railing pillar. On one side is a portion of a standing male figure wearing a tunic and trousers. On the reverse is a lotus-rosette. Mortices broken. Find-place unknown.

J 39. Fragment (ht. 1′ 6″ or 0 m. 455; section 7″ by 6″) of a railing pillar carved on one face with two lotus-rosettes. Reverse plain. On each side three mortices, 7¾″ long. Find-place unknown.

J 40. Fragment (ht. 1′ 3″ or 0 m. 48; section 8″ by 4″) of a railing pillar. On the obverse is the bust of a female figure standing under an *asoka* tree (*jonesia asoka*) of which she clasps a branch with her right hand. Above is a balcony over which two figurines are partly visible On the reverse are a full and a half lotus-rosette. On each side are two mortices for the reception of cross-bars. The fragment was the first Buddhist sculpture found by General Cunningham at Mathurā. He discovered it on the Kaṭrā site in 1853, and deposited it in the Lahore Museum. At my suggestion the Panjāb Government made it over to the Mathurā Museum in July 1905. Cunningham's designation of this sculpture as "a broken Buddhist railing pillar with a figure of Māyā Devī standing under the *sal* tree" is incorrect (*A. S. R.*, Vol. I, p. 237 and III, p. 15, plate XII B.)

*J41. Fragment (ht. 1′ 2″ or 0 m. 355; section 8½″ by 6″) of a railing pillar carved on one side with a prostrate dwarf on whose back a female figure is standing of which only the feet remain. On the obverse is a panel enclosed between pilasters. It shows an owl seated on a stool and two monkeys pouring water on its head. The scene probably refers to the *jātaka* of the owl (Pāli *Ulūka-jātaka*).[1] Below this panel is a symbol, apparently the numeral 30.

At both sides is a mortice, 9″ (?) long. The fragment was found in clearing a well at the village of Jamālpur and rescued for the Museum by

[1] On the *Ulūka jātaka* see *Jātaka* (ed. Fausböll) Vol. II, pp. 352f. No. 270 and transl. Rouse, Vol. II, p. 242.

The story of the owl forms also the frame story of the 3rd book of the *Pañchatantra.*

Lieutenant Colonel W. Vost, I.M.S. (Cf. my *Etudes de sculpture bouddhique* in B. E. F. E. O., Vol. IX, 1909, p. 530).

J 42. Fragment (ht. 2′ 2″ or 0 m. 66; section 8″ by 4″) of a railing pillar carved on two sides. On the obverse is the lower portion of a male figure, presumably a Bodhisattva, facing front. On the reverse are two panels, each representing a figure mounted on a fish or *makara* and enclosed between two Indo-Scythian pilasters which support a *chaitya* architrave. On each side is a mortice, 9″ long, to receive a cross-bar. The pillar slopes at the bottom like nos. J 8 and 9 which possibly indicates that it formed part of the balustrade of a staircase. It was at the Allahabad Library till December 1907 and perhaps came from the Jamālpur site. (Plate XXIV.)

J 43. Fragment (ht. 2′ or 0 m. 61; section 8″ by 4½″) of railing pillar sculptured on two faces. The obverse is carved with a standing male figure of which the head and feet are missing. This figure is clad in a tunic, held round the waist by a girdle, and trousers, the dress being similar to that found on the coins of the Kushaṇa kings. He holds in his right hand a bunch of lotus-flowers and in his left an indistinct object, perhaps a lotus bud. On the reverse are two panels enclosed between Indo-Scythian pilasters. The upper panel which is much defaced contains what seems to be a Buddha (?) figure seated in meditation inside a cave or shrine. The lower panel shows a man seated on a stool under a tree and petting (?) a bird placed on another stool opposite him. Cf. above I 4c. On each side is a mortice, 9″ long. The fragment was preserved at the Allahabad Library till December 1907 and perhaps came from the Jamālpur site. (Plate XXIV.)

J 44. Fragment (ht. 1′ 2½″ or 0 m. 37; section 8½″ by 4″) of a railing pillar carved on one side with a male figure, standing to front, of which only the lower half is preserved. The obverse, almost completely defaced, has a Buddha (?) figure seated in meditation. On both sides mortice holes. It was preserved at the Allahabad Library till December 1907 and probably originates from the Jamālpur site.

J 45. Fragment (ht. 1′ 7½″ or 0 m. 495; section 7½″ by 4″) of a railing pillar carved on two faces. One displays a medallion with a *stūpa*, a rosette partly missing, and a half rosette. On the reverse are two rosettes (one broken) and a half rosette. On both sides are mortices, 6″ long. It belonged to the Allahabad Library collection.

J 46. Fragment (ht. 1′ 9½″ or 0 m. 545; section 6½″ by 6″) of a railing pillar, carved on two faces. One is carved with three rosettes of which two are incomplete. The reverse is defaced, but was probably ornamented in the same fashion. At the sides are mortices, 6½″ long. It was preserved at the Allahabad Library till December 1907 and probably originates from the Jamālpur site.

J 47. Fragment (ht. 1′ 1½″ or 0 m. 44; section 8¾″ by 4½″) of railing pillar carved both back and front. On the obverse is a lotus-flower on which a figure stood of which only one foot remains. On the reverse is a panel, enclosed between two Indo-Scythian pilasters. In the centre a male figure is standing with an indistinct object in his right hand. On both sides mortices. It was kept at the Allahabad Library till December 1907 and came perhaps from the Jamālpur site.

*J 48. Fragment (ht. 2′ 9″ or 0 m. 836; section 9″ by 5½″) of a railing pillar. On the obverse is a standing figure completely defaced. On the reverse two panels much obliterated. In the upper panel are two figures, male and female, standing. In the lower panel are a male figure and a crouching dwarf. These scenes seem to be similar to those on the reverse of No. J 18. On two sides are mortices 9½″ long. On the tenon of the fragment are three symbols.

J 49. Fragment (ht. 9″ or 0 m. 227; section 9½″ by 5″) having on one side four conventional flowers and on the back a defaced standing figure. Mortices on two sides. The carving on the obverse, which is much more recent that on the reverse, evidently dates from a time when the pillar fragment was used as a decorated building stone of some Hindū or Muhammadan building. It belonged to the Allahabad Library collection.

J 50. Fragment (ht. 9″ or 0 m. 277) of a railing pillar carved on one side with a doorway and the lower half of a standing male figure and on the reverse with a defaced figure, apparently an Atlant. Mortices on two sides. It was preserved at the Allahabad Library till December 1907 and perhaps originates from the Jamālpur site.

J 51. Fragment (ht. 2′ or 0 m. 61; section 11½″ by 7½″) of railing pillar carved on both sides. On the obverse is a prostrate dwarf on which stood a figure of which only the feet are preserved. On the reverse is a portion of a panel containing two standing figures, one clad in a long robe. The other appears to be an ogre similar to the one on the bas-relief of the large railing pillar no. J1. The fragment probably belongs to the same railing as the Bhūtēsar railing pillars nos. J 4 and 5. The bas-relief seems to represent some *jātaka*. (Plate XXIV.)

*J 52. Fragment (ht. 2′ 2″ or 0 m. 66; section 9″ by 7½″) of a railing pillar carved on both sides. On the obverse is a prostrate dwarf on which stood a figure of which only the feet remain. On the reverse a somewhat defaced panel contains the figure of an ascetic (?) who holds a staff in his left hand and with his right points towards a bird (?) which is shown across the

a. No. J, 42 ; Ht. 2' 2".

b. No. J, 51 ; Ht. 2'.

c. No. J, 54 ; Ht. 1' 10½".

d. No. J, 43 ; Ht. 2'.

FRAGMENTS OF RAILING-PILLARS.

trunk of a palm-tree. The scene is enclosed between Indo-Persepolitan pilasters; it probably refers to some *jātaka*. Beneath the panel are three inverted letters which I read *Śivara*. This is perhaps the name of the sculptor.

J 53. Fragment (ht. 2′ 1″ or 0 m. 635; section 9″ by 7″) of a railing pillar, carved on both faces. The obverse is completely obliterated. The reverse has a greatly defaced panel, in which two male (?) figures stand between Indo-Persepolitan pilasters. The fragment was preserved at the Allahabad Library till December 1907, and probably originates from the Jamālpur site.

J 54. Fragment (ht. 1′ 10½″ or 0 m. 572; section 8¾″ by 5¼″) of a railing pillar. The obverse is carved with rocks on which a figure is standing of which only the feet remain. On the reverse is a defaced panel containing an elephant driven by a mahaut who holds a goad (Skr. *aṅkuśa*). The scene is enclosed between Indo-Persepolitan pilasters. The fragment belongs to the Allahabad collection. (Plate XXIV.)

J 55. Railing pillar (ht. 2′ 1½″ or 0 m. 647; section 6¼″ by 4″) sculptured with a graceful female figure wearing a bead girdle, a scarf and the usual ornaments. Her high head-dress deserves special attention. She stands under an *aśoka* tree in blossom of which she clasps a branch with her left hand, and leans with her back against its trunk, which she presses with her left foot. The scene evidently illustrates the belief, referred to in old Indian poetry, that an *aśoka* tree can be made to blossom, when touched by the left foot of a fair woman. It recalls a scene in Kālidāsa's play "Mālavikā and Agnimitra," in which the King watches the heroine, while she performs the act just referred to at the request of her mistress the Queen.[1] The reverse of the pillar is decorated with two full and one half lotus-rosette. On both sides are three mortices, 6¾″ long, for the reception of cross-bars. The lower portion of the stone with the right foot of the figure is missing. The sculpture was brought from the garden of the Collector's bungalow and made over to the Museum by Mrs. Last in January 1908. (*Cf.* my *Etudes de sculpture bouddique* in *B. E. F. E. O.* Vol. IX (1909) p. 531.f, fig. 34.)

J 56. Railing pillar (ht. 2′ 6¾″ or 0 m. 782; section 7″ by 3¼″) carved on one side with a male figure standing to front and holding a bunch of flowers over his right shoulder and an indistinct object in his left hand. His dress, consisting of a high conical cap, a tunic, trousers and boots, is

[1] Other references to this custom from Sanskrit literature are *Raghuv.*, VIII, 62 and *Meghadūta* (ed. Stenzler), p. 16, verse 75.

of peculiar interest, as it agrees with that of the royalties portrayed on the Indo-Scythian coinage. He wears, moreover, a flat torque and a belt from which a tassel hangs down in front. The dress of this figure is identical in every detail with that of the human devotees on the Kubera group of Tahkāl near Peshawar, now in the Lahore Museum [1].

Over the figure is a projection carved with a so-called *chaitya* window. On the reverse of the pillar are two complete and two half lotus-rosettes. Both sides have three mortices, 6½" long, for the reception of cross-bars. The top and bottom of the stone are bevelled, from which it may be inferred that the pillar belonged to the balustrade of a staircase. The railing-pillar was acquired at the village of Kōṭā together with Nos. J57 to 62. These pillars, which must have belonged to the same railing, were first noticed and described by General Cunningham. The present specimen seems to be identical with B (and P ?) of his list. (*A. S. R.*, Vol. XX, p. 51). On loan from the Government of India.

J. 57. Railing pillar (ht. 1′ 11″ or 0 m. 602; section 7″ by 3″) sculptured on the front with a female figure standing under a tree with her back to the spectator and looking back over her right shoulder. She is shown in the act of culling flowers. The lower portion of the stone with the feet of the figure is missing. On the reverse are two full and one half lotus-rosette; the lower half rosette is wanting. On both sides are three mortices, 6½″ in length, to receive the cross-bars. This railing-pillar comes from Kōṭā and seems to be identical with A of Cunningham's list. Cf. above sub no. J 56. On loan from the Government of India.

*J58. Railing pillar (ht. 2′ 9″ or 0 m. 863; section 7″ by 3″) decorated on the front with a female figure erect on a prostrate dwarf under a tree of which she clasps a branch with her left hand. Her right hand rests on her hip. The reverse is carved with two full and two half lotus-rosettes. Above the upper half rosette there are two figures (reversed) which I read 48 (?) apparently the serial number of the railing pillar. On each side are three mortices, 6″ in length, for the reception of cross-bars. The top and bottom of the stone are bevelled, from which it appears that the pillar formed part of a staircase. It came from Kōṭā and seems to be identical with D (and O ?) of Cunningham's list. Cf. above sub no. J56. On loan from the Government of India.

J 59. Railing pillar (ht. 3′ or 0 m. 942; section 7″ by 3″) carved on one side with a female figure standing to front and holding with her left hand a necklace which she seems in the act of unloosing. Her face

[1] Cf. my *Note sur une statue du Gandhāra conservée au musée de Lahore*, in *B. E. F. E. O*, Vol. III (1903) pp. 150 f.

and right arm are damaged. Over her is a *chaitya* window. The reverse is decorated with two full and two half lotus-rosettes. On both sides of the pillar are three mortices, 6" long, for the reception of cross-bars. This pillar belongs to the Kōṭā railing and is perhaps identical with F of Cunningham's list. Cf. above sub. No. J56. On loan from the Government of India.

J 60. Railing pillar (ht. 2′ 4" or 0 m. 733; section 7" by 3¼") carved on one side with a male figure standing to front on a cushion (?) He is clad in an ample robe, leaving the right shoulder uncovered, and holds his right hand, adorned with a bracelet, in front of his breast. A scarf hangs over his left hand which rests on his hip. The upper portion of the pillar with the head of the figure is missing. The reverse is decorated with two full and one half rosette. On both sides of the pillar are three mortices, 6" in length, for the reception of cross-bars. The pillar belongs to the Kōṭā railing, but does not seem to occur on Cunningham's list. Cf. above sub no. J56. On loan from the Government of India.

J 61. Railing pillar (ht. 1′ 10" or 0 m. 567; section 7" by 3½") carved on the obverse with a female figure standing to front under a *chaitya* window and balancing a ball on her right elbow. She holds an indistinct object in her right hand; her left arm hangs by her side. The lower portion of the pillar with the feet of the figure is missing. The reverse is decorated with two panels of which the upper one contains a sacred tree and the other a *stūpa*. The third panel is lost with the lower portion of the pillar. On both sides of the stone are three mortices, about 6" in length, for the reception of cross-bars. The pillar was brought from Kōṭā and is apparently identical with G of Cunningham's list. On loan from the Government of India.

J 62. Railing-pillar (ht. 2′ 3" or 0 m. 706; section 6¼" by 3") carved on the front with a female figure standing to the proper left with her back and right foot against the trunk of a tree and playing a harp with a plektron. The head of the figure is lost with the upper portion of the pillar. The reverse is decorated in the same manner as in no. J59. On each side of the stone are two mortices about 6" long. The pillar came from Kōṭā, but does not seem to have been described by Cunningham. On loan from the Government of India.

J 63. Railing-pillar (ht. 3′ 2" or 0 m. 994; section 6¾" by 4") carved on one side with a female figure with elaborate head-dress standing to front under a tree and holding a sword in her right hand. The left rests on the hip. Both feet are missing. The obverse is decorated with two full and two half rosettes. On each side of the stone are three mortices, about 6" long, for the reception of cross-bars. This railing pillar and the next one (No. J 64) which seem to have belonged to the same railing, were found let in a wall on both sides of the inscribed tablet of homage (No. Q. 2). Pandit Radha Krishna secured the three sculptures for the Museum. (*Cf.* V. A. Smith, *Jain Stūpa of Mathurā*; plate CIII)

J 64. Railing pillar (ht. 3′ 2″ or 0 m. 994; section 6″ by 3½″); carved on the front with a female figure standing under a tree of which she clasps a branch with her left hand. She looks in a mirror which she holds in her right hand. The obverse is decorated with two full and two half rosettes. On each side of the stone are three mortices, about 6″ long, for the reception of cross-bars. Cf. above sub no. J 63. On loan from the Government of India.

J 65. Railing pillar (ht. 9″ or 0 m· 235) belonging to a solid miniature railing and carved on the front with a female figure standing with her left hand on the hip and holding a garland in her right hand. The lower portion of the stone with the feet of the figure is missing. The reverse has a standing figure which is entirely defaced. On each side of the pillar two cross-bars can be traced.

J 66. Fragment (ht. including tenon 1′ 9½″ or 0 m. 546; section 7″ by 3⅝″) of a railing pillar carved in front with a male figure, perhaps a Bodhisattva, standing on a cushion. The upper half of the pillar with the head and bust of the figure is lost. Beneath it is a winged dragon running (or flying ?) to the proper right and carrying in its mouth what appears to be a garland. On the reverse are a full and a half lotus-rosette, defaced. On both sides are two mortices, 7⅜″ long, for the reception of cross-bar. The sculpture was found on the top of the Nōnāsur Ṭīlā near the village of Pālī Khēṛā, 3 miles south of Mathurā, and placed in the Museum in December 1908. On loan from the Government of India.

J 67. Fragment (ht. 1′ 3″ or 0 m.38) of a railing pillar carved on one side with the lower portion of a standing male figure and on the reverse with a sunk panel containing two standing male figures in Indo-Scythian dress, each holding a garland. Above and beneath these must have been similar panels, the feet of two figures of the upper panel being preserved. Obtained from Ānyōr near Gōvardhan. On loan from the Government of India.

*J 68. Railing-pillar (ht. 2′ 1½″ or 0 m. 649) carved on one face with a male figure standing to front under a balcony. He holds a bunch of flowers in his right hand which is raised to the shoulder. The reverse is decorated with two complete and one half lotus-rosette. Above the latter there are two letters which I read: *Rama*. They show the sculpture to belong to the Kushaṇa period. Obtained from a *maṭh* in the Gōpālpur Quarter of the City. On loan from the Government of India.

J 69. Fragment (ht. 1′ 5″ or 0 m. 432) of a railing-pillar carved on one side with a female figure, of which only the feet with bangles remain, standing on a cushion. The reverse shows a sunk panel containing a male figurine, perhaps a Buddhist monk, holding a bunch of flowers in his right hand. From Arjunpūra Maḥalla in Mathura City. On loan from the Government of India.

J 70. Railing-pillar (ht. 2′ 1″ or 0 m. 635) carved on the front with a female figure standing with her right arm raised and on the obverse with rosettes. Both sides are defaced. From Arjunpūra Maḥalla in the City. On loan from the Government of India.

J 71. Railing-pillar (ht. 5′ 5½″ or 1 m. 665; section 1′ 1″ by 7½″) carved on the obverse with a female figure, defaced, standing in the act of unloosing her girdle. She is standing on a prostrate dwarf, his chin resting on his hands, and is surmounted by a balcony over which two figures, both defaced, are partly visible. The reverse is decorated with three panels, partly defaced, enclosed between pilasters. The top panel represents a *stūpa* surmounted with a triple parasol. The dome is encircled by four cobras. This scene, which also occurs on a Sārnāth sculpture, probably refers to the relic-tower of Rāmagrāma which, according to a Buddhist legend, was guarded by the Nāgas[1]. The remaining two panels seem each to contain three figures, but are too much defaced to be identified. On both sides of the pillar are mortice holes, 11′ long. The pillar was found by Pandit Radha Krishna inside the Mahōlī Paur (or Gate) of Mathurā City. It must have belonged to the same railing as the Bhūtēsar pillars nos. J4-5. On loan from the Government of India.

J 72. Fragment (ht. 8″ or 0 m. 203) of a railing pillar, with a prostrate dwarf on which another figure was standing of which only the feet remain. It was found inside the Mahōlī Paur of Mathurā City. On loan from the Government of India.

[1] Cf. *A. S. R.* for 1904–5, p. 89, fig. 12.

K.—Railing coping-stones.

K 1. Coping stone (ht. 10″ or 0 m. 253; width 4′ 1″ or 1 m. 24; and thickness 8″ or 0 m. 23) of a railing, carved on each side with a series of ogee arches enclosing sacred symbols. On one side are two such arches, one with a conch and the other with a round object placed on a triple platform. On this side there are portions of two more arches. One of the latter contains half of a Buddhist railing. On the obverse one has a bouquet (?) and the other a figure peeping over a curtain. This side of the sculpture is identical with Cunningham's drawing of a railing coping-stone except that the two last subjects are reversed. This is possibly due to an oversight and the stone may be identical with that reproduced by Cunningham. In any case, it must belong to the same railing. The plate on which Cunningham's coping-stone is pictured is marked *Kaṅkālī Ṭīlā.* In the bottom of the stone are three mortice holes, each measuring about 7″ by 2¾″, placed about 10″ apart. It was preserved at the Allahabad Library till December 1907 and perhaps originates from the Jamālpur site. (Cunningham, *A. S. R.* Vol. III, p. 25, plate VIII).

K 2. Coping-stone (ht. 11½″ or 0 m. 293; width 2′ 5″ or 0 m. 735; and thickness 7½″ or 0 m. 9) of a railing carved on both sides with a series of ogee arches enclosing various subjects. On one side is a complete arch with an almsbowl, which contains offerings, and with two conches, and a portion of a second arch with a fragmentary figure, apparently a flying Deva. The two arches on the obverse have one almsbowl filled with offerings, and the other a half lotus-rosette. In the bottom of the stone are two mortices, each measuring 6½″ by 3″, placed 1′ apart. The coping-stone is of precisely the same type as no. K 1, but some slight difference in the measurements indicates that it may have belonged to a different railing. It was kept at the Allahabad Library till December 1907 and came perhaps from the Jamālpur site.

K 3. Fragment (ht. 8″ or 0 m. 203; width 1′ 9½″ or 0 m. 545; and thickness 6¾″ or 0 m. 17) of a railing coping-stone rounded at the top. On the obverse a human-faced animal to right between naturalistic foliage surmounted by a *chaitya* border. On the reverse is a conventional lotus border surmounted by raised bands on which is a row of *stūpas* (or bell and circle border). Mortice on one end.

K 4. Fragment (ht. 8¾″ or 0 m. 22; width 11½″ or 0 m. 29; and thickness 7¾″ or 0 m. 195) of a coping-stone. Obverse foliage; reverse plain.

K 5. Fragment (ht. 7⅓″ or 0 m. 186; width 2′ 1½″ or 0 m. 668; and thickness 6″ or 0 m. 131) of a coping-stone of a railing slightly rounded at the top and carved on both sides with a series of ogee arches. One side is almost completely defaced. On each side are one complete arch and two half-arches, the stone being broken at one end. The sculpture was obtained from a small Hindū shrine near the Balabhadar Kuṇḍ.

K6. Fragment (ht. 5″ or 0 m. 126) apparently of a coping-stone carved on three sides. Two opposite faces are decorated with ogee arches in one of which is the figure of a goose carrying lotus-flowers. The stone is hollow beneath. Find-place unknown.

K7. Fragment (ht. 4½″ or 0 m. 117) apparently of a railing coping-stone decorated with a running human-faced animal.

L.—Railing cross-bars.

L 1. Fragment (ht. 1′ 3¼″ or 0 m. 385; length 1′ 11½″ or 0 m. 595) of the cross-bar of a railing. On both sides is a medallion with a lotus-rosette. Find-place unknown.

L 2. Railing cross-bar (ht. 11¼″ or 0 m. 295; width 1′ 7″ or 0 m. 495) carved on one side with a medallion containing a lotus-rosette from which a male figure on horseback projects. The sculpture was obtained by Pandit Radha Krishna from a weaver (*kōlī*) who worshipped this figure as Zāhir Pīr or Guggā, whereas the Brahmins believed it to represent Kalki the tenth incarnation of Vishṇu.

L 3. Railing cross-bar (ht. 8½″ or 0 m. 21; width 1′ 4″ or 0 m. 40) partly broken, carved on both sides with a medallion containing a deer. Find-place unknown.

L 4. Fragment (ht. 7½″ or 0 m. 19; width 11″ or 0 m. 28) of the cross-bar of a railing. On the obverse is a medallion with a humped bull (head lost). On the reverse is a crocodile (?). Find-place unknown.

L 5. Fragment (ht. 9″ or 0 m. 23; width 7″ or 0 m. 18) of a cross-bar of a railing carved on both sides with a human-faced animal.

L 6. Fragment (ht. 7½″ or 0 m. 19; width 9½″ or 0 m. 24) of the cross-bar of a railing carved on one side with a medallion containing a winged animal.

L 7. Fragment (ht. 8″ or 0 m. 203; width 9½ or 0 m. 24) of the cross-bar of a railing, decorated with a rosette on each face. It belongs to the Allahabad collection.

L 8-19. Twelve fragments of cross-bars of railings of various sizes decorated with rosettes; five are carved on one side and seven on both sides. Find-place unknown.

317. Fragment (ht. 7½″ or 0 m. 19) carved with a prostrate dwarf on which a female figure is standing of which only the feet remain. It was found in clearing a well at Jamālpur and made over to the Museum by Lieutenant-Colonel W. Vost, I.M.S.

L 20. Fragment (ht. 1′ 8½″ or 0 m. 394) of a railing cross-bar carved on two sides with a lotus-rosette containing a human head with large turban, ear-pendants, torque and necklace. It is identical with the sculpture which Mr. Growse noticed between the villages of Pālī Khēṛā and Dhan-singh and which he describes as, "the central portion of a very large Buddhist pillar, with a head on either side." It was placed in the Museum in December 1908 (*Cf.* Growse, *Mathurā*, p. 124.) on loan from the Government of India.

L, 21. Cross-bar (ht. 10½" or 0 m. 267) carved with an ornamental rosette consisting of a conventional full-blown lotus-flower enclosed within a flowering lotus-stalk. Reverse plain. Found together with no. M 7. The fragments nos. L 22-25 appear to have belonged to the same railing. On loan from the Government of India.

L 22. Fragment (ht. 10¾" or 0 m. 273) of a cross-bar decorated with a lotus-rosette containing a female head wearing a flat torque and elaborate head-dress. Found with no. M 7. On loan from the Government of India.

L 23. Fragment (ht. 8¼" or 0 m. 21) of a cross-bar decorated with a lotus-rosette containing a male figure riding on an animal, apparently a bull. Found with no. M 7. On loan from the Government of India.

L 24. Two fragments (ht. 8½" or 0 m. 216) of a cross-bar decorated with a lotus-rosette containing a male figure, armed with bow and arrows, mounted on a lion. Found with no. M 7. On loan from the Government of India.

L 25. Fragment (ht. 10½" or 0 m. 267) of a cross-bar decorated with a lotus-rosette containing a female head with elaborate head-dress. Found with no. M 7. On loan from the Government of India.

L 26-28. Cross-bar and two fragments of a cross-bar (ht. 6½" or 0 m. 165) decorated on both faces with a lotus-rosette and evidently belonging to the same railing. On loan from the Government of India.

L 29. Fragment (ht. 5" of 0 m. 127) of cross-bar decorated with lotus-rosette. Found with nos. L 21-28. On loan from the Government of India.

L 30. Cross-bar (ht. 9¼" or 0 m. 235) decorated on both sides with a lotus-rosette. One side defaced. From the village of Hākimpur 6 miles south of west from Mathurā, north of the road to Sonk. On loan from the Government of India.

L 31. Fragment (ht. 6" or 0 m. 152) of a cross-bar carved on one face with a winged animal, apparently a lion, walking to the proper right. Head missing. On the obverse is some indistinct carving, apparently a lotus-leaf. Found at the Chaurāsī Jaina temple in February 1910. On loan from the Government of India.

M.—Toraṇa Architraves and Brackets.

M 1. Architrave (ht. 10" or 0 m. 254; width 4′ 9½" or 0 m. 46) of a *toraṇa* carved on two sides. The obverse shows ten figures, apparently Buddhist monks. One in the centre pours out some liquid from a large vessel into a bowl. Four figures follow him each carrying a bowl. At the proper right side are a *stūpa* (?) and a *toraṇa* with a double architrave. A figure is visible in the gateway, holding one of the jambs, but here a corner of the stone is broken. The other half of the relief is occupied by four seated figures of which the one nearest the centre is likewise pouring out some liquid from a jar. At the end are a pillar, a *stūpa* and a tree with garlands hanging down from the foliage. Under these figures, along the whole width of the sculpture, there runs a border consisting of a Buddhist railing and a bell-border. The reverse is decorated with a similar border. But here the Buddhist railing supports a colonnade surmounted by ogee arches alternating with balconies. Between the pillars of this colonnade and over the balconies a number of human figures are visible. The sculpture must be identical with "the peculiarly carved architrave of a Buddhist gateway, richly sculptured on both sides with buildings, figures and trees, including a representation of a gateway itself", which was discovered by General Cunningham on the Kaṭrā site during the cold season of 1862-3. The sculpture was preserved in the Public Library at Allahabad till December 1907. (Plate XXV. Cf. *A. S. R.*, Vol. I, p. 237 and Vol. III, p. 15; Growse, *Mathurā* p. 106).

M 2. Fragment (ht. 7¾" or 0 m. 197; width 2′ 1½" or 0 m. 647) of the architrave of a *toraṇa* carved on one side. The central portion which was over the gateway and is broken off, is decorated with a naturalistic lotus design. The square panel which must have surmounted the jamb of the gate contains a curious half-human figure with a forked tail consisting of two coiled snake bodies. These end in two winged dragons rising on both sides of the figure, which holds their necks with his hands. It is seemingly a blending of two decorative elements: the Triton found in the Graeco-Buddhist sculpture of Gandhāra and evidently derived from a classical source[1], and the rampant dragon or leogryph which as a decorative bracket is met throughout Indian art. The round end of the stone is carved with the curled-up body of a fish-tailed crocodile (Skr. *makara*), such as are found in exactly the same position on the *toraṇa* architraves of Barāhat. The stone is pierced with a round hole at the

[1] *Cf.* also the Sārnāth railing-pillar, reproduced *J. R. A. S.* for 1908, p. 1095, plate IV, fig 2.

PLATE XXV.

(*a*) OBVERSE.

(*b*) REVERSE.

No. M, 1 ; Width 4' 9½"

TORANA LINTEL FROM KATRĀ.

No. M, 2 ; Width 2' 1½".

FRAGMENT OF TORANA LINTEL.

place where it rested on the jamb of the doorway. Besides there is a square mortice above for the tenon of a *toraṇa* figure placed between the two architraves; and two mortices (one round and the other oblong, beneath, the purpose of which is not clear. (Plate XXV*c*. Cf. V. A Smith, *Jain Stūpa*, plate XXIV, fig. 1; and Foucher, *L'art gréco-bouddhique*, Vol. I, pp. 242 f. fig. 124).

M 3. *Toraṇa* architrave (ht. 7½" or 0 m. 19; width 8' or 2 m. 52) sculptured on both faces; each face being divided into five compartments. On the obverse the middle of the central compartment is occupied by a sacred tree, probably the *bodhi* tree, behind (or inside ?) a building, through the gateway of which the trunk is visible, while the foliage is shown emerging from the windows and above the roof. It is interesting to note the attempt at perspective in rendering the edifice, the lines of the bastions which flank the gateway being drawn sloping. The sanctuary is approached by twelve male worshippers elegantly draped in flowing garments and arrayed in two rows of six on each side of the building. The two figures at the head of these two rows, carry each a round vessel in both hands whilst the remaining ten hold each a long garland and a nosegay as offerings.

The two square panels which once must have stood over the *toraṇa* pillars represent two other scenes of adoration: that to the proper right a *stūpa* and the left one a wheel of the law (Skr. *dharmachakra*) each worshipped by two male devotees. The wheel which is supported by three lions seated back to back recalls the lion capital of the Aśoka pillar of Sārnāth. The two projecting ends of the architrave are each decorated with a fish-tailed sea-monster with human bust, a blending of the indigenous *makara* and the Triton of classical art.

On the reverse the central panel depicts the well-known scene of Indra's visit to Buddha in the Indraśaila Cave. (Cf. above Nos. H 11 and N 2 h.) The Buddha, seated inside the cave in the attitude of imparting protection, occupies the centre of the scene. To his left stands Indra, the king of the gods, recognisable from his peculiar-shaped hat which characterises him also in Gandharian representations of this episode. He joins his hands in the attitude of adoration and is attended by two females, probably heavenly nymphs (Skr. *Apsaras*), standing in the same pose. They are followed by three elephants, of which the central one is caparisoned and may be supposed to represent Indra's riding elephant Airāvaṭa. The third animal is only partly visible. On the other side of the cave stands Pañchaśikha, the lord of Gandharvas or heavenly musicians, playing the harp. He is followed by six nymphs, the first of which seems to beat time, the second and fourth have their hands joined in adoration, and the remaining four carry each a garland and a bunch of flowers as offerings. The two square panels which once surmounted the gate pillars contain each a vase of lotus-flowers. The two remaining compartments at the ends of the architrave, are each decorated with a Triton similar to those found in the corresponding panels of the obverse.

The heads of some of the figures in the central panel of the reverse are broken; but for the rest the sculpture is in excellent preservation. It is one of the finest specimens of Mathurā art and displays a pleasing combination of Indian and classical elements. A comparison with the *toraṇa* architraves of Sānchi shows at a glance that the general mode of decoration is thoroughly Indian. There also the central panel commonly depicts a scene of adoration, in which a row of worshippers approaches the sacred object from both sides. But on the Mathurā sculpture the arrangement of the figures and their graceful attitude are due to Gandhāra influence, which is especially noticeable in the scene of Indra's visit to Buddha. The human-headed sea-monsters at the ends of the architrave appear also to be developed from the *makaras* on the ancient *toraṇas* under the influence of Gandhāra art.

The beam is pierced in two places to receive the tenons of the *toraṇa* pillars. The bottom is provided with seven mortices. The central one is 15¼" long. On each side are three of which that in the middle is rectangular and 3" long, and the other two circular and 2" in diameter. In the top are nine mortices of which seven correspond in position to those in the bottom surface. The remaining two, which are rectangular and 3¾" long, are found near the two extremities of the architrave. It is clear that the mortice holes were intended to receive the tenons of sculptures placed between and above the three architraves of the *toraṇa*. This may be inferred from a comparison with the gates of the Sānchi *stūpa*, where such sculptures are still found *in situ*.

The Mathurā *toraṇa* architrave was obtained from a house in the City where it was found let in the wall above the main gate. Pandit Radha Krishna arranged for its removal to the Museum in November 1908. On loan from the Government of India.

M 4. Bracket (ht. 2′ 1″ or 0 m. 654) of a *toraṇa* carved on both sides with a female figure standing under an *aśoka* tree of which she holds a branch with one hand. The lower portion of the sculpture with the feet of the figure is missing. It was obtained from a Pandit who had found it in excavating the foundations of his house near the Dīg Gate of the

City. (For similar *toraṇa* brackets cf. V. A. Smith, *Jain Stūpa*, plates XXXIV and XXXV). On loan from the Government of India.

M 5. Head (ht. 1′ 7″ or 0 m. 497) of a leogryph with protruding eyes and curved horns. The lower jaw is missing. On the top of the head is a tenon. The sculpture probably served the purpose of an ornamental bracket of a *toraṇa*. It was obtained by Pandit Radha Krishna from the Maṭh of Mathurā-nāth Mahādēo near the Kaṭrā. (*Cf.* V. A. Smith, *Jain Stūpa*, plate XXXVII). On loan from the Government of India.

M 6. Head (ht. 6½″ or 0 m. 165) of a lion which must have belonged to a bracket supporting the end of a *toraṇa* architrave. *Svastika* on the right cheek. On loan from the Government of India.

M 7. Fragment (ht. 11¼″ or 0 m. 286; length 2′ 4″ or 0 m. 71) consisting of the end of a *toraṇa* architrave, carved on both faces with a yawning crocodile (*makara*), whose curled-up fish-tail follows the curved outline of the stone. In the mouth of each *makara* we notice the figure of a *kinnara* with leafy girdle. One of these *kinnaras* is armed with sword and shield. The sculpture was found together with the cross-bar fragments nos. L 21—25 in a brick-kiln near the Mathura Junction Railway station. On the *makara* and *kinara* ornament cf. *A.S.R.* for 1906-7, p. 160. On loan from the Government of India.

M 8. Statuette (ht. 10″ or 0 m. 254, including tenon) of a lion seated on its hind quarters. Manes treated in a conventional manner. It probably belongs to a *toraṇa* and stood on the end of the top lintel. Obtained from a Dēvī Maṭh in the Bahādurpura Maḥalla of Mathurā City. On loan from the Government of India.

N.—Stūpas.

*N 1. Drum and dome of a miniature *stūpa* (ht. 1′ 7″ or 0 m. 482) consisting of two pieces which have been refixed. On the four sides of the drum are four Buddha figures seated cross-legged in the attitude of protection (*abhaya-mudrā*), each under a trefoil arch supported by two Indo-Scythian pilasters. Along the top of the drum runs a border of garland-carrying Cupids (cf. above nos. 1, 2 to 6), which is supported by flat brackets. On the top of the plain dome is a square mortice with raised border to receive the *hti* (Skr. *harmikā*) with the pinnacle. The bottom of the drum is flanged so as to fit into the basement. (*Cf. post* no. N 3.) There is an inscription in one line on the dome. The *aksharas* measure ⅝″ to 1″ in height. The character is Brāhmī of the Kushaṇa type. I read it: *Nuśāpriyāye Śuranasya ditu* (i.e. *dhitu*). "[Gift] of Nuśāpriyā, the daughter of Śurana."

The inscription was first edited by Professor J. Dowson. On account of the character of the inscription, the votive *stūpa* must belong to the Kushaṇa period. It was at the Allahabad Public Library till December 1907; its find-place was presumably the Jamālpur site.

(Plate IV. *Cf. J. R. A. S.* N. S., Vol. V, p. 187, No. 20, with facsimile; and *J. A. S. B.* Vol. XXXIX (1870), part I, p. 129, no. 13).

N 2. Drum (ht. 8″ or 0 m. 20; diameter 2′ or 0 m. 62) of a miniature *stūpa* carved with a frieze of eight metopes representing the four principal and four secondary scenes of Buddha's life, namely:—

(*a*) His birth in the Lumbinī garden near Kapilavastu. Māyā Devī is standing in the usual pose with her right hand clasping a branch of the *sāl* tree above her. She is held by her sister Prajāpatī standing to her left. On her right side is a god, probably Indra, who receives the child on a cloth. The infant Bodhisattva is repeated at the proper left side of the panel; round the child's head is a halo with scolloped border. At his sides are the Nāga kings Nanda and Upananda emerging halfway from two masonry wells. The same scene is pictured on Nos. H 1 and 2.

(*b*) His enlightenment (Skr. *bodhi*) or attainment of Buddhahood at Bōdh Gayā. To render this event, the sculptor has chosen the scene of the assault of Māra, the evil one, which immediately preceded the *bodhi*. Buddha is seated in the conventional pose; he stretches his right hand out to the earth in order to call her to bear testimony of his good deeds in former existences. To his left are Māra's seductive daughters. The crouching figure to his right must be Māra himself, behind whom an indistinct figure is visible, perhaps meant for a demon wielding a rock. It is noteworthy that the *bodhi* tree has been altogether omitted and that Māra's daughters are represented by only two figures, whereas in all texts their number is three. (*Cf.* above No. H.6.)

(c) His first sermon in the Deerpark, the modern Sārnāth, near Benares. The technical expression is that here the Buddha began "to turn the wheel of the law." On the sculpture he is actually shown touching the wheel which is placed on a low pillar at his right side. The five mendicant friars who became his converts on this occasion are shown on both sides of the Buddha, but apparently for purposes of symmetry the sculptor has reduced their number to four. *Cf.* above no. H 7 *(a)*.

(d) His death or final extinction (Skr. *parinirvāṇa*) in the *sāl* grove of Kusinārā or Kuśanagara. Buddha is reclining in the traditional pose on his couch between the twin *sāl* trees. There are three mourning figures, one to the right, one to the left and a third behind the couch. (*Cf.* above nos. H 1, 7*b*, 8 and 9.)

(e) The meaning of this scene is uncertain, but presumably it shows Buddha seated in the famous Gandhakuṭī. This shrine, in which he used to dwell, was situated in the Jetavana, a sacred grove near Śrāvastī. The site of this ancient city has been identified by General Cunningham with Sahēṭh-Mahēṭh in the Gonda and Bahraich districts of the United Provinces.

(f) Buddha's descent from the Heaven of the thirty-three gods, where he had preached the law to his mother. This event was supposed to have taken place at Saṅkāśya, the modern Sankisa (Farrukhābād district). In the centre of the bas-relief is the triple ladder. In front of the central one is the figure of Buddha and at his sides are Brahmā and Indra standing with folded hands in the attitude of adoration.

(g) Buddha presented with an almsbowl by the four guardian gods of the quarters or world-protectors (Skr. *lokapāla*). When after his enlightenment Buddha wished to partake of the food offered by the merchants Trapusha and Bhallika, the four guardian gods approached him each with a bowl. As he did not wish to disappoint any of them by refusing his gift, he caused the four bowls miraculously to become one.

(*h*) Buddha worshipped by Indra in the Indraśaila Cave, near Rājagṛiha, the modern Rājgir in Bihār. Buddha is shown in the attitude of meditation inside the cave. The figure crouching to his left must be Indra, apparently holding his attribute, the thunderbolt (Skr. *vajra*), in his left hand. The standing figure with the harp on the other side of the cave is Indra's attendant Pañchaśikha, the king of the heavenly musicians (Skr. *Gandharva*). A fuller representation of this scene will be found on the bas-relief No. H 11 and on the *toraṇa* architrave M 3.

It will be seen by a comparison of the other bas-reliefs quoted that the scenes of Buddha's life are depicted here in as summary a manner as possible. The execution is clumsy and we have noted several inaccuracies in the plastical rendering of the legends. The sculpture, however, is of great interest, as in it the influence of the Graeco-Buddhist school of Gandhāra is more manifest than in any other product of Mathurā art. It reveals itself not only in the individual scenes, but also in the decorative elements. This will be evident at once by comparing this *stūpa* drum with that excavated by Sir Harold Deane at Sikri (Peshawar district) and now preserved in the Lahore Museum. In his discussion of the Sikri *stūpa* drum, M. Foucher was the first to point out its relationship to our Mathurā sculpture which he rightly calls "sa caricature lamentablement indianisée." "Le tore grossier de l'architrave," he says, "la corniche trop lourde aux consoles trop larges, les pilastres massifs à chapiteaux barbares ne laissent aucun doute sur la prétention ni sur la maladresse de l'imitation ; c'est un entablement classique avec frise analogue à celui de Sikri, qu'on a voulu composer."

The sculpture which was first published by Mr. V. A. Smith from photos taken by Babu P. C. Mukharji was found by me in the courtyard of a Hindu temple on the Dhruv Ṭīlā where it was used as a receptacle (*thāmlā*) for the sacred *tulsi* plant. With the assistance of Pandit Radha Krishna I succeeded in acquiring it for the Museum in December 1907. (V. A. Smith, *The Jain Stūpa*; plates CV—CVII. Foucher, *Les bas-reliefs du stūpa de Sikri. J. A.*, series X, Vol. II (1903), p. 323.)

N 3. Votive *stūpa* (ht. 4¾" or 0 m. 124) of miniature size carved on its four sides with Buddha figurines seated cross-legged and holding their hands in the traditional attitudes. The break on the top of the stone indicates that it was originally provided with a pinnacle or *hti*. It was noticed by Pandit Radha Krishna in a *bāghīcha* near the Seṭh's Garden on the right bank of the Jamnā, about 1½ mile south of the City.

N 4. Fragment (ht. 9" or 0 m. 23) presumably belonging to the square basement of a miniature *stūpa*. It is carved on one side with a cornice supported by two Atlantes alternating with clumsy brackets. The Atlant to the proper right is squatting with his feet wide apart; and his arms crossed on his chest. The other one who supports the cornice with his right hand has the appearance of a Triton of classical art, his body ending in a double snake tail. Similar figures occur in Gandhāra; they are evidently meant for Nāgas and afford another example of the adaptation of classical types to Indian conceptions. Find-place unknown.

N 5. Fragment (ht. 11¼" or 0 m. 285) consisting of the corner portion of the square basement of a miniature *stūpa*. It is carved on two sides with a Buddha figure seated cross-legged in a niche with his right hand raised in the attitude of imparting protection. The niches alternate with dwarf pilasters which support a bracketed cornice. The top of the stone is flanged to receive the *stūpa* drum. Find-place unknown.

N 6. Fragment (ht. 5½" or 0 m. 14; width 1′ 7½" or 0 m. 495) of a cornice with four brackets and an acanthus border. The sculpture must have belonged to a miniature *stūpa*. It was preserved at the Allahabad Public Library till December 1907 and perhaps originates from the Jamālpur site.

N 7. Fragment (ht. 3½" or 0 m. 09; width 18" × 4" or 0 m. 405) of a circular stone with plain mouldings and mortice on the top. It belonged to the Allahabad collection.

N 8. Fragment (ht. 7" or 0 m. 18) of a pinnacle probably placed on the top of a miniature *stūpa*. The lower portion, broken off at the bottom, is a cube carved on three sides with chapels and on the fourth vertical side with a half-nude female figure standing under an *aśoka* tree of which she clasps a branch with her right hand. The lower portion of this figure is lost. The opposite side was hollowed in the shape of a niche, perhaps meant to contain a lamp. This cube is surmounted by an octagonal pinnacle separated from it by an octagonal neck. The top of the pinnacle is missing. The fragment was preserved at the Allahabad Public Library till December 1907 and perhaps originates from the Jamālpur site.

N 9. Hollow cube (ht. 8½" or 0 m. 216) carved on each of its sides with a Buddha figure seated cross-legged between two Indo-Scythian pilasters. Two of the figures are sitting in the attitude of meditation; the two others have the right hand raised towards the shoulder to express the imparting of protection. One of the two meditating and one of the two other Buddha figures is placed on a conventional lotus. All four have a halo with scolloped border. One of the figures is broken. It was obtained by Mr. Growse from the Mahāvidyā Ṭīlā (*J.A.S.B.*, Vol. XLVII (1878), pt. 1, p. 120; plate XX).

N 10. Fragment (diameter 3′ 9″ or 1 m.143) of a parasol which may have stood either over a *stūpa* or over a statue. It is carved on the lower surface with three conventional borders of a lotus-petal, foliated and garland design. There is a circular hole in the centre to receive the umbrella staff. The fragment was preserved at the Allahabad Library up to December 1907 and came probably from the Jamālpur site.

N 11. Fragment (ht. 2′ 6″ or 0 m. 762) of a parasol which may have overshadowed either a *stūpa* or a statue. It is decorated with six concentric bands of different design, separated by narrow raised rims. The central one is of an elaborate foliated pattern surrounded by a garland border. The outer-most band which is raised has a festoon pattern. This fragment also belongs to the Allahabad collection transferred to Mathurā in December 1907.

O.—Lion figures.

O 1. Figure (ht. 3′ 4″ or 1 m. 15) of a half engaged lion standing with his right paw in front. The upper jaw is missing. The sculpture was broken in five pieces in transit from Allahabad where it was preserved up to December 1907.

O 2. Figure (ht. 3′ 1½″ or 0 m. 952) of a half engaged lion standing to proper left with his left paw in front and mouth open. Back, except head, plain. Find-place unknown.

O 3. Figure (ht. 2′ 10″ or 0 m. 863) of a half engaged lion standing. His left paw, which was advanced, is broken. Tongue injured. Curly moustache. Find-place unknown.

O 4. Figure (ht. 2′ 11½″ or 0 m. 901) of a half engaged lion standing to proper right with his right paw in front and open mouth. Back except head, plain. Find-place unknown.

O 5. Figure (ht. 2′ 10″ or 0 m. 89) of a half engaged lion standing with his left paw in front. Upper jaw broken. Pandit Radha Krishna found this sculpture in the store godown of the Agra Delhi Chord-line Railway and secured it for the Museum. It is said to have been excavated by a railway engineer.

O 6. Figure (ht. 2′ 9″ or 0 m. 837) of a half engaged lion. Legs and lower jaw broken. It was preserved at the Allahabad Public Library till December 1907 and perhaps originates from the Jamālpur site.

O 7. Figure (ht. 2′ 8″ or 0 m. 837) of a half engaged lion standing turned to the proper right with his left paw in front. Head defaced and paws broken. It was obtained from the Janambhūmi shrine [1] near the Kaṭrā and probably once belonged to one of the Buddhist sanctuaries on that site.

O 8. Figure (ht. 2′ or 0 m. 61) of a half engaged lion standing turned to proper right. *Svastika* on right cheek. Find-place unknown.

O 9. Figure (ht. 1′ 10″ or 0 m. 576) of a complete lion. Head, paws and tail broken. It was brought to the Museum from a garden near the Balbhadra Kuṇḍ.

O 10. Figure (ht. 2′ 1″ or 0 m. 635) of a complete lion standing over miniature elephant (?). The right fore paw which was raised, and the head and the tail, are broken. The mane is indicated by schematic curls. Find-place unknown.

O 11. Figure (ht. 1′ 5″ or 0 m. 43) of a half engaged lion standing to front with open mouth. Paws beneath knees missing. Find-place unknown

[1] This shrine is believed to mark the birth-place of Kṛishṇa.

O 12. Fragment (ht. 1′ 7″ or 0 m. 482) of a lion figure. Hind-quarters, right fore-leg and face missing. It was preserved at the Allahabad Public Library till December 1907. Perhaps it came from the Jamālpur site.

O 13. Figure (ht. 2′ 8½″ or 0 m. 825) of a complete lion, much worn. The fore-paws rest on each other. Find-place unknown.

O 14. Fragment (ht. 6¼″ or 0 m. 16) consisting of the fore-paws of a lion standing with his right one in front. Evidently it belongs to a sculpture like nos. O 1—12. Find-place unknown.

O 15. Fragment (ht. 11″ or 0 m. 28) consisting of the leg of a lion figure. Find-spot unknown.

O 16. Figure (ht. 3′ 2″ or 0 m. 995) of a half engaged lion standing turned to proper right and with his left paw in front. Top of head broken. It was acquired from a *chaupāl* near the Kōṭvālī.

O 17. Fragment (ht. 4½″ or 0 m. 115) with lion's head facing. Find-place unknown.

O 18. Fragment (ht. 4¼″ or 0 m. 107) of lion's head. *Svastika* marked on right cheek. Find-place unknown.

O 19. Figure (ht. 2′ 2″ or 0 m. 66) of a half engaged lion with protruding eyes, the head turned to the right. Legs broken and lower jaw damaged. Obtained from a *bāghīcha* between the Pōtrā kuṇḍ and the Kaṭrā. On loan from the Government of India.

P.—Miscellaneous Architectural Sculptures.

(*Buddhist period.*)

P 1. Fragment (ht. 2′ or 0 m. 61; width 4′ or 1 m. 22) which must have formed the proper right half of a door-lintel. In the centre is a panel containing a row of six standing figures of which five carry lotus flowers, whilst the sixth, apparently a woman, has her hands folded in the attitude of adoration. This panel is surrounded by two plain decorative bands. To the proper right of it is a small panel with a flying figure and a rosette. Both panels are enclosed within decorative borders in bold relief and a raised outer border of an elegant *aśoka* design. Beneath the stone has a mortice to fit it to the doorjamb. The sculpture was preserved at the Allahabad Public Library till December 1907 and perhaps came from the Jamālpur site. (Plate II *a*.)

P 2. Fragment (ht. 2′ 10″ or 0 m. 863) of a proper left doorjamb, evidently belonging to the same doorway as no. P 1. The front is carved with two panels each containing two standing figures, male and female. In the upper panel both figures hold a bunch of lotus-flowers in the right hand. In the lower panel the male figure holds likewise a bunch of lotuses; the female stands with folded hands in the attitude of adoration. The figures are standing on a Buddhist railing under an ogee arch which encloses a balcony with a miniature figure. A similar arch is seen under the lower panel.

To the proper left of these panels are four decorative bands of the same design as are found on the door-lintel no. P. 1. The proper right side of the stone which was turned to the passage of the doorway is decorated with a graceful vine border. This sculpture also belonged to the Allahabad collection. It came perhaps from the Buddhist site of Jamālpur. (Plate II b).

P 3. Fragment (ht. 2′ 11″ or 0 m. 889) of a pillar consisting of the top portion of the shaft which is sixteen-sided below and circular above (diameter 1′ 2″), a grooved bell, a flat torus, and a square capital (1′ 2″ by 1′ 2″), the four faces of which are each decorated with two lions couchant surmounted by foliage. The fragment belonged to the Allahabad collection.

P 4. Fragment (ht. 11¾″ or 0 m. 298) of a pillar, consisting of the top portion of the shaft which is sixteen-sided below and circular above (diameter 1′ 2″). Cf. No. P. 3. Allahabad collection.

P 5. Fragment (ht. 11½″ or 0 m. 292) of pillar consisting of the grooved bell and flat torus of the capital. Allahabad collection.

P 6. Fragment (ht. 1′ ½″ or 0 m. 317) of a pillar consisting of the top portion of the capital (1′ 2″ square in horizontal section), the four faces of which are each decorated with two lions couchant placed back to back and surmounted by foliage. Allahabad collection.

P 7. Fragment (ht. 2′ or 0 m. 61) of a pillar consisting of part of the shaft, eight-sided below and sixteen-sided above. The top is circular (diameter 1′ 2″). Allahabad collection.

P 8. Fragment (ht. 8¾″ or 0 m. 222) of doorjamb (?) with figure standing to front; head lost. Ornamental border on proper left side. Find-place unknown.

P 9. Sculpture (ht. 1′ 6½″ or 0 m. 484) carved with a much defaced male figure emerging half-way from the foliage of a tree. The attitude of this figure is very similar to that of the spirit of the *sāl* tree shown on the bas-relief of Buddha's Nirvāṇa No. H 8. There is, therefore, reason to assume that it likewise represents a tree spirit or dryad. The sculpture was found by Pandit Radha Krishna close to the bungalow of the Permanent Way Inspector, R. M. Railway, near the village of Hansganj on the left bank of the Jamnā opposite Mathurā City.

P 10. Fragment (ht. 2′ 1″ or 0 m. 654, including tenon) of a doorjamb carved on the front face with two sunk panels, each containing a figure. The upper figure is a male standing with an offering of flowers in both hands; the lower one is a female crouching with a child in her lap. Evidently this figure is identical with no. F 26. Along the two figures is a vertical raised border decorated with foliage issuing from a vase. The proper right face is carved with a half lotus-rosette and a festoon. The sculpture was acquired from the village of Mahōlī.

P 11. Fragment (ht. 1′ 2½″ or 0 m. 38) of a doorjamb carved on the front face with a male figure, probably a Bodhisattva, standing to front with his right hand raised to the shoulder. His head is encircled in a halo with scolloped border. Along this figure runs a raised vertical band decoratively carved. The proper left face of the stone has part of a lotus-rosette and a festoon. Obtained from Mahōlī. On loan from the Government of India.

P 12. Pillar-base (ht. 1′ 2″ or 0 m. 355) carved with foliated ornament and pierced with a round hole 3½″ in diameter. A portion of it is broken. It was found in a field between the villages of Pāli Khēṛā and Dansingh together with nos. L 20 and P. 13 and placed in the Museum in December 1908. On loan from the Government of India.

P 13. Lamp-stand (ht. 1′ 6″ or 0 m. 457, including tenon) consisting of an elongated cube carved in low relief with *chaitya* windows and provided with a niche on one face and vertical grooves on two of the remaining three faces, and an upper member in the shape of a *liṅga* surrounded with a band. Find-place same as No. P. 12.

P 14. Lower portion (ht. 1′ 2″ or 0 m. 355) of a doorjamb, proper right side, carved with a male figure, standing with a staff in his right and a lotus-flower in his left hand. On the projecting portion is a boyish figure in low relief holding with both hands a stalk with flowers and foliage. Obtained from Sitōhā, 3 miles from the City on the road to Gōvardhan. On loan from the Government of India.

P, 15. Capital (1′ 1″ or 0 m. 33) rectangular in horizontal section, pierced vertically and carved on the four sides. One of the two long sides is carved with a group consisting of an elephant to right, mounted by a *mahaut*, and some seven small figures, apparently children, and a boar to left carrying two female figures. A large bell is suspended from the boar's neck. On the opposite side there is a group of two seated and some standing figures too much defaced to be recognized. Each of the two short sides has a female figure seated with children, probably Hāritī the goddess of abundance and fertility.

The sculpture was obtained by Pandit Radha Krishna from a weaver in the Kēsabpūra Maḥalla of the City. On loan from the Government of India.

P 16. Fragment (ht. 8½″ or 0 m. 215; length 2′ 2¾″ or 0 m. 68) of a lintel decorated with a row of five lion's heads, the surface beneath being carved in a foliated pattern, in which on the proper right end there is a figurine standing with a garland in each hand and enclosed within an ogee-arch. Obtained together with no. P 17 from Rāl, 8 miles north-west of Mathurā City. On loan from the Government of India.

P 17. Fragment (ht. 3′ 1½″ or 0 m. 954) of a proper left door-jamb decorated with a sunk panel containing a male figurine leaning on a staff. On the proper left side is a raised rim carved in flat relief with foliage and scrollwork, in which a conch and a lion's head are introduced. The sculpture seems to belong to the Gupta period. It was obtained from Rāl together with No. P, 16. On loan from the Government of India.

P 18. Fragment (ht. 11″ or 0 m. 28) consisting of a grooved ogee arch, in which a Buddha figure is seated cross-legged in the attitude of meditation. It was obtained from the Rāj Ghāṭ in Mathurā City together with No. H 1 in January 1908.

P 19. Building stone (ht. 7″ or 0 m. 177) carved on one side with a half lotus-rosette enclosed between vertical bands. It was preserved at the Allahabad Public Library till December 1907 and perhaps originates from the Jamālpur site.

*P 20. Pillar-base (1′ 11½″ or 0 m. 587 square; ht. 1′ 1¾″ or 0 m. 35). Torus decorated with lotus petals and with four projecting lion figures of which one is missing. The corner of the stone is broken. Circular mortice in the top. There are two inscriptions. The first inscription runs round the top of the torus. I read it *D[ā]naṁ bhikshusya Buddhiśreshṭhasya cha[tu]rvvi[dha]sya bhaja . . . . . kasya saṅghe ch[ā]turddiśe sa 47 gri 4 di 25.* "Gift of Friar Buddhiśreshṭha Chaturvidha (?) Bhaja . . ka to the universal Community . . . . in the year 47, the 4th [month of] summer, the 25th day."

The second inscription, which is cut on one side of the base, is indistinct. I read it tentatively: *Dānaṁ Buddhiśreshṭhasya bhapranakasya.* The stone was preserved at the Public Library at Allahabad till December 1907.

*P 21. Pillar-base (1′ 8¼″ or 0 m. 514 by 1′ 9¼″ or 0 m. 54; ht. 1′ or 0 m. 305). Torus decorated with lotus petals, but without projecting lion figures. Mortice in the top and two small mortices in the corners of the top of the square base. There are two inscriptions on two faces of the basement. *Aya[ṁ] ku[ṁ]bhaka dā[naṁ] saṅgha-prakṛit[ā]n[āṁ] Bhadraghosha-pra[mukhānāṁ.]* "This pillar-base is the gift of the Superiors of the Community, among whom Bhadraghosha ranks first." The same legend occurs on nos. P. 25 and 26.

The second inscription, which consists of two lines, is mostly obliterated. In the first line I read the word *saṅgha* and at the beginning of the second line *dharmadeya.*

*P 22. Pillar-base (1′ 11½″ or 0 m. 597 by 1′ 10¾″ or 0 m. 578; ht. 1′ 1½″ or o m. 343). Plain torus decorated with four projecting lion figures of which one is broken. The following inscription in two lines is cut on the face of the square basement.

1. *Ayaṁ ku[ṁ]bhako dānaṁ bhikshunaṁ Surīyasya Buddharakshitasya cha prahanīk[ā]na[ṁ]. Anena*

2. *deyadharmma-parityāgena sarvveshāṁ prahanīkānaṁ arogyadak[sh]inōye bhavatu*[1].

"This pillar-base is the gift of the Friars Śurīya and Buddharakshita the *prahanikas.* May, by the munificence of this pious donation, health be bestowed on all *prahanikas.*"

The pillar-base was discovered by Mr. Growse "plastered and whitewashed and imbedded in one of the side pillars of the Tahsili gateway." It had probably been excavated in 1877-8 on the Jamālpur site.

(Dowson No. 23; Growse, *Mathurā*, 2nd ed., p. 154; 3rd ed., p. 165, *Ind. Ant.*, Vol. VI, p. 218, No. 3; Senart, *J. A.* Series VIII, Vol. XV.

---

[1] The grammatical construction of the second sentence of the inscription is faulty. A similar formula is found on pillar-base M 2g in the Calcutta Museum. (Dowson No. 12).

p. 121, note; D. R. Bhandarkar, *J. B. B. R. A. S.*, Vol. XX, p. 269, note 2; Lüders, *Ind. Ant.*, Vol. XXXIII, p. 155, note 100).

* P 23. Pillar-base (2′ ½″ or 0 m. 622 square; ht. 1′1½″ or 0 m. 343) Torus decorated with lotus-petals, but without projecting lion figures. Mortices in the corners of the top of the square basement. One corner broken. The following partly defaced inscription runs along the top of the torus: *Sa . . . . ja[mi]trasya Vojyavatikasya . . . . hishaṇḍasya sitakalagatānāṁ pujāye bhavatu sadhyivihārisya Dha[rmade]vasya arogya-dakshiṇāye. . . . .* "May health be bestowed on the Sadhyavihāri Dharmadeva"[1].

*P 24. Pillar-base (1′ 10¼″ or 0 m. 565 by 1′ 11½″ or 0 m. 597; ht. 1′ ¾″ or 0 m. 325). Torus decorated with lotus-petals and with four projecting lion figures, three of which are broken. The following inscription is cut on the top of the torus: *Dānaṁ saṅgha-prakṛi*[2]*tana* [*ṁ*] *Bhad*[*i*]*la-pramukhana*[*ṁ*]. "Gift of the Superiors of the Community among whom Bhadila ranks first."

*P 25. Pillar-base (1′ 10½″ or 0 m. 57 by 1′ 9½″ or 0 m. 546; ht. 10½″ or 0 m. 266). Torus decorated with lotus-petals, but without projecting lion figures. Mortices in the corners of the top of the square basement The following inscription is cut on the face of the basement: *Ayaṁ* [*kuṁbhako dānaṁ*] *saṅgha-prakṛitānaṁ Bhadraghosha-pramukhā*[*naṁ*]. "This pillar-base is the gift of the Superiors of the Community among whom Bhadraghosha ranks first." The same legend is found on nos. P 21 and P 26.

*P 26. Pillar-base (2″ or 0 m. 601 by 1′ 9½″ or 0 m. 343). Torus decorated with lotus petals, but without projecting lion figures. Mortices in the corners of the top of the square basement. The following inscription is cut on the face of the basement of which a corner with the concluding portion of the inscription is lost: *Ayaṁ* [*kuṁbhako*] *dānaṁ saṅgha-prakṛitānaṁ Bhadraghosha-*[*pramukhānaṁ*]. "This pillar-base is the gift of the Superiors of the Community among whom Bhadraghosha ranks first." The legend is evidently the same as that of nos. P 21 and P 25.

*P 27. Pillar-base (1′ 10¾″ or 0 m. 578 by 1′ 10¼″ or 0 m. 565; ht. 1′ ½″ or 0 m. 318). Torus decorated with lotus-petals and with four projecting lion figures one of which is broken. The following inscription is cut on the face of the basement: [*Siddhaṁ*] *Daja* (*Dānaṁ*) *bhikshuno Bhadrasya*

---

[1] The name *Dharmadeva* occurs also *Ind. Ant.* Vol. XXXIII, p. 101.

[2] The *ka* has both an *i* stroke above and a *ṛi* stroke beneath.

Bhadragh[o]shasya cha "Gift (?) of the two Friars Bhadra and Bhadraghosha." The same legend occurs on no. P 28.

*P 28. Pillar-base (1′ 10¼″ or 0 m. 565 by 1′ 10⅞″ or 0 m. 58; ht. 1′ 1″ or 0 m. 33). Torus decorated with lotus-petals and with four projecting lion figures, all of which are broken. The following inscription is cut on the face of the square basement: [*Siddhaṁ*] *Dānaṁ* (?) *bhiksho Bhadrasya Bhadraghosha*[*sya cha*]. "Gift of the Friars Bhadra and Bhadraghosha." The same legend is found on no. P 27.

*P 29. Pillar base (1′ 11″ or 0 m. 584 by 1′ 11½″ or 0 m. 597; ht. 1′ 3″ or o m. 381). Torus decorated with lotus-petals and with four projecting lion figures, three of which are broken. On the face of the square basement is an inscription, the concluding portion of which is missing. It was published by Prof. Dowson and re-edited by Prof. Lüders, who reads it: *Dānaṁ Saṅgha-sthavirasya bhadanta*... "Gift of the elder of the Congregation, the venerable........................." The stone was preserved in the Public Library at Allahabad till December 1907. (*Cf.* Dowson No. 21; Lüders, *Ind. Ant.* Vol. XXXIII, p. 155, No. 37.)

*P 30. Pillar-base (2′ or 0 m. 61 by 1′ 10½″ or 0 m. 571; ht. 1′ ½″ or 0 m. 292). Torus decorated with lotus-petals and with four projecting lion figures, one of which is destroyed. The following inscription is cut on the face of the square basement: [*Dā*]*naṁ Viśvasikasya Sūśyalasya ku*[*ṁ*]*bhako sabharyyakasya supu* [*trrakasya*..............] "A pillar base the gift of the Viśvasika ([1]) Sūśyala with his wife [and sons.....................]." The stone was noticed by my photographer at the entrance of the Tahsil gate in December 1907.

*P 31. Pillar-base (1′ 11½″ or 0 m. 596 by 2′ or 0 m. 61; ht. 1′ ½″ or 0 m. 311). Torus decorated with lotus-petals and with four projecting lion figures two of which are broken. The following inscription is cut on the face of the square basement. *D*[*ā*]*naṁ bhiksho*[*ḥ**] *Saṅghadevasya Vakuḍatev*[*â*]*sikasya*. "The gift of Friar Saṅghadeva, the disciple of Vakuḍa (i.e., Vakula)."

*P 32. Pillar base (1′ 10¼″ or 0 m. 562 square; ht. 1′3¼″ or 0 m. 375). Torus decorated with lotus-petals and with four projecting lion figures. The following inscription is cut on the face of the square basement: *Ja......a yi*(?) *k*[*uṁ*]*bhako d*[*ā*]*naṁ bhik*[*shu*]*sya Saṅghavarmma*[*sya*] *Vaddha* (?) *sya cha*. "A pillar-base the gift of Friar Saṅghavarman and of Vaddha (Vṛiddha ?)."

[1] The word *Viśvasika* which also occurs in the inscription on pillar base M 2 g. in the Calcutta Museum (Dowson No. 13) is apparently a title.

*P 33. Pillar-base (1′ 11¼″ or 0 m. 59 by 1′ 10½″ or 0 m. 572 ; ht. 1′ 2″ or 0 m. 356). Torus decorated with lotus-petals and with two projecting lions and one elephant. The following inscription, partly defaced, is cut on the face of the square basement: *D[ā]nam bhikshus[ya] Buddhamitra-s[ya]* "The gift of Friar Buddhamitra............"

*P 34. Pillar-base (1′ 10½″ or 0 m. 57 by 1′ 11″ or 0 m. 584 ; ht. 1′ 1½″ or 0 m. 342). Torus decorated with lotus-petals and with four projecting lion figures, all of which are damaged. One corner is missing with the concluding portion of the inscription cut on the face of the square basement. *D[ā]nam bhikshu[sya] Dattasya* 37 (?) *saṅghe ch[ā]t[urdiśe* ....] "The gift of Friar Datta to the Universal Community".. .... (Dowson no. 27).

*P 35. Pillar-base (1′ 10½″ or 0 m. 57 by 1′ 10¾″ or 0 m. 577 ; ht. 1′ 1½″ or 0 m. 342). Torus decorated with lotus-petals and eight symbols and with projecting lion figures which are damaged. One corner is missing with the beginning portion of the inscription cut on the face of the square basement. The remainder reads : ....*datta* 126 *saṁ* 47[1] *va.* 1 *di.* 11. "..........................in the year 47 ; in the first month of the rainy season ; on the 11th day" (Dowson No. 7 ; Cunningham, *A.S.R.* Vol. III, p. 34, no. 14.)

*P 36. Pillar-base (1′ 10½″ or 0 m. 57 by 1′ 10¾″ or 0 m. 577 ; ht. 1′ ¾″ or 0 m. 323). Torus decorated with lotus-petals and with four projecting lion figures of which three are destroyed. Inscription on the face of the square basement almost entirely obliterated.

*P 37. Pillar-base with indistinct inscription on the face of the square basement. It reads: *Dānaṁ saṅghaprakṛitānāṁ Bhaddila-pramukhā-nāṁ sarva-satvānāṁ hita[sukhārthaṁ]* ; "Gift of the Superiors of the Community, among whom Bhaddila ranks first, for the sake of the happiness and welfare of all creatures." (Cf. above no. P 24.)

*P 38. Pillar-base with indistinct inscription in two lines on the face of the square basement. It reads: *[Saṁ]* 47 *gr* [*i*] 4 *di* [20] *asyapurv-vāyāṁ [bhikshusya]*.. "[In the year] 47 ; in the 4th month of summer ; the 20th (?) day ; on that date as specified above [of Friar].................."

*P 39. Pillar-base with obliterated inscription on face of square basement.

*P 40—53. Fourteen pillar-bases similar to nos. P 20—39 but without inscriptions.

P 54. Fragment (ht. 3′ 6″ or 1 m. 065) of an Indo-Persepolitan

---

[1] Professor Lüders reads 77.

pilaster of highly decorative design consisting of the top portion of the round shaft, decorated with lotus-buds and conventional Garuḍas separated by double festoons, and of a grooved bell-shaped capital surmounted by four lions couchant which support an abacus decorated with a palmette and two defaced female figurines. The pilaster projects from a post carved on both sides with a decorative border in which two grotesque figures and a dragon are introduced. The sculpture was preserved at the Allahabad Library till December 1907 and perhaps originates from the Jamālpur site. (Plate II*d*).

P 55. Fragment (ht. 3′ 6″ or 1 m. 065) of the shaft of a highly decorated, semi-circular pilaster (diameter 9″) rising from a vase. The shaft is carved with a pattern of interlaced double garlands, the triangular spaces being filled with lotus-flowers and palmettes, and the square ones with Garuḍas conventionally treated. The design is the same as that on the shaft of no. P 54 which must have belonged to the same building. Find-place unknown. (Plate II*c*.)

P 56. Fragment (ht. 1′ 7″ or 0 m. 48) of an Indo-Persepoltan pillar, consisting of a bell-shaped capital carrying four winged lions couchant, which support the upper member which is decorated on three sides with a palmette ornament in low relief. One of the narrow sides of the upper member is plain, but has a vertical groove. A similar groove divides one of the broad sides. Find-place unknown.

P 57. Fragment (ht. 10″ or 0 m. 255) of a small Indo-Persepolitan pillar consisting of an abacus supported by four winged lions couchant. The obverse is decorated on the two long sides with a palmette. One of the narrow sides is carved with a fernlike ornament and the fourth side is marked with a groove. The sculpture was kept at the Allahabad Library till December 1907 and perhaps came from the Jamālpur site.

P 58. Fragment (ht. 1′ 6″ or 0 m. 457) of a bas-relief with a portion of an Indo-Persepolitan pilaster consisting of a semi-octagonal shaft and ornamented bell-capital, carrying two winged lions couchant. The upper member is missing. To the right traces of drapery. Find-place unknown. (*J. A. S. B.*, Vol. XLVII (1878) Pt. 1; plate XX).

P 59. Fragment (ht. 9½″ or 0 m. 24) of a sculpture carved on one side with the upper portion of an Indo-Corinthian dwarf pilaster and on the reverse with a foliated design. Find-place unknown.

P 60. Bracket (ht. 1′ 1½″ or 0 m. 242; length 2′ 9″ or 0 m. 833, including tenon, with projecting figure of an elephant. Trunk and legs broken. Find-place unknown.

P 61. Bracket (ht. 7½" or 0 m. 19; length 1′ 5" or 0 m. 435 including tenon) with projecting figure of a winged *makara*. Allahabad collection.

P 62. Bracket (ht. 6½" or 0 m. 165; length 1′ 10" or 0 m. 555 including tenon) with projecting figure of a lion. Allahabad collection.

P 63. Bracket (ht. 5½" or 0 m. 139; length 1′ 1" or 0 m. 33) with projecting figure of an elephant. The trunk which was raised is broken. Find-place unknown.

P 64. Central member (ht. 11½" or 0 m. 293) of an Indo-Persepolitan capital with four human-headed winged lions couchant. The head of one is missing. It is pierced from top to bottom by a round hole, 4" in diameter. It was found in cleaning a well at Jamālpur and made over to the Museum by Lieut-Col. W. Vost, I.M.S.

P 65. Abacus (ht. 10½" or 0 m. 267) carved on both sides with the figure of a Triton flanked by two lions rampant which support the volutes. It was also found in the Jamālpur well.

P 66. Capital (ht. 2" or 0 m. 28) of an Indo-Persepolitan corner pilaster, decorated on two adjoining sides with two lions couchant. It was also found in the Jamālpur well.

P 67. Stele (ht. 2′ 2" or 0 m. 66), square in section, with five niches in two opposite sides. The niches are flanked by Indo-Scythian pilasters and separated by Buddhist railings. Each of the top niches is surmounted by an ogee arch. On the sides which have five niches a figure is carved on each side of the central niche, whilst on the remaining two sides of three niches the central niche is placed between two figures peeping over a curtain. The sculpture which probably served the purpose of a lamp-stand (Hindī *dīpdān*) was preserved at Allahabad till December 1907, and came perhaps originally from Jamālpur.

P 68. Fragment (ht. 3′ or 0 m. 914) of a doorjamb carved on both sides with a male figure standing and holding a long staff in one hand. Allahabad collection.

P 69. Fragment (ht. 1′ 7¾" or 0 m. 505) carved with a quadruple decorative border, one showing a vine pattern. Find-place unknown.

P 70. Fragment (ht. 1′ ¾" or 0 m. 32) the raised portion carved with a triple decorative border of which the one on the proper left has an acanthus design and the adjoining one a vine pattern. The sunk portion is decorated with naturalistic lotus-flowers.

P 71. Fragment (ht. 1′ 10¾" or 0 m. 575) of a doorjamb (?) carved on the obverse with two panels, much defaced. In the upper one are two standing figures, in the lower one is a seated figure. The narrow sides are decorated on the proper right with a male and female figure and on the proper left with two dragons rampant. The sculpture was obtained by Pandit Radha Krishna from a shrine at Sītalā Ghāṭī in Mathurā City.

P 72. Fragment (ht. 6" or 0 m. 459) carved with a double border of an *aśoka* and lotus design respectively. Find-place unknown.

P 73. Fragment (ht. 1′ 2½" or 0 m. 367) of the facing of a doorjamb (?) decorated with vertical bands and the figure of a Bodhisattva in royal dress, and halo with scolloped border, seated cross-legged with his right hand raised in the attitude of imparting protection. In his left hand he holds a vessel. On the narrow sides are portions of two figures of which the lower one is a Buddha. Find-place unknown.

P 74. Fragment (ht. 1′ 11" or 0 m. 585) of the capital of an Indo-Persepolitan pilaster with defaced figures of winged lions couchant. Find-place unknown.

P 75. Fragment (ht. 10" or 0 m. 255) of a doorjamb (?) carved on one side with a panel containing two half-nude figures, male and female standing with folded hands in front of four men placed in a row. The first one is seated on a stool; of the others only the head is visible. Over the panel is another scene of which only the portion of a figure seated on the ground is preserved. Both are enclosed between vertical decorative borders. On the adjoining face is a male figure standing and holding a garland in both hands. The head is missing. The fragment was preserved at the Allahabad Public Library till December 1907, and perhaps originates from the Jamālpur site.

P 76. Half-figure (ht. 4" or 0 m. 104) of a winged lion couchant. From shrine of Mathurā-nāth Mahādēo at the Dīg Gate.

P 77. Fragment (ht. 6½" or 0 m. 165) of a doorjamb (?) decorated, with two male figures standing to front and holding a bunch of flowers in their right hand. Remnants of standing figure on proper right side. It was found in clearing a well at the village of Jamālpur and made over to the Museum by Lieutenant-Colonel W. Vost, I.M.S..

P 78. Fragment (ht. 2′ 10½" or 0 m. 877) of a doorjamb, proper right side. The front is divided into three sunk panels, in each of which there are two figures, male and female, standing with hands joined in the attitude of adoration. Of the lower-most figures only the heads remain. Each couple is standing on a Buddhist railing supported on three brackets and is surmounted by a roof with *chaitya* window. On both sides of these panels there is a raised border carved with a foliated design. The side face of the jamb is decorated with a lotus-rosette and bands mostly defaced. It was obtained by Pandit Radha Krishna from the village of Kerāvarī two miles from the left bank of the Jamnā on the road to Rāyā. On loan from the Government of India.

P 79. Stele (ht. 7′ 4″ or 2 m. 237) carved with five females, placed one over the other, of which the lowermost one is totally, and the next one partially defaced. These panels are separated by railings surmounted by *chaitya* windows, in three of which standing figurines are half visible. To the proper right runs a narrow bamboo border, to the proper left a flat band carved in low relief with palmettes and symbols.

The uppermost panel contains three female figures, two of which are seated on low stools opposite each other, the one apparently receiving a cup from the hand of the other. The third figure, evidently a maid-servant, is standing somewhat back with a fan in her right hand. In the upper corner the foliage of a tree is visible.

The second panel contains a similar scene showing three female figures making music. Two are seated, of which one plays the harp, and the other appears to hold castanets in her right hand. The third, standing, plays the flute. At her side is the foliage of an *aśoka* tree.

In the third panel one female is seated on a stool, the second rubbing her left foot and the third standing with a dish in her left hand. The next two panels are too much defaced to be identified.

The slab was discovered by Pandit Ram Chandar inside the Mahōlī Paur (or gate) of the City, where it was used as the corner stone of a dwelling house. It was subsequently acquired for the Museum by Pandit Radha Krishna. On loan from the Government of India.

Q. Inscribed Slabs and Tablets.

*Q 1. MORA WELL INSCRIPTION. Slab. (ht. 11′ 2″ or 3 m. 506, width 2′ 11″ or 0 m. 916) inscribed with a fragmentary inscription in four lines. The inscription was discovered by General Cunningham in 1882-83 at the village of Mora 7 miles west of Mathurā City, where it formed part of the terrace of an ancient well. It was then incomplete, but it appears from Cunningham's facsimile that it has since become much more mutilated. In the following transcript I enclose within round brackets the portions found only in the facsimile:—

1. *Mahak(sha)t(rapasa Rājūvulasa putra)* . . . . .
2. *Bhagavatā Vṛi(sh)ṇe(na paṁcha Virānāṁ pratimā śaila-ṭrivagra)* . . . .
3. *yastoshayā ś(ai)le (śrimadgrahamatula muda-dhasa)* . . . . .
4. *archā daśaṁ śailaṁ pachajvala(ta iva parama vapusha)* . . . .

In January 1908, I had the slab removed to the Museum under supervision of Pandit Radha Krishna. (*A. S. R.*, Vol. XX, p. 48f.; plate V, no. 4). On loan from the Government of India.

*Q 2. Tablet of homage or *āyāga-paṭa* (1) (ht. 2′ 4″ or 0 m. 733; width 1′ 9¾″ or 0 m. 569) carved with a complete *stūpa* surrounded by a railing and approached by means of a flight of steps and an ornamental gateway (Skr. *toraṇa*). This *toraṇa* is of the usual type with three architraves, the projecting ends of the one beneath being supported by lion-brackets. The *stūpa* is flanked by two pillars of Persepolitan style, the one to the proper right carrying a wheel and the other a sitting lion. On each side of the *stūpa* are three worshipping figures. The two flying figures above possibly represent *munis* who were supposed to have the power of transporting themselves through the air. They are naked and carry in the left hand a piece of cloth and a waterpot or almsbowl, whilst their right hand is applied to the forehead in token of respectful salutation (Skr. *namaskāra*). The second pair of figures may be identified with *suparṇas* or *kiṁnaras* corresponding to the harpies of classical art. They have birds' tails and claws. The one to the proper right carries a bunch of flowers, the other a garland. The two female figures leaning in a graceful attitude

(1) "An *āyāga-paṭa* is an ornamental slab, bearing the representation of a Jina or some other object of worship, and the term may be appropriately rendered by "tablet of homage or of worship," since such slabs were put up in temples, as the numerous inscriptions on them say "for the worship of the Arhats" . . . . "Among the Jainas they probably went out of fashion at an early period, as the inscriptions on them invariably show archaic characters, and are in no case to be dated." Bühler, *Ep. Ind*, Vol. II, pp. 311 and 314. For other specimens of *āyāga-paṭas cf.* V. A. Smith, *Jain Stūpa*, plates VII—XIII.

against the drum of the *stūpa*. I suppose them to represent nymphs (*yakshī*). They resemble the so-called dancing-girls found on railing-pillars. On each side of the staircase is a niche containing a standing figure, the nature of which cannot be ascertained. That to the proper right seems to be a male figure accompanied by a child, that to the left a female.

On the dome is a Prakrit inscription in six lines, 7¼" to 8¼" long. It reads:

TEXT.

1. *Namo Ārahato Vardhamānasa Ārāye*[1] *gaṇikā-*
2. *ye Loṇaśobhikāye dhitu śamaṇaśāvikāye*
3. *Nādāye gaṇikāye Vasu[ye] Ārahāto devik[u]la*
4. *āyāga-sabhā prapā śil[ā]pa[ṭo] patisth[ā]pito Nigathā-*
5. *nāṁ Araha[tā]yatane sa[hā] m[ā]tare bhaginiye dhitare putreṇa*
6. *sarvena cha parijanena Arahata pujāye.*

TRANSLATION.

"Adoration to the Arhat Vardhamāna. The daughter of the matron (?) courtesan Loṇaśobhikā (Skr. Lavaṇaśobhikā), the disciple of the ascetics, the junior (?) courtesan Vasu has erected a shrine of the Arhat, a hall of homage (*āyāgasabhā*), a cistern [and] a stone slab at the sanctuary of the Nirgrantha Arhats together with her mother, her daughter, her son and her whole household in honour of the Arhats."

I take *ārāye* (Skr. *āryāyāḥ*) and *nādāye* (Skr. *nandāyāḥ*) to be titles denoting certain ranks among courtesans. It should be remembered that in the *Mṛichchhakaṭikā* the courtesan Vasantasenā is addressed as *ajjukā*.

This inscribed tablet was first noticed by Bhagavan Lal Indraji who published a rough sketch of it together with a transcript and translation of the epigraph. Subsequently Mr. V. A. Smith published a photograph of it. The exact whereabouts of the sculpture were, however, unknown, until Pandit Radha Krishna rediscovered it let into the wall of a small *liṅga* shrine at the well of the name of Mukund Kuān not far from the Lachhmangaṛh Ṭīlā outside the Holi Gate. The Pandit secured it for the Museum in April 1908 together with the two railing pillars nos. J 63 and 64. It is asserted that the three sculptures had been dug up from a field near the village of Mahōlī (Plate V. Cf. *Actes du sixième congrès international des Orientalistes tenu en* 1883 *à Leide*, part III, section II, pp. 142—144, with plate; Smith, *Jain Stūpa*, plate CIII; Burgess, *Ancient Monuments*, plate 155, no. 2; Lüders, *Ind. Ant.*; Vol. XXXIII,

[1] Professor Lüders reads *Adāye*.

pp. 152 f., and *Z. D. M. G.* Vol. LVII (1904), p. 868).

On loan from the Government of India.

*Q 3. Fragment (ht. 1′ 6¼″ or 0 m. 463) consisting of the upper proper left corner of a tablet of homage (*āyāga-paṭa*). Of the central panel, enclosed in a double rope border, only two flying figures with garlands which occupy the spandrels remain. Along the proper left side is a narrow panel which contains a column with Persepolitan bell capital and two winged lions couchant, surmounted by an elephant standing to the right. The whole is enclosed within a decorative vine border.

On the back is a fragmentary inscription in two lines, 14½″ by 5½″ long, enclosed within a border carved in low relief. It was first published by Mr. Growse and re-edited by Professor Lüders. It reads:

1.... [*nā*]*ye Mogalī-putasa Puphakasa bhayāye*

2. *Pūsāye pasādo.*

"Gift of Pūsā (Skr. Pushyā), the wife of Puphaka (Skr. Pushpaka), the son of Mogalī"......

Judging from the character, the tablet must belong to the 1st century B.C. Mr. Growse notes that it was found in the Kaṅkālī Ṭīlā (*Mathurā*, pp. 177f., *Ind. Ant.*, Vol. VI, p. 218, no. 4, and *J. A. S. B.*, Vol. XLVII (1878), Pt. I, p. 119, plate XX; Lüders, *Ind. Ant.*, Vol. XXXIII, p. 151, no. 28.)

*Q 4. Slab (length 3′ 6″ or 1 m. 10; width 3′ 4″ or 1 m. 047 and thickness 6″ or 0 m. 157) with traces of an inscription of four lines in Brāhmī characters of the Kushaṇa period. The slab was found together with the inscribed Nāga image no. C13 at the village of Chhaṛgaon, 5 miles south of Mathurā. All that can still be traced is:

1... ... .[[*ra*]*jati*[*raja*] ... ...

2...... .... [*pu*]*rvayya* ... ...

8.................................*kā sa sa va pi da ra va*

4. ....[*pri*]*jati* ... ...

Apparently the inscription contained a date. It must have been contemporaneous with the inscribed Nāga statue.

*Q 5. Gupta inscription. Fragment (ht. 11¾″ or 0 m. 302; width 11″ or 0 m. 288) of a tablet, broken in two pieces, with portions of ten lines of an inscription in Gupta character. It contains the genealogy of the Gupta emperors and must belong to the reign of Chandragupta II Vikramāditya. The stone was discovered by General Cunningham in 1853 at the Kaṭrā where it formed part of the pavement immediately outside the Kaṭrā gateway. The inscription was first published by Cunningham and re-edited by Dr. Fleet (*Gupta Inscr.*, p. 26, no. 4). On loan from the Government of India.

*Q 6. Tablet (1′ 7″ or 0 m. 498 by 1′ 1½″ or 0 m. 353), broken in two pieces, with an inscription in thirteen lines of corrupt Sanskrit. Line 11 is written vertically along the proper right margin. Lines 12 and 13 are written in the top margin, the last line being a short one. The character is Nāgarī. The letters, which are raised, are irregular and badly formed; and measure about ¾″ in height. The inscription apparently records the construction of some sanctuary by an individual of the name of Nārāyaṇ Dās. The date is the Vikrama year 1612, Chaitra *ba ti* 10, Sunday, corresponding with

Text.

1. *Svasti Śrī atha saṁvatsare smin*
2. *Śrī-nṛipati-Vikramāditya-śāke saṁvat*
3. 1612 *varshe Chaitra va. di.* 10 *dasamī Ravi-*
4. *dine Vijai-Sikaṁdara-rājye Tivārī Nihaṁ-*
5. *dātasya putra Gopāladāsasya sishya Nārāya-*
6. *ṇadāsa dharmmārthena kāritaṁ vihāravāsī Ḍhala*
7. *ti Rāī to vā sta ṇu|| Taj janma tāni karmmā-*
8. *ṇi tad āyus tan mano-vachaṇ|| nṛiṇāṁ yena*
9. *hi viśvātmā sevyate Harir Īśvaroḥ||* 1-*Pha*
10. *syu'a dhari ga rī vā vā dā daasha nu*
11. *dahulakarī Dādū Brāhmaṇa*
12. *Likhitaṁ Keso Miśru gaṇiko śishya.*
13. *śrī-Gopāla jaya.*

TRANSLATION.

"Hail! Good fortune! In this year, the year 1612 of the illustrious prince Vikramâditya, in [the month of] Chaitra, the tenth (10th) day of the dark fortnight, on Sunday, in the victorious reign of Sikandar, Nārāyaṇ Dās, the pupil (?) of Gopāl Dās, the son of Tivārī Nihaṁ (?) Dat (Dās ?), caused for the sake of religious merit.........to be made ....

"That is [true] existence, those are [true] deeds, that is [true] life, and that is [true] thought and speech of men [that namely] by which the Soul of the Universe, the Lord Hari, is served ....

....

written by Keso Misru...

"May Srī Gopāl be victorious!"

The tablet is said to originate from Brindāban. The date of the inscription corresponds to Sunday the 17th March 1555 A.D. The king in whose reign it is dated, is Sikandar the younger brother of Shēr Shāh Śūr and last of the line of Afghan kings of Delhi. He was defeated by Humāyūn in the battle of Sirhind which took place on the 18th of June 1555, viz., three months after the date of the present inscription.

*Q 7. Stele (ht. 5′ 6″ or 1 m. 728) with a sunk panel, 1′ 11½″ high and 1′ wide, containing a rudely carved male figure walking to the right and holding a large bow. The lower portion of the panel bears a Nāgarī inscription in six lines which I read:

1. *Saṁvat 1420 varshe Maṁgoḍalā janmasthāna*
2. *stha-kāyastho Māthurāṁ nvayu* (?) *Bhāskara-pau-*
3. *tra-Vikrāta Pithau Siṁgha-suta.......*
4. ||1||*Aśvana-māse site pakshe daśam* [*yāṁ*]
5. *Somavāsare gomihesa.......saṁ*[*ga*]
6. *me Amarasiṁgho nāma*

The inscription contains the name of the village (?) of Mangoḍalā situated 13 miles from the City in the direction of Bharatpur (*Cf.* Growse, *Mathurā*, p. 4) and the date Saṁvat 1420, Aśvina *su. ti.* 10, Monday corresponding to the 18th September 1363 A.D.

The stone was obtained by Pandit Radha Krishna from the village of Maglora (?) On loan from the Government of India.

*Q 8. Tablet (ht. 1′ 4″ or 0 m. 42; width 1′ 1¾″ or 0 m. 36) of buff-coloured sandstone containing a Sanskrit inscription in nine lines of Bengali characters. Pandit Binode Bihari Bidyabinode has supplied the following reading:

1. 1702 *Śaka uraṅgakā....*
2. *gate Rayanamāsi*||*Śrī Utla-*
3. *ma rā*(?)*ma Srī ma*[*tahāṭi ?*] *ka*
4. *Śrī Lakhirāma Śrī Ravā*
5. *ni Śrī Virachandra Srī Lakhi*
6. *rāma Śrī Govodhana Śrī U*
7. *rāvi Śra*(*Śrī*) *prānnātha Śrī ki*
8. *ttivāsa Śrī Vishṭo*
9. *rāma.*

*Q 9. Square pillar (ht. 4′ 6¼″ or 1 m. 40) carved on one end with a half lotus-rosette on each face and inscribed on two sides.

*Q 10. *Satī* slab (ht. 10¾″ or 0 m. 282) with two figures, male and female, standing to front, hand in hand. It has a fragmentary Nāgarī inscription in two lines, one above and the other beneath the figures. Both sides of the stone are broken. It was obtained from a shrine near the Balbhadra Kuṇḍ. On loan from the Government of India.

*Q 11. Slab (7" or 0 m. 178 square) inscribed with three lines in Nāgarī. Obtained from a *bāghicha* near the Kanskā Ṭīlā at Mathurā City. On loan from the Government of India.

*Q 12. Undressed stone with indistinct carvings and Nāgarī (?) inscription apparently consisting of five lines of writing. On loan from the Government of India.

*Q 13. Monolithic column (ht. 19′ 7" or 5 m. 954; width 1′ 2" or 0 m. 356; thickness 1′ or 0 m. 304) square in section up to a height of 8′ 7" and octagonal above. It is inscribed with the following inscription in seven lines, 1′ 2" in length :—

Transcript.

1. *Siddhaṁ* 11 *Mahārājasya r*[*ā*]*jāt*[*t*]*irājāsya deva*[*pu-*]
2. *trasya Shāher=Vvāsishkasya rājya-saṁvatsare* [*cha-*]
3. *turviṁśe* 24 *gr*[*ī*]*shmā-māse chaturtthe* 4 *diva*[*se*]
4. *triṁśe* 30 *asyām purvvāyāṁ Rudrila-puttreṇa Droṇa-*
5. *lena brāhmaṇena Bhāradvāja-sagottreṇa mā*[1]-
6. *na* (?) *chchhandogena ishṭvā sattreṇa dvādaśar*[*ā*]*ttreṇa*
7. *yūpaḥ pratishṭhāpitaḥ*[1*]*Priyan'ām=Agnaya*[*ḥ*].

Translation.

"Success! In the reign of the King, the King of kings, His Majesty, Shāhi Vāsishka, in the twenty-fourth (24th) year, in the fourth (4th) month of summer, on the thirtieth (30th) day—on this date Droṇala, the son of Rudrila, a Brāhmiṇ belonging to the *gōtra* of Bharadvāja and a......chanter of holy hymns, while performing a sacrifice in a [solemn] session of twelve days (lit. nights), has set up this sacrificial post. May the [three] Fires be propitious."

The pillar was discovered by Pandit Radha Krishna in June 1910 at the village of Īsāpur or Hans Ganj on the left bank of the Jamnā opposite the City. (Cf. *J.R.A.S.* for 1910.)

---

[1] Possibly an *akshara* is lost after *mā*.

R. Brahmanical Architectural Sculptures.

R 1—29. Remains from a Hindū temple at Sahār, Chhātā *pargana*. (Cf. Growse, *Mathurā Notes*, *J.A.S.B.*, Vol. XLVII (1878), part I, pp. 117f., plate XV.)

R 1. Fragment (ht. 5′ 10½″ or 1 m.79) of a profusely carved door-jamb, which must have stood on the proper left side of the entrance to the temple. Beneath are two projecting figures too much defaced to be identified. The remaining portion is decorated with four vertical borders. That nearest the entrance (proper right side) is carved with an elegant foliated design. The second border contains four erotic groups placed one over the other, and each consisting of a male and a female figure standing under a canopy. Under the lowermost group is a four-armed flying figurine supporting with two hands the canopy above and holding a lute (Skr. *vīnā*) with the other two hands. The third band is carved in the shape of a pilaster. Both in its base and capital the well known device of the vase with overhanging foliage has been introduced. The square shaft is decorated with a bell hanging down from a grotesque mask. The fourth band is carved with a simple relief pattern.

R 2-10. Eight pillars and pilasters with plain square shafts recessed along the corners and with elaborately carved capitals of the pot-and-foliage type.

R 11—12. Two specimens of an abacus.

R 13-15. Three bracket capitals (ht. 1′ 2″ or 0 m.356). The four brackets are each decorated with a projecting four-armed male figure. These figures support with two hands and with their feet the slab on which the architrave rested. Their remaining two hands are placed on their knees. All the four figures are defaced. Between two of them there projects an elephant of which the trunk is broken. Under it is a figurine seated cross-legged. On the three remaining sides are standing Nāga (?) figures.

R 16—19. Four capitals of different shape.

R 20—29. Ten ornamental building-stones carved in the shape of chapels in which figures of deities are placed. No.* R 21 has a fragmentary Nāgarī inscription dated Saṁvat 1428 (A.D. 1371-2).

R 30. Fragment (ht. 9″ or 0 m. 235) of a building-stone carved with an ornamental pediment.

R 31. Fragment (ht. 1′ 2¾″ or 0 m. 385) of a doorjamb carved with a standing figure of a river goddess carrying a vase in her right hand.

R 32. Ornamental building-stone (ht. 1′ 8¾″ or 0 m. 544) decorated with a diaper pattern. It was obtained by Mr. Growse from Mahāban and probably belonged to a mediaeval Hindū temple. (*Mathurā Notes*, *J.A.S.B.*, Vol. XLVII, 1878, part I, p. 119, plate XX).

R 33-34. Two pillar bases from Sahār (?) carved in the shape of stepped pyramids (*Ibidem*, plate XV, but cf. Introduction).

R 35—36. Two square pillars (ht. 3′ 6″ or 1 m. 068) with bases and capitals of the pot-and-foliage type. One pillar has on one side over the lower vase a female figurine seated to the proper left. The other pillar had presumably a similar figure, which, however, is defaced. The centre of the shaft is marked with a rim from which a double festoon hangs down on each side. Mr. Growse who obtained these two pillars from the Kaṅkālī Ṭīlā ascribes them to about the year 400 on account of the absence of a grotesque mask (*Mathurā*, p.118 ; *Mathurā Notes*, p.119, plate XX).

R 37. Grotesque mask (ht. 1′ 6″ or 0 m.458) with protruding eyes, pointed nose and a wide mouth with a moustache. It probably belongs to a Brahmanical temple.

R 38. Building-stone (ht. 8½″ or 0 m. 215) profusely decorated with carvings.

R 39. Building-stone (ht. 10″ or 0 m. 254) apparently the moulded base of a pilaster.

R 40. Building-stone (length 2′ 9″ or 0 m. 533); purpose uncertain.

R 41. Pilaster (ht. 1′ 7″ or 0 m. 497) with portion of architrave, profusely carved, probably belonging to some mediaeval Hindū temple. It was discovered by Mr. Growse in opening out the new paved way along the river bank in the City. (*Mathurā Notes*, p. 119, plate XX).

R 42. Building-stone (ht. 6″ or 0 m. 15 ; width 1′ 2″ or 0 m. 356) carved on two sides with *chaitya* windows.

R 43. Fragment (ht. 11½″ or 0 m. 29) of an ornamental lintel decorated with horizontal borders of various design. A projecting chapel which originally must have occupied the centre contains a figure of Śiva seated on the bull Nandi and holding a trident and a snake. With his right arm he clasps Pārvatī who is seated on his knee. Both figures are injured. On each side stands a female attendant. It was obtained by Mr. Growse " in the progress of repairs of the Chhatthi Palna (or Assi Khamba) at Mahaban, being part of the Hindū temple[1] there which was destroyed by Aurangzeb." (*Mathurā Notes*, p. 120, plate XX).

R 44. Fragment (ht. 1′ or 0 m. 305) carved with a corpulent dancing figure in high relief. Find-place unknown.

R 45. Fragment (ht. 1′ 1″ or 0 m. 33) of a doorjamb, containing two dancing figures placed one over the other.

---

[1] In the Lucknow Museum are two pillars said to have belonged to the same temple. They both bear inscriptions dated *Saṁvat* 1227 (A.D. 1170-1). Cf. above p. 17.

R 46. Fragment (ht. 1′ 6½″ or 0 m. 47) of a sculptured stone apparently belonging to the doorway of some Brahmanical temple. It is carved with three figures. The surface is much disintegrated. It was preserved at the Allahabad Public Library till December 1907, but it is doubtful whether it belongs to Mathurā.

R 47. Sculpture (ht. 1′ or 0 m. 304) apparently the pediment of a Brahmanical miniature temple or chapel. The centre is occupied by an ornamental niche containing a corpulent male figure which holds a staff over his left shoulder. It is flanked by two squatting female figures of which that to the proper right holds a child in her lap. That to the proper left, which is defaced, is four-armed. Beneath these three figures there is a row of nine squatting figurines representing the Sun, the Moon, the five planets Mars, Mercury, Jupiter, Venus, and Saturn, the Eclipse-demon Rāhu (depicted as a bust) and the Comet Ketu. These nine figures called *Nava-Grahas* are usually placed over the entrance of Brahmanical temples. On both sides of this row is a projection containing a pair of dancing female figures carrying various attributes. There is, moreover, at both ends of the sculpture a standing figure which is mostly defaced. Along the top of the stone is a row of eight flying figurines of which four are placed to the right of the central figure and four to the left.

It was purchased by Pandit Radha Krishna from a Khatrī, Girdhar Lāl, who is said to have found it in the Jamnā near the old Foṛt of Kaṇs. On loan from the Government of India.

R 48. Building-stone (length 3′ or 0 m. 942 ; ht. 8″ or 0 m. 21) with a four-armed supporting bracket-figure, partly broken, on one side and a plain bracket of geometrical design at the other end. The stone apparently first belonged to a Brahmanical temple and was afterwards used in a Muhammadan building. It was noticed by Pandit Radha Krishna let into the wall of a house in the Kakōr Ghāṭī in Mathurā City and subsequently purchased for the Museum.

R 49. Fragment (ht. 2′ or 0 m. 61) of a sculptured building-stone, which Mr. Growse obtained from Shērgaṛh in the Chhātā *parganā*, where he found it imbedded in one of the towers of a fort built according to tradition by the Emperor Shēr Shāh. It probably belongs to a mediaeval Brahmanical temple (*Mathurā Notes*, p. 119, plate XX).

R 50. Fragment (ht. 1′ 1½″ or 0 m. 353), probably lower portion of the proper left doorjamb of a doorway, carved with two standing figures, male and female, which are much defaced. It was obtained by Pandit Radha Krishna from the Jōgīpura Quarter of the City close to the Holi Gate. On loan from the Government of India.

R 51. Fragment (ht. 1′ 3″ or 0 m. 393), probably lower portion of the jamb of a doorway, carved with two partly defaced standing figures. It was obtained by Pandit Radha Krishna from the Jōgīpura quarter of the City close to the Holi Gate.

R 52. Fragment (ht. 11″ or 0 m. 288), probably lower portion of the jamb of a doorway, carved with two standing figures, male and female, which are partly defaced. It was obtained from a cowherd who is said to have found it on the Brindāban road.

R 53. Building stone (ht. 1′ 8″ or 0 m. 523), apparently base of a pillar, carved in front with a partly defaced female (?) figurine kneeling to proper left and holding a vessel (?) in her right hand. It was found by Pandit Radha Krishna in the village of Jaisinghpura, 1 mile from the City on the Brindāban Road. According to a local tradition, it had once formed part of the Kēsab Dēv temple destroyed by Aurangzeb in A.D. 1661.

R 54. Stele (ht. 3′ 11″ or 1 m. 23) carved in the shape of a *śikhara* temple surmounted by an *amalaka* stone. Style late mediaeval. The four faces beneath the *śikhara* bear the following figures enclosed between square dwarf pillars:—1. Male figure with pointed beard seated on horseback and apparently receiving a cup from a female figure behind. 2. Male figure lying on a couch under a tree with a female figure rubbing his feet. 3. Male deity with pointed beard seated on a cushion; attributes indistinct. 4. Male figure seated with a female figure on his left knee.

The sculpture is said to be a sepulchral monument erected in memory of a Rājpūt warrior who is probably represented by the first figure. The other three figures seem to be Śiva (with Pārvatī), Brahmā, and Vishṇu (with Lakshmī). The stone was obtained by Pandit Radha Krishna from the neighbourhood of the village of Behach, Dīg Tahsil, Bharatpur State. On loan from the Government of India.

(For a description of a similar sepulchral monument cf. Cunningham, *A.S.R.*, Vol. XXI, p. 120, and Führer, *Monumental Antiquities*, pp. 139 f.)

R 55. Bracket (ht. 8″ or 0 m. 209) with Atlant. Legs broken; circular hole in body. Obtained from the town of Kāmī in Bharatpur State.

R 56. Lower portion (ht. 3′ or 0 m. 914) of proper left doorjamb with figure of the river goddess Gaṅgā (the Ganges) standing on a crocodile (Skr. *makara*) and turned to the proper right with her right hand (which is broken) raised to the shoulder and her left hand resting on the head of a girl who is standing behind her. She is accompanied by two male figures: one a boy—apparently an attendant—standing behind her in uncertain action, and the other standing to front with his right hand raised to his shoulder and holding a staff in his left hand. Behind the boy attendant rises a lotus-stalk and over his head we notice a flower on which two miniature figures, apparently male and female, are seated. On each side there is a full-blown lotus-flower. The stalk ends in a defaced Nāga figurine which is provided with a seven (?)-headed serpent-hood and joins hands in the attitude of adoration.

On a level with this Nāga there are three figurines supporting three vertical bands of carving. To the proper right we have a band with two dancing figures: the one Kārttikeya (?) seated on a peacock (?) with a staff in his left hand, and over him Chāmuṇḍā (?) with a long necklace and a staff resting in her left arm. The central projecting band is carved with a female figurine holding a *chaurī* in her left hand and standing under a pediment of a miniature chapel. Beneath is a capital of the pot-and-foliage type. The third raised band to the proper left is decorated with croll-work. The three raised bands are separated by deep vertical recesses. To the proper left runs an inner border of scrollwork over the Nāga figure.

The sculpture, which came from the bungalow once occupied by Mr. Growse, was presented to the Museum by Mr. J. Ingram.

R 57. Proper right doorjamb (ht. 5′ or 1 m. 52) decorated with the figure of a river-goddess, probably Yamunā (the Jamnā) standing on a tortoise and turned to the proper left, *viz.*, the side of the doorway. The animal on which she stands is uncertain and may be a crocodile in which case the figure would represent Gaṅgā (the Ganges). The river goddess is accompanied by a female attendant of smaller size, apparently holding a lotus-stalk, while a male figure is standing to front with his left hand raised. There is, moreover, a broken figure of a child standing to his right with one hand placed on his shoulder and with the other apparently holding his hand. The action of this figure is uncertain. We notice further a miniature figure kneeling (or flying ?) to the proper left of Yamunā and holding an offering in both hands.

Over each of the two larger figures there rises a vertical raised band, supported by a four-armed Gandharva, flying to the proper left, who holds a mace or sword in two hands and with the remaining two hands supports the pedestal above.

The two raised borders which are separated by a flat sunk band of scroll-work are each decorated with four amatory couples. To the proper left of the inner border there runs a narrow line of busts of dancers and musicians, sixteen in number, the lowermost figure being turned towards the temple entrance with hands folded in adoration.

R 58. Fragment (ht. 7⅞" or 0 m. 20; length 2′ 3¾" or 0 m. 705) consisting of the proper left half of a lintel with defaced seated male (?) figure in the centre, a row of six flying figures carrying garlands (Gandharvas and Apsaras ?) and a male and female figure standing. Obtained together with no. F 38 from the village of Dhangaon 6 miles south-west of Mathurā. On loan from the Government of India.

S. Mughal Architectural Remains.

S 1—35. White marble remains from Aurangābād [1], apparently belonging to some building of the Mughal period.

S 1. Fountain basin (2′ 4″ or 0 m. 71 square) with raised border and depression, circular in outline, and carved in the scalloped fashion in vogue during the Mughal period.

S 2. Stand (3′ 7″ or 1 m. 092 square) consisting of a slab resting on four detached legs of an ornamental kind.

S 3.—Stand (2′ 1″ or 0 m. 635 square).

S 4. Broken screen (5′ 3″ by 2′ 8″) pierced in a hexagonal design.

S 5—6. Two tapering shafts (ht. 3′ 8″) of pillars, fluted with twelve flutings and ending on both sides in a calice of twelve leaves.

S 7—8. Two tapering shafts (ht. 3′ 8″) similar in shape and design to the pillars nos. S 5—6.

S 9—10. Two pillar bases (ht. 2′ 5″ and 2′ 6″) with a central bulbous portion of twelve flutings.

S 11—12. Two bases of pilasters (ht. 2′ 5″ and 2′ 6″) with a central bulbous portion of twelve flutings.

S 13—35. Twenty-three carpet-weights (Persian *mīr-farsh*) each consisting of an ornamental boss resting on a square base.

S 36. Building stone (ht. 1′ 5½″ or 0 m. 458 ; length 4′ 2″ or 1 m. 31) with a bracket on each side. It probably belongs to a building of the early Mughal period. It was found on the road leading from the Holi Gate to the Kōṭwālī and presented to the Museum by Seṭh Bhik Chand, Honorary Magistrate of Mathurā.

S 37. Red sandstone fragment (ht. 1′ 1½″ or 0 m. 34) of the fluted shaft of pillar rising from a border of foliage. Probably it belongs to some building of the Mughal period. It was preserved at Allahabad till December 1907, but it is doubtful whether it originates from Mathurā.

S 38. Red sandstone fragment (ht. 7½″ or 0 m. 19) carved with the figure of a peacock. The stone seems to belong to some Hindū or early Mughal building[2]. It was kept at Allahabad till December 1907, and it is uncertain whether it originates from Mathurā.

S 39. Base (ht. 1′ 6″ or 0 m. 471) of a pillar, early Mughal in style. Allahabad collection.

---

[1] Aurangābād is a village 4 miles to the south of Mathurā, which is named after Aurangzeb who here enticed his brother Murād Bakhsh. The ancient name of the place appears to have been Rūpnagar. Cf. Manucci, *Storia do Mogor* (transl. Irvine), Vol. I, pp. 298ff. and Valentijn, *Nieuw Oost-Indiën*, Vol. IV, p. 302.

[2] A frieze of similar peacocks occurs on the early Mughal buildings in the Lahore Fort.

S 40. Carpet-weight (ht. 6½″ or 0 m. 165) consisting of a boss on an octagonal base. It was preserved at the Allahabad Public Library till December 1907; origin unknown.

S 41. Figure (ht. 10″ or 0 m. 253) of an elephant, trunk and legs broken, probably belonging to a bracket of some Hindū or early Mughal building. It also belonged to the Allahabad collection; origin unknown.

S 42. Figure (ht. 6¾″ or 0 m. 171) of an elephant probably belonging to a bracket of some Hindū or early Mughal building. Allahabad collection; origin unknown.

S 43. Bas-relief (ht. 1′ 3½″ or 0 m. 393; width 2′ 2¼″ or 0 m. 666) in a sunk panel representing a horseman pursued by an elephant mounted by two men of whom one holds a goad (Skr. *aṅkuśa*) and the second an object in the shape of a dumb-bell [1]. The sculpture must belong to the early Mughal period (*circa* A.D. 1600). Pandit Radha Krishna obtained it from Gōvardhan where it was being worshipped as Jāhir (i.e., Zâhir) Pīr or Guggā, the Cid Campador of Hinduism. When found, it was covered with plaster. On loan from the Government of India.

[1] A very similar scene occurs among the tile mosaics on the Lahore Fort which will shortly be published in the Journal of Indian Art and Industry.

T.—Terra-cottas and Miscellaneous Antiquities.

T 1. Terra-cotta plaque (ht. 9¼" or 0 m. 235) with a squatting corpulent male figure wearing a garland round his shoulders, heavy ear-rings, a necklace and bracelets. The two hands are empty; the left rests on the knee. Find-place unknown.

T 2. Terra-cotta fragment (ht. 8½" or 0 m. 216) containing the left leg and right foot of a standing male (?) figure wearing a *dhōtī* and a garland (Skr. *mālā*) hanging down along his knee. Workmanship rude. Find-place unknown.

T 3. Terra-cotta fragment (ht. 9" or 0 m. 228) with a corpulent female figure seated to front on an ornamental chair and holding in her left arm a male child facing and wearing a string of beads round its neck and its loins. Her right hand is raised to the height of her shoulder with the open palm of the hand turned outward. She wears a wreath on her head, heavy pendants in her ears, a row of bracelets and a *tilaka.*

T 4. Terra-cotta fragment (ht. 6" or 0 m. 152) consisting of a headless female figure with a girdle, bracelets and heavy bangles standing to front with a bulbous flower-vase to her right. Find-place unknown.

T 5. Terra-cotta fragment (ht. 7" or 0 m. 178) consisting of a rudel modelled female figure, the arms and legs of which are missing. Find-place unknown.

T 6. Terra-cotta fragment (ht. 1′ 4″ or 0 m. 407) consisting of a female figure, presumably a Nāgī, carrying a flower vase on the palm of her left hand, which is raised to a level with her shoulder. Right arm and legs below knees missing. Nose, chin and breasts damaged.

Nos. T 6—14 were found in 1905 at Malpur by Mr. H. L. Battersby, P. W. D., Assistant Engineer, Agra-Delhi Chord Railway, when making a cutting through the south-west corner of the site of the ancient city of Mathurā. They were presented to the Museum by Major Ashworth, R.E., in charge of the construction at Mathurā of the Agra-Delhi Chord Railway.

T 7—10. Four large-sized bricks (15" by 8½" by 2"; 15¾" by 9" by 3" 16½" by 9" by 2" and 16¾" by 9" by 2¼").

T 11. Six balls of baked clay, perhaps used in slings.

T 12. Stone stool (ht. 6" or 0 m. 152).

T 13—22. Ten fragments of stone stools.

T 23—24. Two fragments of terra-cotta drains.

T 25. Fragment (length 7" or 0 m. 183; thickness 1¾" or 0 m. 046) of a carved brick decorated with scrollwork. Obtained from the village of Mahōlī near Mathurā.

T 26. Figurine (ht. 6" or 0 m. 157) of a female wearing an elaborate headdress and standing with a pitcher in her right and an indistinct object in her left hand. Obtained from the village of Rāyā.

T 27. Fragment (ht. 9" or 0 m. 23) consisting of male figure, of which the head and legs are broken, standing with a sword in his left hand. He wears a necklace, bracelets and a *dhōtī* fastened to the loins with a belt. Obtained from the village or Sitōhā, three miles from Mathurā on the road to Gōvardhan. On loan from the Government of India.

T 28. Head and bust (ht. 2¾" or 0 m. 07) of a female figurine [1] with elaborate head-dress in which lotus-flowers have been introduced. Left breast broken. From the ancient site of Gosna, three miles from the City on the road to Rāyā. On loan from the Government of India.

T 29. Fragment (ht. 2⅛" or 0 m. 053) of a male figurine wearing a diadem and apparently winged. From Gosna. On loan from the Government of India.

T 30. Head and bust (ht. 3¾" or 0 m. 095) of a female figure with heavy earring in right ear and lotus-flowers on her head. From Gosna. On loan from the Government of India.

T 31. Head and bust (ht. 2¾" or 0 m. 07) of a female figurine with heavy earrings in both ears surmounted by lotus-flowers. From Gosna. On loan from the Government of India.

T 32. Male figurine (ht. 3½" or 0 m. 09) holding a bird in his right and a fruit in his left hand. Legs missing. From a *maṭh* in the Gōpālpur Maḥalla of the City. On loan from the Government of India.

T 33. Head and bust (ht. 3" or 0 m. 075) of a female figurine with heavy earring in left ear. From Airā-khēṛā. On loan from the Government of India.

T 34. Head (ht. 2⅛" or 0 m. 055) of female figurine. From Mōrā site. On loan from the Government of India.

T 35. Head (ht. 2½" or 0 m. 063) of female figurine. From Gaṇēsrā. On loan from the Government of India.

T 36. Fragment (ht. 2" or 0 m. 05) of bearded figure. From Gaṇēsrā. On loan from the Government of India.

---

[1] A terra-cotta very similar to the Gosna figurines nos. J28 and 30-31 was found by Cunningham on the site of Taxila. Cf. *A.S.R.*, Vol. XIV, p. 14f; plate IX, no. 1.

U. Sculptures excavated from the Sitōhā and Gaṇēsrā Tanks.

In June 1908, Pandit Radha Krishna cleared the ancient tanks of Sitōhā and Gaṇēsrā three miles west of the City in the direction of Gōvardhaṇ and Dīg and obtained 99 pieces of sculpture. Nos. 1-37 were found in the Sitōhā and nos. 38-99 in the Gaṇēsrā tank. They are too much defaced and water-worn to allow of a detailed description. The great bulk are statuettes in buff-coloured sandstone, representing Brahmanical deities. We recognize Vishṇu (nos. 8, 10, 37, 57—59, 70, 79 and 86); Sūrya (no. 41), Jagannātha (no. 17), Lakshmī (no. 32), Śiva and Pārvatī (nos. 3, 23, 53, 81 and 94), Gaṇeśa (nos. 2, 18, 43 and 61), Gaṇeśa with four Śaktis (no. 47), Durgā slaying Mahisha (nos. 13, 24, 51, 64, 89 and 91). The only piece which is certainly Budhist is no. 72 (ht. 4" or 0 m. 101). It is the upper half of a Buddha figurine seated with the right hand raised at the level of the shoulder and the left hand placed on the knee. It has a halo with scolloped border. Judging from the style, it must belong to the Kushaṇa period. Other sculptures which may be assigned to the same period are nos. 30, 45, 50, 55, 68, 84 and 93. No. 30 (ht. 9½" or 0 m. 248) represents a male figure, carved in the round, standing with his right hand raised to the shoulder and the left placed on the hip. The attitude is that of the Bodhisattva figures of the Kushaṇa period. No. 50 (ht. 6" or 0 m. 157) is the upper half of a slab carved with a figure of the goat-headed Nemesa, carrying a child on each shoulder (Cf. above E 1). No. 55 (ht. 8" or 0 m. 21), which is carved in the round, is a headless female figure seated on a bench with ornamental back against which a round cushion is placed. A child crouches between her feet. The subject is apparently the same as that of the inscribed fragment no. G 10. No. 84 (ht. 11½" or 0 m. 302) is the upper portion of a Nāga statuette with a seven-headed serpent hood, standing in exactly the same attitude as the Nāga images of the Kushaṇa period (C 11-13). No. 68 (ht. 8½" or 0 m. 216) is a fragment carved on both faces with a *chaitya* arch containing a human bust. It deserves notice that in general the older sculptures are made of spotted red sandstone.

The sculptures of this section have not been exhibited, on account of their slight interest, but will be shown on application to the Curator.

V. Ancient Brasswork [1].

V 1. Water-vessel (*jambu*) decorated with floral and geometrical designs. Purchased at Brindāban.

V 2. Round dish (*rakābī*) decorated with foliated design. Purchased at Mathurā.

V 3. Stand, decorated with a kneeling winged Garuḍa figure, and used in worship. Purchased at Brindāban.

V 4. Square idol-stand (*singhāsan*) used in worship. Purchased at Brindāban.

V 5. Pump (*pichkara*) decorated with an elephant's head and used to sprinkle colour water on the occasion of the Holi festival. Purchased at Mathurā.

V 6. Pair of mirror-stands (*kalas*) used to decorate the corners of idol-stands (*singhāsan*) and idol-cars (*rath*). Purchased at Brindāban.

V 7. Sacrificial box (*chauprā*) decorated with four peacocks and containing three divisions for rice (*akshat*), incense (*dhūp*), red-lead (*sindūr*) and other articles employed in worship. It is said to be mainly used in the Dekhan and was purchased at Brindāban.

V 8. Idol pedestal (*chaukī*) on four legs. Purchased at Mathurā.

V 9. Attar-holder (*attardān*) worked *à jour* and decorated with floral ornament. A piece of cotton-wool drenched with attar is placed in the cavity. Purchased at Mathurā.

V 10. Sacrificial bowl (*panchpātrā*) meant to contain the water in which the idol is washed. It is decorated with geometrical designs. Purchased at Mathurā.

V 11. Sacrificial spoon (*āchmanī*) used to sprinkle the water contained in the *panchpātrā* on the right palm of the devotee who sips it. The handle is wrought in the shape of a cobra. Purchased at Mathurā.

V 12. Tortoise used as a toy which is placed before the idol. It must originally have been surmounted by a bird the feet of which are still extant. Purchased at Brindāban; but probably Japanese work.

V 13. Collyrium-holder (*surmedānī*) in the shape of a fish. Purchased at Brindāban.

V 14. Stag (*bārasinga*) used as a toy. Purchased at Brindāban.

V 15-16. Two elephants (*hāthī*) used as toys. Purchased at Mathurā.

V 17. Idol of Vishṇu, four-armed, standing on a detachable stand. Purchased at Brindāban.

V 18. Idol of Vishṇu, four-armed, standing. Purchased at Mathurā.

[1] The objects under this heading were all given on loan by the Government of India.

V 19. Idol of Lakshmī-Nārāyaṇa defaced. It shows the four-armed Vishṇu seated with his spouse Lakshmī on his left knee. Purchased at Mathurā.

V 20. Idol of Balarāma or Baladeva (usually called Dāuji), the elder brother of Kṛishṇa. He is standing in front of the serpent Śesha-nāga of which he is supposed to be an incarnation and holds a cup in his left hand and an indistinct object, perhaps a plough, in the right. Purchased at Mathurā. (Cf. above *sub.* no. D 36).

V 21. Figurine defaced, probably Garuḍa, the bird of Vishṇu, kneeling with hands folded. Under his left knee two cobras are traceable. Purchased at Mathurā.

V 22. Figurine of a four-armed goddess, perhaps Lakshmī, seated on a tortoise. In the head-dress is a cavity for the reception of a precious stone.

V 23-29. Seven figurines of Bāl Mukund also called *Makkhan-chōr* "Butter thief" or *Laḍu Gōpāl* "Sweetmeat Gōpāl." It represents the infant Kṛishṇa crawling and holding in his right hand a lump of butter (or sweetmeats) which he has taken away from his foster-mother Yaśodhā. They were purchased partly at Mathurā and partly at Brindāban.

V 30. Copper idol-throne (*singhāsan*) with high back, detached. From Gōvardhan.

V 31. Brass scissors (*sarautā*) used to cut *areca* nuts. From Gōvardhan.

V 32. Brass elephant (*hāthī*) on square pedestal. It must have held some object in its trunk. From Brindāban.

V 33. Two brass deer (*hiran*), lying. Horns apparently broken. From Brindāban.

V 34. *Surāhī* decorated with a foliated design. Very ornamental. Obtained from Mathurā City.

V 35 and 36. *Hukkas* with floral design. From Mathurā.

V 37. *Hukka* smaller than the above. From Mathurā.

V 38. *Hukka* of the same pattern as above. From Brindāban.

V 39. *Hukka* plain. From Brindāban.

V 40. *Hukka* with floral design. From Mathurā.

V 41. Pair of palankins. From Mathurā.

V 42. Vessel with spout. From Mathurā.

V 43—44. Vessel with spout. From Mathurā.

V 45. *Lōṭā* of brass surrounded with images of the Sun. From Mathurā.

V 46. *Lōṭā*, smaller than the above. From Mathurā.

V 47. *Jambhu* of the Deccan style. From Mathurā.

V 48. *Jambhu* smaller than the above. From Mathurā.

V 49. *Jambhu* same as above in size, but different in pattern. From Mathurā.

V 50. Flower-pot. From Brindāban.

V 51. Small water vessel with spout, ornamental. From Mathurā.

V 52. Small water vessel with spout, ornamental, smaller than the above. From Mathurā.

V 53. Old lamp stand. From Brindāban.

V 54. Old lamp stand, smaller than the above. From Mathurā.

V 55. Spouted vessel of good workmanship. From Delhi.

V 56. Wide-mouthed bell (*ghaṇṭī*) slightly ornamental. From Mathurā.

V 57. Wide-mouthed bell (*ghaṇṭī*) smaller than the above. From Brindāban.

V 58. Vessel to hold Ganges water (*gangājalī*). From Mathurā.

V 59. Pump (*pichkara*) decorated with flower on one side. From Mathurā. Cf. sub no. V, 5.

V 60. *Ārtī* with serpent-headed handle. From Brindāban.

V 61—63. *Ārtī*, handle with female figure. From Brindāban.

V 64. *Ārtī* without decoration. From Mathurā.

V 65 and 66. Vishṇu badge. From Brindāban.

V 67. Hanumān badge. From Brindāban.

V 68. Sacrificial bowl (*panchpātrā*) large. From Mathurā.

V 69. Sacrificial bowl (*panchpātrā*) small. From Mathurā.

V 70—71. Female head. From Agra.

V 72. *Chilam*. From Mathurā.

V 73. *Chilam*. From Brindāban.

V 74—75. Tripod. From Mathurā.

V 76. Small idol-throne (*singhāsan*). From Brindāban.

V 77. Cup with four wheels and a bull's head. From Brindāban.

V 78. Conch stand. From Brindāban.

V 79. Fragment of an Indian lamp.

V 80. Sand-holder used for blotting.

V 81. Small dish, floral ornament.

V 82. Idol-car (*rath*) drawn by elephants containing an idol of Vishṇu. From Mathurā.

V 83. Car (*rath*) drawn by horses. From Mathurā.

V 84. Śiva's bull Nandi. From Mathurā.

V 85. Śiva's bull Nandi. From Brindāban.

V 86—87. Cow. From Brindāban.

V 88—89. Horse on four wheels. From Brindāban.

V 90—91. Horse without wheels. From Brindāban.

V 92—94. Elephant (*hāthī*) on wheels with rider. From Mathurā.

V 95—96. Elephant (*hāthī*) mounted, but without wheels. From Brindāban.

V 97. Elephant on wheels, not mounted. From Brindāban.

V 98. Elephant without wheels, unmounted.

V 99. Fantastical beast (*simurgh*) on wheels holding a flower-like object in one of its paws.

V 100. *Pūjādānī*, mounted with a peacock, used to place various objects used in worship. From Mathurā.

V 101. Copper conch-shell (*sankh*). From Mathurā.

V 102. Sacrificial spoon (*āchmanī*) with serpent head. From Brindāban.

V 103. Sacrificial spoon (*āchmanī*) plain. From Brindāban.

V 104. *Argha*. From Brindāban.

V 105—106. Peacock. From Gōvardhan.

V 107. Peacock. From Mathurā.

V 108. Image of Dēvī standing. From Mathurā.

V 109. Image of Kṛishṇa dancing. From Brindāban.

V 110. Image of Kṛishṇa singing. From Brindāban.

V 111—114. Duck. From Agra.

V 115. Collyrium-holder (*surmedānī*) of good workmanship. From Brindāban.

V 116. Small pocket *hukka* (*hukkiya*) of good workmanship. From Agra.

V 117. Image of Sākhī Gōpāl, i.e., "Gōpāl the witness," worshipped in a temple near Jagannāth, Orissa. From Mathurā.

V 118—119. Image of the infant Kṛishṇa crawling, called Bālmukund. From Brindāban.

V 120. Vishṇu image. From Brindāban.

V 121. Vishṇu image. From Brindāban.

V 122—123. Brass images. From Brindāban.

V 124. Small copper image. From Brindāban.

W.—MISCELLANEOUS OBJECTS.

W 1. Chinese chess-board, with backgammon board inside, of sandal-wood inlaid with ivory, and twenty-nine chessmen of ivory.

Presented by the Court of Wards' Estate of Raja Seth Lachman Das through Mr. D. Calnan, I.C.S., Collector, Mathurā, on the 14th September 1908

W 2. Conch-shell (Skr. *śaṅkha*) obtained from a *sādhu*.

X.—COINS [1].

X 1. Buddhist cast copper coin.

Obverse : Lion facing sacrificial post.

Reverse : *Chaitya* and two symbols.

X 2. Copper coin of Soter Megas. Common type.

X 3. Copper coin of Wemo Kadphises. Common type.

X 4. Copper coin of Huvishka. Elephant rider type. Deity uncertain.

X 5. Four copper coins of the late Indo-Scythian or Kushaṇa type.

X 6. Gold coin of the Scytho-Sassanian or Kushaṇo-Sassanian type.

Obverse : King, standing to left at altar with trident in left hand, wearing richly ornamented coat and conical cap; small trident over altar; *svastika* between king's legs. Below king's left arm a monogram. Corrupt Greek legend intended for *Shaonana Shao Bazodeo Koshano.*

Reverse : Śiva and bull, in degraded style. Legend *Oasho*.

(V. A. Smith, *Indian Museum Catalogue*, p. 91, plate XIV, 12.)

X 7. Copper coin, late Indo-Sassanian. Common type.

X 8. Gold coin of the later Kushaṇa type.

Obverse : Kushaṇa king standing at altar. Legend to left *bha* (?); under arm *sena* (V. A. Smith reads *sita*); to right *shaka*.

Reverse : Throned Ardokhsho. (V. A. Smith, *Indian Museum Catalogue*, p. 89; plate XIV, 6.)

X 9. Gold coin of the later Great Kushaṇa type.

Obverse : Kushaṇa king standing at altar. Legend to left *bha*; under arm *sya* (?); to right *shaka*.

Reverse : Throned Ardokhsho. (Cunningham, *Coins of the later Indo-Scythians*, p. 32, nos. 6 and 7.)

X 10. Gold coin of the later Indo-Kushaṇa or Little Kushaṇa type (Cunningham, *op. cit.* p. 72; plate VI, II.)

X 11. Gold coin of Nara-bālāditya, probably Narasiṁha-gupta of the Imperial Gupta Dynasty.

---

[1] For the particulars given in this section I am indebted to Mr. R. Burn, I.C.S.

Obverse: King standing to left, grasping bow with left hand; right hand extended across Garuḍa standard. Legend *Nara* und.r left arm.

Reverse: Goddess seated on lotus. Legend indistinct (V. A. Smith, *op. cit.* p. 119).

X 12. Gold coin of Govinda-chandra-deva of Kanauj. (Cunningham, *Coins of Mediaeval India*, plate IX, 16).

X 13. Gold coin of Kumāra-pāla-deva of Delhi. (Cunningham, *op. cit.* plate IX, 3.)

APPENDIX I.

LIST OF INSCRIPTIONS [1].

MAURYA PERIOD (3rd and 2nd centuries B. C.)

C 1. Parkham statue (LL 150).

SATRAP PERIOD. (1st century B.C.)

Q 1. Mōrā stone slab; fragmentary inscription of the reign (?) of the Great-Satrap Rājūvula. (LL 14).

Q 2. Holi Gate tablet of homage. (LL 102.)

Q 3. Tablet of homage; fragmentary inscription. (LL 97).

J 7. Railing pillar inscription. (LL 98).

KUSHANA PERIOD (1st and 2nd centuries A.D.).

Dated.

B 71. Jina fourfold image; inscription, dated in the year 5. (LL 20).

Q 13. Sacrificial pillar inscription of the year 24 in the reign of Vāsishka.

A 49. Buddha image inscription of the year 28 in the reign of Vāsi (?)-shka. (LL 33).

A 71. Pedestal of Buddha statuette; inscription of the year 31 (?) in the reign of Huvishka.

A 63. Lākhanū Bodhisattva image; inscription of the year 35 in the reign of Huvishka.

B 70. Jina four-fold image; inscription of the year 35 (LL 19).

C 13. Chhargaon Nāga image of the year 40 in the reign of Huvishka.

E 25. Male figure in Indo-Scythian dress; inscription, dated in the year 42 (?).

P 20. Pillar base; inscription of the year 47.

P 35. Pillar base; inscription of the year 47. (LL 65).

P 38. Pillar base; inscription of the year 47.

B 29. Jina (?) image; fragmentary inscription of the year 50 in the reign of Huvishka. (LL 51).

E 20. Fragments of female figure from Mōrā; inscription, dated in the reign of Huvishka.

A 66. Anyōr Buddha statuette; inscription of the year 51.

C 21. Nāga statuette; inscription of the year 52.

B 2. Jina image; inscription of the year 83 in the reign of Vāsudeva (LL 68).

B 3. Jina image; fragmentary inscription of the year 83. (LL 69).

B 4. Jina image; inscription of the year 84 in the reign of Vāsudeva.

[1] The letters LL refer to the List of Brāhmi inscriptions published by Professor H. Lüders in the *Epigraphia Indica*, Vol. X, Appendix.

B 5. Jina image; inscription of the year 90 (?). (LL 73).

G 38. Pedestal; fragmentary inscription of the reign of Vāsudeva (?).

Undated.

A 1. Kaṭrā Bodhisattva inscription.

A 2. Anyōr Buddha inscription (LL 13).

A 50. Buddha (?) image; fragmentary inscription.

A 56. Bodhisattva (?) pedestal; inscription defaced.

A 64. Dhūnsarpārā Buddha image; fragmentary inscription.

B 14. Jina (?) statuette inscription (LL 123).

B 18. Jina image; fragmentary inscription.

C 16. Nāga image inscription.

C 28. Yaksha and Yakshī figure.

G 10. Jamālpur fragment inscription.

G 39. Fragment inscription.

G 42. Pedestal fragment inscription.

G 43. Kōtā pedestal fragment inscription (LL 15).

G 47. Base of female figure.

J 1. Railing pillar inscription (?).

J 13. Railing pillar inscription.

J 15. Railing pillar inscription.

J 21. Railing pillar inscription.

J 36. Railing pillar inscription.

J 41. Railing pillar inscription.

J 48. Railing pillar inscription.

J 52. Railing pillar inscription.

J 58. Railing pillar inscription.

J 68. Railing pillar inscription.

N 1. Votive *Stūpa* inscription (LL 136).

P 21, 34, 36, 37 and 39. Pillar base inscriptions (P 22, LL 126; P 29, LL 120).

Q 4. Slab; fragmentary inscription.

GUPTA PERIOD. (4th and 5th centuries A.D.)

B 15. Jina (?) statuette; inscription of the Gupta (?) year 57[1] (A.D. 376-7). (LL 45).

B 31. Jina pedestal; inscription of the Gupta (?) year 97 (?) (A.D. 416-7).

A 48. Buddha image; inscription of the Gupta year 135 (A.D. 454-5).

Q 5. Slab fragment of Chandragupta Vikramāditya (*circa* A.D. 400).

A 5. Buddha image; inscription of about the 5th century A.D.

---

[1] According to Professor Luders, the date is to be referred to the era of Kanishka.

MEDIAEVAL AND LATER INSCRIPTIONS.

B 22. Jina statuette ; inscription of the Vikrama year 1104 (A.D. 1047).

B 24. Jina statuette ; inscription of the Vikrama year 1234 (?) (A.D. 1177).

B 21. Jina statuette ; fragmentary inscription.

B 23. Jina statuette ; fragmentary inscription.

Q 7. Stele ; fragmentary inscription of the Vikrama year 1420 (A.D. 1363).

R 21. Chapel ; fragmentary inscription of the Vikrama year 1428 (A.D. 1371—2.)

Q 6. Stone tablet ; inscription of the Vikrama year 1612 (A.D. 1555 or 1556) and of the reign of Sikandar Sūrī.

D 52. Sculpture with three-headed figure ; inscription of the Vikrama year 167[3], Śaka 153[8] (A.D. 1616).

D 32. Midhauli stele inscription.

Q 8. Tablet inscription dated Śaka 1702 (A.D. 1780).

Q 9. Pillar inscription.

Q 10. *Sāti* slab inscription.

B 25. Jina statuette ; inscription of the Vikrama year 1826 (A.D. 1770).

APPENDIX II.

Dr. J. F. Fleet has favoured me with the following note on the date of the slab inscription Q 6. It will be seen that, if the year corresponds to A.D. 1556, the epigraph would be posterior to the defeat of Sikandar Sūrī at Sirhind.

" Saṁvat 1612 : Chaitra vadi 10 Ravidine."

" This date may fall in A.D. 1554, 1555, or 1556. In these three years, the given *tithi* can be connected with a Sunday only as follows :—"

" A.—In Vikrama saṁvat 1612 current, whether Chaitrādi, Āshāḍhādi, or Kārttikādi, the *Pūrṇimānta* Chaitra vadi 10 began at about 3-0 p.m. (afternoon) on Sunday, 17th March, A.D. 1555. But, even if we accept the current year, what reason was there for using the *tithi* with the weekday on which it began, instead of with the weekday (Monday) on which it was current at sunrise ? The *tithi* is not a special one devoted to some festival or rite : so there is no reason of that kind. Does the inscription record a death ? If so, the reason may be found there."

" B.—In Āshāḍhādi or Kārttikādi Vikrama saṁvat 1612 expired, the *Amānta* Chaitra vadi 10 ended at about 1-0 p.m. (midday) on Sunday, 5th April, A.D. 1556. The *tithi* therefore answers quite regularly to this date. I should prefer this result, as far as I am in a position to decide without knowing the purport of the record : especially if the inscription is a Jain record."